ALASKA
OVER
ISRAEL

OPERATION MAGIC CARPET,
THE MEN AND WOMEN
WHO MADE IT FLY, AND
THE LITTLE AIRLINE
THAT COULD

DARRAGH
METZGER

A TFA Press Original

Lynnwood, Washington

.   .   .

Cover Photos courtesy of
JDC Archives and Alaska Airlines

Map by Daniel Fried,
courtesy of the Alaska Jewish Museum

Cover Design, Print Layout and eBook by
N.D. Author Services [NDAS]
www.NDAuthorServices.com

DEDICATION

To all the men and women who worked on Operation Magic Carpet, especially those whose names have not survived in any record I could find. I know there are so many of you who cared passionately about the airlift and gave everything to make it a success. Please know that what you did saved countless lives and changed history. Your deeds are recorded where it counts most.

And to Mom and Dad,
without whom this story, too,
would not have happened, and
certainly would have been left untold.

ACKNOWLEDGMENTS

I started work on this project somewhere around the very tail end of 2007 or early 2008, and puttered away at it as circumstances permitted. So many people have helped me over the years—or at least tried to—that it would take another book to list them all. Now, almost ten years later, I am finally able to say, "Thank You. This book would not have been possible without you."

Naturally, I'll start out by thanking my husband, Dameon, my two brothers, my sisters-in-law, and my nieces and nephews for all the love, support, encouragement, and ceaseless nagging that kept me on track, even when the situation seemed hopeless and I thought I'd never be able to do it. My brothers also supplied valuable intel; Chip with his pilot's-eye perspective on some of the technical details, Tim with his inside scoop on some family history I hadn't known. Love you all to pieces, one and all. Thank you, thank you, thank you.

Sam Silver was not only an invaluable source of information and anecdotes, he became over the years a close personal friend. He was impatient to see this in print, and I'm so sorry I didn't quite get there in time. I miss him still. Thank you also to Susan Silver, his daughter, for her friendship, support, and the photo of Sam in his free-wheeling youth. I will always value both.

More than anyone else Archie Satterfield made this entire project possible by giving me unstinting and open-handed access to all his notes, his tapes, and his memories of all the things he never recorded or wrote down before his death in 2011. Since most of the Alaska Airlines employees he interviewed way back when are long dead, he alone is the reason that knowledge and those stories are not lost. I agree with you, Archie; your publishers should have let you call your book, "A Breed Apart." A much better title than "The Alaska Airlines Story," and maybe would have opened it to the widespread readership it deserved. You are a rare bird, Archie, and you are missed.

Elgen Long not only sat with me for an hour or two in Anchorage and video-taped the entire interview, he answered an additional extremely long and involved list of questions, and sent me a free copy of his book when it finally went to print. Even provided me with a map of the route he'd produced for his own book. Thank you, sir! You are a gentleman and a scholar. I still think you should write your complete memoirs. What a read it would make!

Leslie Fried, Curator of the Alaska Jewish Museum, who put together the Operation Magic Carpet exhibit that became such an overwhelming success at the museum's opening. Thank you for allowing me to be a part of the experience and for all your support, encouragement, and unstinting access to any information I requested. Honestly, if it hadn't been for you, I don't know if I'd ever have finished this book.

To Robyn Russell, Senior Archivist, and Joann Henszey, Oral History, Alaska and Polar Regions Collection, at the Elmer E. Rasmuson Library, U of A Fairbanks, a huge Thank You for digging out Archie's buried research and going above and beyond to make sure I had copies of anything I could possibly need. Then doing it again when the first batch went missing. Your dedication and professionalism, and friendly on-site know-how, really saved my bacon more than once.

The helpful crew at the Seattle Public Library, particularly Steve, deserve a round of applause and a Thank You as well. How those guys do it, I've no idea. While I'm at it, a huge Thank You to Leon Seaman, a kindly random stranger at the UW library who shared his account to e-mail files to me.

Misha Mitsel, the JDC Senior Archivist, for providing almost instant responses to any query or question I fired off, and getting me the photos I could not otherwise obtain.

Shirili Green, who did her best to put me in touch with former Yemenite passengers before her passing. Not her fault time and illness caught up with her first. A lovely lady.

Ann Shilling and Brenda Cooper waded through my very rough first drafts and provided absolutely invaluable feedback. Thank you from the bottom of my heart; you made this a better book.

Deborah Fisher of the Clarion West Writers' Workshop, for her encouragement, and especially for getting me a place to stay in Fairbanks so I could do my research. I therefore also heap vast amounts of Thanks and gratitude upon Andre and Sheri Layral, who opened up their home in Fairbanks to provide a complete stranger with said place-to-stay so I could research to my heart's content. And for introducing me to Allie and Timmy, who provided endless amusement and opportunities for ear-scratching in my off-hours.

I just can't say "Thank You" often enough to the entire crew at Alaska Airlines, those still employed and those enjoying a well-earned retirement, for helping me out with photos, info, record searches, contacts, memories, and offers of help in every way, shape, and form. And, of course, stories about my dad, many of which made it into this book. Thanks, Smokey Schnee,

Chuck and Gail Spaeth, Ron Suttell, Paula Marchitto, Susan Ewbank, Mike Tobin, Don Conrard, and Gayle Christiansen, daughter of the late Maynard Christiansen, who shared a lot of years at ASA with Dad.

I'm sure I've left out dozens of people; it's not intentional, I assure you, just bad record-keeping and an over-stuffed memory. Please know that everything you've done has helped me get to this point.

ABOUT THE AUTHOR

Darragh Metzger was born and raised in Anchorage, Alaska, entering the world via her parents' house. Her mother walked into the hospital carrying the infant forty-five minutes after Darragh was born, so she knew from a tender age that she had a legacy of hardiness to live up to. She now lives in Seattle, Washington, where she makes her living in theater, writing in her free time. An amateur musician, she also sings, arranges music, and writes songs for two music groups.

Though she no longer flies, she still loves stories about aviation, and hopes one day to be able to produce a book consisting of all the stories she's collected from bush pilots and pioneer aviators.

Her publishing credits include plays, articles, interviews, short stories, and nine novels, several of which were previously released by another publisher and are now available from TFA Press in updated and revised editions.

ALSO BY DARRAGH METZGER

Available as trade paperbacks, e-book for Kindle, and all other e-book formats at Smashwords.com:
The Strawberry Roan
Stories of the Season
Stories of the Seasons
Tales from Opa

The Triads of Tir na'n'Og series:
Ironwolfe
The Triads
The Red Triad
The Green Triad
The Blue Triad
The Ironlords
The Gate

Additional titles available in all e-book formats at Smashwords.com (Short Stories):
"A Box of Magic"
"And To All A Good Night"
"Masque of Moonlight and Shadows"
"Return of the King"
"Trick'ed Treat"

CONTENTS

PROLOGUE

OPERATION ON WINGS OF EAGLES

A.K.A.

OPERATION MAGIC CARPET

"You yourselves have seen what I did to Egypt, and how I bore you on wings of eagles, and brought you to Myself." Exodus, 19:4

"But those who hope in the Lord will renew their strength. They will soar on wings like eagles; they will run and not grow weary, they will walk and not be faint." Book of Isaiah 40:31

In May of 1948, Israel, still called Palestine on the maps of the world, jumped the gun and threw the United Nations into turmoil by bypassing all arguments for and against and declared itself an independent state.

Jews around the world heeded the call to return to their ancient homeland. In China, displaced refugees from Hitler's persecution and Stalin's equally lethal, if less well-publicized, pogroms[1], huddled in ghettos in

Shanghai to escape Mao's communist army and prayed for rescue.

In the country known as Yemen—when it was known at all—dwelt several tribes of almost-forgotten Jews who according to one legend had followed the Queen of Sheba from Jerusalem back to her homeland. Lost among the Arabic and fiercely Islamic inhabitants, the Yemenite Jews had existed in virtual isolation for centuries, living lives of near-servitude, persecution, and utter misery.

Now at last, they heard the call they had awaited for two thousand years: a king named David[2] had returned to the Holy Land, and it was time for the scattered tribes to return to Israel. They packed up their ancient scrolls, their Torahs, their small belongings, and trekked across miles of trackless desert and barren, robber-infested mountains toward the ancient port city of Aden within the British Protectorate, where a refugee camp had been established.

Meanwhile, in an event that didn't even make the news back in the States, a tiny, struggling American airline known as Alaska Airlines bid on and won a charter privately financed by the American Jewish Joint Distribution Committee (JDC) in New York to ferry stranded and endangered Jews to their new homeland. With inadequate aircraft and virtually no preparation, pilots and crew undertook an incredible feat of humanitarianism, risking their own lives every time they lifted from the runways in Aden or Shanghai to fly planeloads of Jewish refugees through Muslim territory to the besieged new nation. Warren Metzger, Marian Liscomb, Bob Maguire, Clark Cole, Sam Silver, Larry Currie, Elgen Long, Bob Platt and others took on what they thought was just another dicey job, little suspecting that they were about to create a new aviation legend.

Hired by Alaska Airlines only a few months before, Warren Carl Metzger had just finished flying the Berlin Airlift and was one of several pilots to accept the offer of another more dangerous mission. He knew just enough of the region to be aware that the country of Yemen existed, and he wondered if what the newspapers said was true: the Yemenite Jews were the legendary "Lost Tribe" of Israel. It was a chance to fly as Captain of one of the great C-46s he'd helped modify for the task and to be involved in the making of history. It seemed to him that, after two thousand years, the Jews had been given a mighty tough row to hoe. He wanted to see for himself what was going on "over there."

Marian Frances Liscomb jumped at the chance to fly as a stewardess on the trips from Shanghai and Hong Kong in rescuing Jews fleeing the Chinese Communists and getting them to Israel. She recognized the danger, but the pull of humanitarianism—and the lure of adventure—was strong; danger added spice to life. True to her Irish heritage, she never backed down from a good fight.

In doing so, they helped fulfill a more than two thousand years old prophecy: they bore the scattered children of Israel to the Holy Land "on wings of eagles."

And they started an adventure of their own: a romance that was to last the rest of their lives.

1. A pogrom is a violent riot aimed at the massacre or persecution of an ethnic or religious group, particularly a riot aimed at the massacre or persecution of Jews. The term originally entered the English language in order to describe 19th-and 20th-century attacks on Jews in the Russian Empire. Similar attacks against Jews at other times and places also became retrospectively known as pogroms. https://en.wikipedia.org/wiki/Pogrom
2. David Ben-Gurion, first Prime Minister of Israel.

CHAPTER ONE:
WARREN

Everybody who knew him liked Warren Metzger. He was easy enough to like: tall, a little too thin, handsome in a boy-next-door sort of way, with an often disorderly thatch of black hair and twinkling eyes that every year lost more of their childhood brown and edged further toward green. He had a natural warmth and genuine kindness in him that people instinctively responded to. He laughed easily at himself as often as anything else and spontaneously generated a seemingly bottomless supply of puns and jokes he was apt to spring on anyone who didn't get away fast enough.

He had a beautiful singing voice but was more likely to burst out in a Spike Jones classic—complete with sound effects—or an off-color sea chantey than one of the sentimental love songs popular in his youth, or the lovely, melodious hymns his mother encouraged her boys to learn.

Like the classic absentminded professor, he was always losing socks, keys, and lighters, spilling food on books or his clothes, or forgetting to change out of his best shirt before working on his car. Women found these little quirks either endearing or exasperating; more than one promising romance dissolved in the wake of one of his unconscious gaffs.

However, all habits of distraction vanished in the cockpit of an airplane. In the sky, he was focused, alert, fully engaged and joyfully alive in a way he never managed when earthbound. "There's nothing else like it," he wrote to a friend in a burst of uncharacteristic enthusiasm. "I'd rather fly an OX-5 [an early plane engine almost universally loathed by pilots] than drive a new Rolls Royce."

In 1948, he was twenty-nine years old and had already flown more types of aircraft and put in more hours in most of them than many pilots a decade older. Once in the air with him, other pilots quickly saw past the boyish, good-natured clown and learned to respect his skills, reflexes, and judgment.

"Warren was a hell of a pilot," said Chuck Spaeth, a friend and fellow pilot voicing an opinion universal among those who flew with Warren.

'Smokey' Schnee, another fellow aviator retired from Alaska Airlines, concurred. "He was an incredible pilot. He could handle a plane with a touch like a feather, like it was part of his body."

Growing up in Alberta, Canada, Warren couldn't remember when he hadn't wanted to fly. A neighboring rancher with the last name of Ross had owned a plane, using it to cover the distance between his remote property and the nearest real towns, Stirling or Maybutt, once or twice a month (Lethbridge was actually closest, but it hardly fit the definition of a town). Each time that plane flew over the endless, rolling acreage where Warren tended the family cattle or labored in the wheat and hay fields, he would stop and look up, mouth agape, filled with a sense of excitement and longing that went bone-deep. The open plains of Alberta, where the Rocky Mountains were only a blue-hazed rumor on the horizon, were nothing to the wide-open skies above, where only birds and God dwelt. He belonged up there. He just knew it.

His parents—George Lewis ("Lew" to everyone, including his wife) and Elsie Metzger—were less than thrilled with the prospect.

Lew and Elsie both came from a long line of farm and ranch stock in their native Ohio, where they had grown up on neighboring farms. Lew had older brothers to inherit his father's spread, and buying a sufficient amount of land on his own was out of the question. He worked hard and saved his money, but even at the very dawn of the twentieth century, Ohio was settled, civilized and coveted ground. Nothing affordable appeared in the surrounding region.

Just a few hundred miles north, land was plentiful and considerably less expensive. Hearing of an abandoned farm with neighboring, virtually untouched acreage in Alberta, Lew said goodbye to his then-fiancée, Elsie Limbaugh, and headed north. The land was as perfectly situated as rumor claimed.

Lew promptly bought several thousand acres with his own savings, boosted by loans from his parents and other relatives. He built the initial house, barn and outbuildings before sending for Elsie. They married quietly at the Maybutt United Church, rolled up their sleeves, and set to work.[1]

Elsie popped out Earl, the eldest son, in 1915, then Glen in 1917, and finally Warren in 1919, and then took in a niece, Mary Duncan, to raise as her own. She brought them up in a sturdy, dirt-floor house without running water or electricity. She also fed and managed a rotating crew of hired hands, raised turkeys for her own income, and kept a large garden to feed the household.

Lew experimented with other crops, but his mainstays were cattle and wheat, and he did well with them. He paid off the initial loans, built up a moderate savings, acquired more acreage, and made improvements on his investment. When his sons were old enough to help, he built a second, larger house with wooden floors and, eventually, electricity. He moved in his growing family, letting the head hand and his family take over the original house.

Lew and Elsie were of the same mind: farming and ranching were respectable, time-honored occupations with a guaranteed future. Land was wealth. When you had land, you were someone. And you would never, ever starve. The greatest things parents could give their children were a solid future, meaningful work, and a path to a good life if not to fabulous wealth. Lew, never forgetting the lessons of his youth, planned to divide his land among his three sons.

If Earl and Glen ever thought to set their feet upon another path, they suppressed those yearnings early on and settled more-or-less peacefully into the role of future farmers under apprenticeship to Lew. Glen took to it better than Earl, but both became successful farmers and ranchers, building onto what Lew had begun. A family photo taken when the three boys were in their teens shows Earl and Glen already looking like farmers; younger and less-weathered versions of Lew. Warren, standing in the back, looks slightly out of place; the cuckoo in the Metzger nest.

Warren was different. As a child, he built make-believe planes out of logs and lumber scraps, and wore an aviator's helmet and scarf as he sat astride the rough bark. His imitation of the engine's noise was sometimes so loud that, when his mother called everyone in to supper from the porch, she would then have to go out behind the barn and almost shout into his ear before he heard her.

Despite its questionable suitability in the bitter cold Canadian winters, Warren sometimes wore the helmet for the ride to school aboard one of the horses. He dressed his dog, Teddy, in it—complete with scarf and goggles—for family photos.

He even tried to convince some of the horses to wear wooden wings and play airplane. Most apparently went along with it except for Babe. "Babe and I," Warren wrote, "had a mutual dislike for each other." Horses and boy seemed to have survived the experience intact. Let his brothers have the farm, till the soil and watch the weather; he had his head in the clouds and his dreams higher still. Somehow, some way, he was determined to make them into reality.

But flying lessons and airplanes cost money. Lew and Elsie loved their sons, but justifying the expense was as far beyond the family budget as it was beyond their ken. Warren would have to find his own way.

He studied hard under Miss Jedson at the local one-room schoolhouse and got good grades, hoping to be accepted into the Royal Military College in Ontario, the Canadian equivalent of Westpoint. From there, it would be a straight shot to the Royal Canadian Air Force and earning his wings as a pilot.

As graduation neared, his hard-won letter of acceptance finally arrived. There was one hitch: he needed three years of Latin, and he'd only completed two. He could make it up with an approved class offered through summer school, but this meant being held back until Second Round.

Swallowing his disappointment, he signed up for summer classes but hedged his bets by applying to Tri-State University in Indiana as well. Tri-State had a top-notch Aeronautical Engineering program, and that was a path to the sky that even his parents acknowledged might be worth the effort. Even during the depths of the Great Depression, which Canada had not evaded, Engineers could find jobs and make a decent living.

Lew and Elsie were not happy with either choice, but losing Warren to a career outside of farming was beginning to look infinitely better than losing him to the Royal Canadian Air Force. By 1936, the clouds of war were gathering over Europe. Canada, still by-and-large a loyal member of the British Empire, watched with growing apprehension as Germany kicked sand in England's face over and over again, taunting what was then the world's only super power. Led by determined pacifists, England kept hunching its shoulders and turning the other cheek while Germany flexed its growing muscle and swallowed Europe in bite-sized chunks.

In Lethbridge and the surrounding farms, at church, at the local feed stores, at the grocers and the cattle lots, Lew and Elsie and their neighbors debated the great events occurring across the water. Just how far would Baldwin let Chancellor Hitler go? And how long would it be before the situation changed? If England went to war, there was no doubt in anyone's mind that Canada would do her duty and send her sons to fight.

Lew and Elsie had never surrendered their American citizenship, but Earl, Glen, and Warren had been born on Canadian soil, subjects of the Crown as well as U.S. citizens. They were vulnerable.

A kindly fate dealt Warren an ace. He received a letter of acceptance to Tri-State University in the fall semester and planned on leaving the following Sunday for Indiana. Another letter from the Royal Military College followed before his plans were fixed. An opening had occurred, and he was accepted into the First Round. Classes started immediately; if he were to accept, it would mean leaving that Saturday.

It was an opportunity not to be missed, and few children could pass up such a fortuitous, God-given shot at parental blackmail.

Warren laid both letters before his parents. Elsie and Lew knew what the letters signified: if Warren went to the Royal Military College, he'd graduate as an officer in the Royal Canadian Air Force and very possibly face German planes in the skies over Europe shortly thereafter. Baldwin had been replaced by Chamberlain as Prime Minister of England, but Chamberlain's appeasement policies had proved no more successful against

Herr Hitler than had Baldwin's. Lew and Elsie's memories of the horrors of World War I were still vivid. Neither wanted that future for their sons.

Warren played his ace. "If I can have money for flying lessons," he told them, "I'll go to Indiana."

His parents made the best of a bad bargain and paid. Warren sent a letter to the Royal Military College telling them to offer the position to another hopeful candidate. He set out for Tri-State and the skies above Indiana. Taking flying lessons between classes, he soloed in 1938 and received his pilot's license the same year in Angola, Indiana.

Warren excelled, graduating with a Bachelor of Science in Aeronautical Engineering in 1940. And promptly joined the Royal Canadian Air Force.

To assuage parental fears, he transferred to the U.S. Army Air Corps in 1941. That conciliatory act landed him soon after in Houston, Texas, forever after synonymous in his mind with miserable heat, smothering humidity, and cockroaches the size of his father's draft horses.

.   .   .

"High Flight" is quite possibly every pilot's favorite poem. Written by John Gillespie Magee, Jr., of the Royal Canadian Air Force shortly before his death in 1941, it speaks for all pilots but most especially the eager young military pilots of the early days of World War II, when aviation was shaking the last dew from its wings and proving itself to the skeptical old school military establishment. Given the same literary leanings and gifts, any one of those eager young men could have written it, for it put into words the passion every one of them carried in his heart. Almost to a man, they lived to fly, any time they could, any way they could.

All planes were a way to the heavens, but every pilot developed his preferences. In some cases, those preferences were determined by physical limitations. The pilots of fighter planes tended to be physically smaller to squeeze into the cockpits of the day. Bombers were bigger, and so therefore were their pilots. The speed and agility of the smaller planes was a heart-stopping, adrenaline-pumping thrill, but the gravity-defying raw power and majesty of the "big birds" won their share of admirers and addicts as well.

A rush of aggression that overwhelmed judgment could save a fighter jock's life but could get a bomber pilot and his entire crew killed. Lacking a fighter plane's maneuverability, a bomber required steady nerves and a cool head at the controls.

At six-foot-two-inches in his bare feet, Warren could barely squeeze himself into a fighter plane. He proved able to keep a steady hand and a detached calm under the most trying conditions his instructors could throw at him. He was a natural for bomber training. Commissioned in May of 1942, he went to Kelly Field in San Antonio, Texas, for six weeks of advanced training in the B-10, A-20, B-34 and—his personal favorite—the Martin B-26.

From there, he shipped off to El Paso. He'd been assigned to tow targets for anti-aircraft guns in between flying reconnaissance missions, hunting for German subs in the Caribbean and the Gulf of Mexico. With the posting came another, far juicier opportunity: an offer to test-fly experimental aircraft.

Warren couldn't believe his luck. To be among the first to fly newer, bigger, faster, more powerful airplanes? It was every pilot's dream come true!

The choice cost him dearly. On August 19, 1942, Warren taxied down the runway behind the sluggish controls of a fighter-style plane equipped with a new "remote control" piloting system[2]; he was supposed to take over if it failed.

Like many autopilots even today, this one relied on vacuum powered gyroscopes to stabilize the aircraft. The chief weakness of this particular installation was an unfortunate tendency for the gyroscope to "tumble" at slow speeds and high bank angles, conditions regularly encountered on an approach to landing. So it was that, upon being turned to "final" at little more than 100 feet of altitude, Warren's plane suddenly lost its kinship with the sky and turned back into several thousand pounds of metal, rubber, and wire; remote control died and took the manual controls with it. The plane bucked, shuddered, and spun down, smashing into the runway and scattering pieces of itself across the harsh Texas landscape.

The knowledge that he had no control over his craft and that he was going to die hit at the same moment, but the trip down was too fast for fear. A fleeting thought whipped through his mind: "So this is what it was like for J.J." —J.J. Lamb, Warren's best friend, had died in a similar crash in March. The ground smashed into him like a giant fist; the thunder of impact and the shriek of dying metal drowned out thought. The belts and harnesses tore free, and he was flung from the spinning wreckage to tumble along beside it in a terrible, unstoppable dance.

He never lost consciousness; he was aware of a horrifying, jarring pain; the feeling that something inside was twisting, bending, tearing in ways the human body was never meant to endure. Sun and earth spun around him like a whirlwind, as if a tornado held him in its grip. And then the sky was above him. The cruel August sun seared down on his lacerated flesh like a brand with the side of his face pressed against the hard, unyielding earth.

After a while, he heard voices and sirens. Real or imagined? He could not tell. His head still seemed filled with the cacophony of the crash. Someone spoke overhead, high-pitched and frantic. "Metzger? Metzger? You alive? Jesus Christ, he's alive!" Someone else moaned over and over, "Oh my God, oh my God—" He wanted to tell them he was all right but couldn't answer, couldn't make the words come. It was a lie anyway; he was hurt and he knew it, but they sounded so damned upset.

Discipline overrode horror. Other voices barked out orders. One of the mechanics knelt over him, spreading his arms and his shirt over Warren's head in a pathetic attempt to shield him from the sun. Someone else assured him over and over that an ambulance was on the way. Sirens wailed, help finally arrived, and he was whisked off to the hospital.

In the weeks that followed, Warren thought more than once that he'd have been better off if he'd died with his aircraft. Repeated operations—piecing together bones like jigsaw puzzles and fusing vertebrae—were unable to fully restore feeling and function to his legs or ease the constant pain. Increasingly heavy doses of morphine helped somewhat, until he realized he was looking forward to his daily allowance and asked the doctors to cut him off.

Strangely, it wasn't until his prospects looked darkest that he rallied. Warren didn't have much of a temper, at least not by the standards of his more volatile family. But when the doctors told him he would most likely never walk again, fury overrode his pain-filled lassitude and drove him to prove them wrong.

Months later, he took his first shaky steps under his own volition. The doctor in charge of his case updated the warning: "Be grateful you can walk; that's enough of a miracle for one lifetime. You'll never fly again."

Nearly a year after the crash, Warren walked out of the hospital and climbed back into the cockpit of a plane. He looked like a walking skeleton. His right leg, withered to little more than bone, never regained flesh and remained weak for the rest of his life. He was never cleared to return to combat duty nor test pilot status, but at least he was allowed to fly. He spent his flight hours towing targets and teaching other pilots.

Among his other assignments, he was given command of a squad of WASP recruits in Sweetwater. He found the experience enlightening. On the one hand, he felt that women pilots were being given short shrift; their skills were comparable to male pilots on every level, but they were rarely given the chance to prove it, adequate compensation, or even the basic safety considerations that their male counterparts expected and enjoyed. Much like the few Negro pilots he encountered, women pilots were definitely treated as "second-class citizens." It grated against his natural sense of fairness.

On the other hand, the WASPS were under the protection of the flamboyant aerial pioneer Jackie Cochran, whose love affair with General "Hap" Arnold was considered a secret only in polite company. Just as open a secret was the unofficial order which came down from General Arnold that no woman pilot could possibly be found guilty of "pilot error." Warren found the inevitable return of his reports, with demands that he revise his conclusions about the reasons for various mishaps, infuriating. And every bit as unjust to the male pilots as unthinking prejudice was to the women.

Warren was careful not to cross the lines of rank with his female subordinates. Not that some of them weren't attractive or showed no interest in the handsome young officer, but he wasn't willing to risk the consequences of discovery. Not all of his fellow commanders were as scrupulous.

One such commander, embroiled in an affair with a WASP whom Warren thought to be one of the worst pilots he'd ever encountered, concealed her incompetence in his reports. This happened despite the resulting and—to Warren—appalling number of accidents. He couldn't bring himself to squeal on his friend, but he bent his efforts to persuading the other man to at least keep the young lady out of the air. For a short time, it worked.

One day, several of Warren and his counterpart's superior officers, some of whom loudly harbored severe doubts as to the wisdom and viability of the entire program, came to the hanger for an inspection. Immaculately turned out, Warren and his co-commander squired their superiors from hanger to planes to barracks, which were, of course, in perfect order. All seemed to be going well.

As they strode across the tarmac on the way back to the hanger, the WASP in question planted herself belligerently in front of them, fists planted on shapely hips. Glaring at her erstwhile lover, she announced loudly and in full earshot of the other officers, "I can fly, too, you know."

No one wanted the publicity of a court-martial. Warren's friend vanished—probably to spend the rest of his military career in a Quonset hut at Point Barrow watching for unauthorized flights over the North Pole. The young lady departed the WASPs. After a brief investigation, Warren was absolved from complicity but found himself re-assigned to other duties.

For a while, he continued to hold his own, passing his flight tests, periodically requesting to be returned to combat duty or test-pilot status, while the war roared past beyond the horizons on all sides. In late autumn of 1944, it looked like his patience was finally rewarded. He was sent to Louisiana to take combat training in the Martin B-26 Marauder.

Six months of grueling physical training brought heretofore concealed weaknesses to light. His half-healed body wasn't working right, and he could no longer hide it from his superiors. He was sent to William Beaumont Hospital in El Paso for more operations and various treatments.

Finally, Warren had enough; he was given honorable discharge in June of 1945 and started looking for a civilian career in aviation.

He took a job selling Hudson automobiles to make ends meet; he firmly believed they were the best car on the road, a conviction in which he was probably correct. This helped make up for his natural lack of aggression when it came to snaring potential customers.

His enthusiasm for the car remained undimmed. For the rest of his life, he was never without a Hudson or two. However, the experience of selling them confirmed in him two things: that God had never intended him to be a salesman, and that he just could not face a life on the ground. He spent the better part of a year sending resume after resume into circulation, knocking on every door he could think of and hoping one of them would open.

Finally, one did. World Wide Aviation hired him to ferry a C-47 from England to Montreal, where it was to undergo an overhaul at the Air Canada factory to be reborn as a DC-3, suitable for civilian use.

The initial flight led to a steady job ferrying assorted former military aircraft—newly refitted and customized —from the factory to their new owners around the world. Warren found himself living in Montreal and flying from there to Oslo, Brussels or London, or from Montreal to South America or South Africa, or dozens of other destinations that had heretofore been only names on maps to him. Aircraft of every variety made their way in and out of the Air Canada factory, and from there to his capable hands. It was, in many ways, a pilot's dream job. There was one drawback, and as time passed, it became more and more difficult to ignore.

Between assignments, there were sometimes weeks of down time. Of course, he didn't get paid during those times, but more importantly, he loathed Montreal with a passion that grew in proportion to the amount of time he had to spend there awaiting assignments. Though Charles de Gaulle's infamous "Vive le Québec libre!" speech to French Canadians was twenty years in the future, the separatist movement was already strong in Montreal. French Canadians bitterly resented their fellow Canadians of English persuasion and vice-versa. Warren felt more like an unwanted foreigner than he had in South America—though at least the French Canadians hadn't thrown him in jail for failing to pay a bribe, as had happened to him once in Argentina.

He couldn't quite bring himself to actively look for another job, where he would be far less likely to fly virtually brand-spanking-new airplanes to exotic locations all over the world. He loved the opportunities to meet up with other pilots everywhere he landed, usually friends or acquaintances from his war days. However large on a global scale, aviation was, after all, a relatively small community. And he was hardly unaware of the advantages that being a young, handsome pilot gave him as far as the opposite sex was concerned. Women threw themselves at him on a regular basis, and he was more than happy to catch them. But it grew harder and harder to make the return trip to Montreal, where he felt utterly alone and isolated.

He settled into a semi-stable relationship with a young lady named Kay. Greatly daring and in defiance of the prevailing social mores of the times, the two eventually moved in together, though they kept the relationship discreet. But neither of them was ready for marriage. Since both held jobs that required frequent travel (just as well; Kay hated Montreal as much as Warren did), the relationship fell into a comfortable holding pattern, despite Kay's desire for Warren to quit flying and find a more settled job in another city.

Aware that they were wasting Warren's talents when he wasn't in the cockpit, WWA began utilizing his other skills. They hired him to perform stress analysis on some of the planes. It wasn't flying, and it paid poorly, but at least it gave him a chance to use his degree. More importantly, it enabled him to get his name entered into the prestigious rosters of the Royal Society of Aeronautical Engineers. Who knew where that might lead? He no longer cared; just so it was out of Montreal.

During a brief layover in London, he ran into another pilot he knew from El Paso. Paul "P.D." Liscomb was a slight man with a soft voice and unassuming manner; few knew of the medals he'd won during the war, or that he was the pilot who had been awarded the singular honor of ferrying the Japanese delegates to the USS Missouri for Japan's surrender. Behind Paul's quiet exterior lay a wicked sense of humor and a gift for uttering unexpected witticisms or intricate puns with a completely straight face. Usually, these left his audiences blinking for a second or two, trying to decide if he were serious or figure out exactly what he'd said.

Since Warren had an equally powerful and unfortunate addiction to puns, they quickly sized one another up and cemented their friendship. They met seldom, but when they did, innocent bystanders ended up with sore ribs and streaming eyes.

Liscomb listened to Warren's complaints about his situation with some sympathy, since he'd spent time in Montreal himself, but he secretly thought Warren should be more appreciative. In Liscomb's opinion, anything was better than being out of work; a situation that seemed imminent in his own future. Airlines were popping up everywhere like mushrooms, but most died just as quickly. He'd already lost two such jobs in the last two years, and the freight company he currently flew for was about to go under as well. He'd just interviewed with a tiny company that had recently changed its name from Alaska Star Airlines to simply Alaska Airlines.[3] The company was in constant financial difficulty, making employment precarious at best, but he was grateful just to have the chance of a job. Steady flying jobs were scarce, and he had a wife and a very small son to support.

Liscomb didn't think too much about Warren's situation until a week or two later during a follow-up interview, when he learned that Alaska Airlines needed some stress analysis done as soon as humanly possible on a couple of C-46s the company was modifying for human transport. Liscomb mentioned to James Wooten, the new President of Alaska Airlines, that he happened to know someone listed in the Royal Society of Aeronautical Engineers who was looking for a job. Wooten listened, nodded, and looked up Warren's credentials. Then he picked up the phone.

Warren answered the phone on a bitter January day in 1948 and heard Jimmy Wooten's voice for the first time on the other end of the line. Wooten's pitch was simple and straightforward: would Warren be willing to move to Everett, Washington, and do some stress analysis for Alaska Airlines?

It wasn't a job as a pilot, but with a foot in the door, it could easily lead to one. And it would get him out of Montreal. "Hell, yes," said Warren.

1. Stirling Sunset Society, Stirling: its Story and People 1899-1980, Calgary: Friesen Printers, 1981.
2. The second aircraft in most new aviators' training progression was the Vultee BT-13, the "Vultee Vibrator" as it became known. A very successful trainer throughout WWII, it was adequately powered and agile but notoriously unforgiving. It was the platform for the system Warren was assigned to help test. Autopilots and remote control had been around since the first World War; nevertheless, the integration of those systems was still a work in progress in 1942.
3. The official abbreviation for Alaska Airlines is still ASA.

CHAPTER TWO: MARIAN

In 1922, the post-World War I generation was living the high life. The average income was $2,067, and a new car cost about $390.[1] The Teapot Dome scandal was just casting its shadow over the administrative accomplishments of President Harding, not yet dimming the shining glow of his progressive efforts on behalf of women's rights and the plight of people then referred to as the American Negroes.

For most people, the Great Depression wasn't even a shadow on the horizon, though already some economists were crying out that the Federal Reserve, created in 1913, was leading the U.S. down the path to ruin. In magazines and newspapers, the Save The Surface Campaign[1] ran advertisements that admonished the public:

> You owe it to the man without a job to find one for him, if you have work that needs to be done... every extra day's work you cause to be done now takes men off the streets; every dollar you use now for worth-while purposes puts money into circulation. Every dollar you put into circulation employs men

—checks business depression—hastens business prosperity.

It was a slow year for women in aviation, but two events worth noting did occur. Lilian Gatlin became the first woman to fly across the United States, accomplishing this feat in 27 hours and 11 minutes.[2] She was, however, only a passenger, despite her passionate devotion to aviation in general. Women pilots were still a rarity, and were to remain so for many years.

And Marian Frances Liscomb was born in a hospital in New Brighton, Pennsylvania.

Admittedly, few took note of this second momentous event. Paul Etheridge Liscomb and his wife, Mary, had been trying for another child since the birth of their son, Paul Darragh—known within the family as "Bun" and to outsiders as "P.D." —seven years earlier, and had all but given up. This second pregnancy had already lasted a full month beyond its natural term, and despite the doctor's reassurance, they were both concerned for the health of their little girl. Mary, especially, could not take her daughter's welfare for granted. She spent much of Marian's childhood hovering anxiously nearby, ready to spring into maternal action at a moment's notice. She needn't have worried, at least not on that score.

Baby Marian, a name soon shortened to "Babe," was a frisky little handful almost as soon as she entered the world, which she had done in her own time and on her own terms, foreshadowing what was to come.

Once she learned to walk, Babe wasted no time in evading the protective and watchful eyes of her mother and father, the three aunts who lived with them, and her older brother—and finding ways to get into trouble. Life in the formerly settled Liscomb household changed forever.

Both Paul and Mary came from socially prominent families, if somewhat astray from the main branches.

Mary's mother, Edith Darragh, was the only child of Thomas Lyon Darragh, a former riverboat captain who had gone on to become a wealthy and influential businessman. She was also the many-times-great-granddaughter of John Darragh, an Irish immigrant who became the second Mayor of Pittsburgh. Beautiful if somewhat tempestuous, Edith at sixteen had already established herself as a promising concert singer when she abruptly ran away from her well-placed home to elope with Harry Fry, the dashing heir to the Fry Glass fortune. Both sets of parents objected strenuously and expended large amounts of money and influence to see the marriage annulled. Chastened, Edith returned to her parents, who tried very hard to brush the entire affair under the rug.

She foiled their efforts to avoid scandal by producing a daughter, Mary Hurst Fry, a few months later. For a time, Edith seemed destined to a life in the shadows of society's censure. But then along came Charles Bayly, a rising politician who owned a music store in Washington D.C. He fell in love with her despite her somewhat questionable past and married her in short order.

Edith settled into the life of a politician's wife, playing the glamorous hostess for bigwigs from D.C., occasionally singing for charitable events, and producing baby Baylys, whom little Mary thought of as her brothers and sisters. Charles, however, never adopted her.

Mary never met or had any contact with her real father. As hard as she tried to fit into her stepfather's family, something was missing. She was quite literally the red-headed stepchild.

Paul Etheridge Liscomb's father, George, had been a raging and highly abusive alcoholic. "His booze had boxing gloves," said those who knew him. He ruled his household with an iron fist, driving his son to flee the house forever the second he came of age, and forbidding his daughters, Adessa and a younger daughter, another Mary, to consort with men or to marry. Mary

Liscomb rebelled and hit the stage, while Adessa sought her own fulfillment in scholastic endeavors, earning several degrees over the course of her long life. But both remained single, even after their father's death.

The young Paul used his intelligence and family connections to establish himself in a minor governmental position. As soon as he could afford a house, he invited his two sisters and another female relative, Hannah, to live with him and escape Papa Liscomb's brutality. His mother, Ella, joined them after George's death.

The five of them rubbed along happily enough for several years until Ella Liscomb's death. Paul's sister Mary left the stage and took a respectable and very highly-paid secretarial position. Adessa taught school for a time and then took a better-paying secretarial position with the school district.

Paul's job evidently paid well enough for him to dress in the latest fashions and regularly attend theater and sporting events. Handsome and dapper, he was a popular fellow who made friends easily, one of whom was Henry Arnold, whom he called "Benny," but who later became better known as General "Hap" Arnold. Like his pal Benny, Paul had an early fascination with airplanes and flight, though he never learned to fly.

Then Paul E. Liscomb met Mary Fry—quiet, pretty, and nearly two decades younger than he. He was smitten and, surprisingly, so was she. Perhaps she was searching for a father's love. For whatever reason, she married him in 1912 and moved in with him and the other Liscomb women. It was not a smooth adjustment.

The arrival of little Paul Darragh Liscomb, a.k.a. "Bun," in 1915 gave all the Liscomb women at least one common interest. They doted on the boy, a naturally well-behaved child who learned early the value of remaining outwardly docile and obedient.

But as little Bun grew, it became increasingly obvious that the family simply had to find new living arrangements. The Liscomb house in town wasn't big enough for a man and four women, let alone any children. His long-time friendship with a prominent lawyer named Stewart McConnell paid off with an offer to take over a house on Patterson Heights in Beaver Falls. "The Cottage" had once been part of a much larger estate originally owned by Harry Traver, the designer of some of the country's greatest roller coasters. McConnell had purchased what remained of the estate, including the original manor house, separated years previously from "the Cottage" by the tree-lined, brick-paved street.

"The Cottage" had a mere thirteen rooms, a full attic and basement, a broad staircase with stained-glass windows overlooking the landing, and a shaded porch wrapped around a third of the house. Ancient walnut, maple, and chestnut trees like those along the street shaded the expansive lawn. A gracious remnant of a passing era, "the Cottage" was ideal in every way. The Liscombs accepted with alacrity, purchased it, and moved in when Bun was four.

Baby Marian's arrival three years later was far from unwelcome, but she did rather upset the order of things. Being neither quiet, docile, nor obedient, "Babe" seemed to have more in common with her flamboyant grandmother than her gentle mother. Certainly, she did not share her mother's habit of yielding control to the strong-willed and forceful Paul Sr. Babe loved her father, but they fought a furious and life-long battle of wills, neither willing to give an inch.

For the most part, however, the Liscomb home was content. Even the ghosts—three the Liscombs knew of for certain—were benevolent specters who appeared now and again to move through the rooms and hallways in clothes of bygone eras, as if checking on the whereabouts and welfare of the current inhabitants. They only occasionally moved furniture or knick-knacks.

The ghosts didn't frighten Babe, who regarded them as just another of her home's secret delights. She never tired of exploring the house, especially the attic, de-spite it having been declared forbidden territory to her and her brother. The horded miscellany of generations of ancestors was stored up there; she came from a long line of packrats who found it difficult, if not im-possible, to throw anything away. She rummaged end-lessly, looking for mysterious treasures from the past and invariably found—and played with—such fabulous finds as antique pistols, knives, and swords. She found a cannon ball an ancestor had brought back from Get-tysburg and promptly rolled it down the elegant, curved stairs as an experiment. The damage cost a for-tune to repair, and Babe was severely punished. Gen-uinely contrite, she refrained from sneaking back into the attic for several weeks afterward.

Even as a very small child, she could successfully lose herself for hours, causing a great deal of anxiety and hand-wringing until she chose to re-appear. She found orphaned or injured animals and brought them home, hiding them in closets and drawers, where her mother and aunts invariably found them to their mu-tual and not always pleased surprise. Despite severe warnings and threats of dire punishment, she caught frogs in the neighbor's fishpond, trapped fireflies in jars, and followed copperhead snakes winding their way through the woods on the hill below the house, looking for their "hidey-holes."

Her mother all but despaired of ever turning her wild daughter into a proper lady. But it wasn't possible to stay angry with Babe. The mischievous sparkle in those big, hazel eyes, the dimpled smile, and the belly laugh that seemed too big for such a small body, in-variably melted adult anger. For all the chaos Babe brought to her long-suffering household, she was a charming child with a warm and generous heart, who grew into an increasingly pretty and charismatic young woman. She genuinely loved people and, invariably, they loved her back.

She loved the smell of her father's Lucky Strike and Chesterfield cigarettes. She started smoking when she was twelve, hiding in the basement where she was sure no one would notice. After catching her at it, her father forbade her to do it again, so she simply took her new vice into the attic instead. After catching her the second time, he forced her to smoke an entire pack at one sitting, thinking to make her sick. When that didn't work, he finally gave up. They compromised, and she agreed not to smoke in the house. By the time she was an adult, the sweet soprano voice she'd inherited from her mother and grandmother had devolved into a "whiskey baritone." It worked well for the blues, swing, and torch songs she preferred, however.

Her willfulness and sense of adventure backfired when she was fourteen. After having been forbidden to try the stunts with her bicycle that her brother and his friends regularly performed at her age, she took to practicing out of sight at a neighbor's. The resulting accident left her bedridden for the better part of a year and unable to hold down any food except for tiny amounts of Ovaltine.

Her mother saved her life, remaining almost ceaselessly by her bedside to keep a steady supply of the life-giving fluid trickling down her daughter's throat every hour.

The undiagnosed internal abscess finally burst as Babe was on her way to the operating table in a last-ditch effort to discover what was wrong. In a few months, she was fully recovered, though the experience cost her most of her teeth before she reached the age of 30, forcing her to wear dentures for the rest of her life.

The experience did little to curb her adventurous spirit or her boundless energy. Once she was restored to health, Babe was ready to tackle new adventures. One of those was starting up a neighborhood newspaper for which she sold advertising space, wrote articles, and drew whatever artwork was needed. She solicited articles from her parents' social and political connections and infused several of her friends with journalistic enthusiasm, sending them forth to garner tidbits from every corner of Beaver County. Eventually, she had over a hundred subscribers before school-work forced her to cut back her operation.

At some point before Marian was born, her father had become half-owner of a highly successful car dealership selling Buick, Studebaker, LaSalle, Plymouth, DeSoto, and Cadillac cars. The business suffered during the Great Depression, but the family continued to live comfortably, if not at the level of extravagance some of their friends and relatives enjoyed. Babe was able to indulge her love of horses; she showed Saddlebreds for high-end breeders from Virginia to New York and won countless ribbons on her own mare, Lady Esther. And when Bun was caught flying a neighbor's plane illegally at fourteen years old, Paul, instead of punishing the boy, contacted a friend with a small plane at Lake Chautauqua. Paul paid for lessons, so that Bun could legally earn his license.

Bun wasn't the only Liscomb to pick up his father's interest in aviation. Although Baroness Raymonde de Laroche had become the first woman to obtain a pilot's license in 1910, women pilots remained a rarity in 1939. When Babe demanded an equal chance to learn to fly, her father thought it a ridiculous request and refused. Undaunted, Marian took a job as neighbor Stewart McConnell's secretary at one dollar an hour and worked until she had enough money to pay for her own lessons.

She soloed in 1940 after her eighteenth birthday, the same year as her brother. When she proudly showed her new pilot's license to her father, he growled that it was a waste of money. But he secretly obtained a copy, had it framed, and gave it to her as a belated birthday present to hang on her bedroom wall.

The Great Depression had not yet released its grip on the country, and Marian very much wanted to keep

Lady Esther in oats and herself in the air. She tried finding a job as a pilot, even if it meant just carrying mail or dusting crops. Unfortunately, she found no one willing to take on a female pilot, at least not one with her limited experience. She took a turn as a singer for a local swing and jazz band, where her smoke-roughened voice served her well, but their few bookings didn't pay the bills, and she threw in the towel after a few months. She continued to show horses, but while the various owners and breeders were grateful, few of them paid her in actual money. More often, they simply added to her collection of trophies, tack or oats, though one breeder rewarded her with a second horse; a flashy strawberry roan gelding named Frost King, whom she called "Rusty."

Finally, she took a job at Curtis Wright in 1941 as a propeller inspector. This meant spending hours in a dark room examining x-rays of new propellers, looking for defects. The job paid well enough but lacked any semblance of excitement, and the factory was hardly a wellspring of glamour. At that time, no one knew or cared about the effects of long-term x-ray exposure, but Babe complained of eyestrain and headaches; she lost weight and her rosy complexion paled from all those hours sitting in the dark.

The Great Depression ended abruptly and at long last, thanks to a most unwelcome savior: the attack at Pearl Harbor, which pulled the U.S. into the bloody embrace of World War II. Nonetheless, Marian was as eager as every other young American to do her part. She tried to join the Women's Flying Training Detachment, which later merged with the Women's Auxiliary Ferrying Squadron to become the Women Airforce Service Pilots, or WASPs. To her great disappointment, she was turned down. Only much later did she learn that her father and brother, who was by then an officer in the Army Air Corps, had undermined her. Both had used their mutual influence with General Arnold (whose relationship with Jackie Cochran, the WASPs flamboyant "queen bee," was not exactly a secret), to ensure Marian's application was rejected. Marian spent the war years crouched in the darkroom at Curtis Wright, staring at X-rays of propellers while dreaming of the sky.

Marian's best friend, Meck—Madeline Mecklem, the daughter of one of her mother's friends—also worked at Curtis Wright in the "white collar" section of the upper offices. On sunny days, the two girls spent their lunch breaks at the municipal swimming pool, conveniently located a short distance from the plant.

On a summer day in 1945, a day Marian later referred to as "the beginning of my life,"[3] they were lounging by the pool when what looked like a DC-3 flew overhead.

"There's something I'd like to do," said Meck, pointing upward.

Marian opened one eye, following her friend's finger to the plane. "Fly a plane?"

"Frankly, yes." Meck, following Marian's lead, was working on obtaining her pilot's license. "But actually, I was thinking about being an Airline Hostess."

The idea had never occurred to Marian; it suddenly seemed like a great one, or the next best thing to being a pilot.

"Where would you like to go, and with what company?"

Meck laughed. "I never really thought about it. I guess I'd like to see the world first, then maybe Mars, or the moon..."

Marian snorted and jumped to her feet, quickly hauling Meck to hers. "Come on, let's get back to the salt mines."

Inwardly, however, a new dream was taking shape. Meck might be kidding, but Marian had already decided: if she couldn't get into the sky one way, then there was always another. Becoming an Airline Hostess sounded like just the ticket.

A few weeks later, World War II effectively ended. Though Bun was still three weeks away from ferrying the Japanese dignitaries to the USS Missouri to sign the documents of surrender, the fighting was officially over. Curtis Wright celebrated by closing the Beaver plant, and Marian was suddenly out of a job.

She donned a tailored wool suit that showed off her shapely figure, and she and Meck drove to Pittsburgh, where she knew two major airlines had branch offices. They applied at Pennsylvania Central and TWA, and went back to Beaver Falls to wait.

Pennsylvania Central—shortly to become Capital Airlines—responded first and gave them an interview date with the Chief Hostess, who would be in Pittsburgh specifically for that purpose. When the big day arrived, the girls dressed to the nines. This time they took the train to Pittsburgh, arriving breathlessly at the William Penn Hotel only to find twenty or thirty other girls already waiting.

One by one, the applicants were ushered into a private room. The rest waited, growing increasingly nervous. But once in the presence of the Chief Hostess, Marian's terror vanished.

"She was a very good-looking girl," Marian recalled, "with the ability to put you at your ease immediately." The interview process was far more extensive than Marian had assumed. "I learned later that there were about twelve hundred girls interviewed in a three-day period, and out of these were chosen nineteen. I was one of those lucky nineteen."[3]

Meck wasn't as lucky that day but later interviewed for TWA and was accepted there for Hostess training. Meanwhile, Marian was told to return the next day to take some examinations that were necessary to qualify for a position as Hostess.

"There were twenty-one of us there to take these tests," she later recalled, "and there were almost as many tests there to take us." She dug in, working furiously for hours. "There were intelligence tests and personality tests and ability tests and tests to see whether you could pass the tests."

She thought she did well but couldn't be sure, and when it was all over, she learned she would have to wait to find out. She waited for over a week.

Just as she thought her nerves would snap, a letter finally arrived. She opened it with shaking hands, afraid to read the verdict. The response, however, was what she'd prayed for. "I was to report to Washington, D.C., to begin my Hostess training December 1st, and would I please arrive a day or so early so that I could be settled and ready to work in school the morning of the first. I would, and did."

Reluctantly, she sold Rusty, arranged for a fellow equestrienne whom she trusted to look after Lady Esther, kissed her parents good-bye and dashed off to Washington D.C. in a frenzy of excitement. She breezed through classes for the first two weeks until her turn for the required physical examination came up. This, she knew, would be a problem.

Capital Airlines had a maximum height requirement of five feet, six inches, and a minimum of five feet, two inches. In her bare feet, Marian stood just over five foot one. She'd "fudged" by an inch on her application, but now she'd have to make good.

The physician running the examinations was a man still a few years shy of middle age. On the day of the exam, Marian lined up against a wall with the other girls while the doctor carefully measured them against pre-drawn marks on the wall. Just before he reached her, she stealthily released the top button on her blouse and widened the neckline as much as she dared without being too obvious. When he reached her, she looked directly into his eyes, smiled, and silently drew in a deep breath.

The doctor had seen a lot of very pretty girls over the previous two weeks, but few with Marian's combination of beauty, curves, and high-wattage smile. He smiled back and utterly failed to notice that she'd risen up on her toes just far enough to achieve the minimum height.

Hostess school was not for the weak. The girls were required to study the history of aviation, the theory of flight, aerodynamics, and the differences in makes and models of airplanes. They studied weather patterns, radio ranges, first aid, and maps, particularly those covering routes flown by Capital. They also had complete courses in psychology in respect to dealing with the public, and a great many of the graces that were once part of what was called "charm school."

"The idea," Marian recalled, "was that we were to think of the airplane as our own living rooms, and our passengers as invited and welcome guests therein."

Simply walking in high heels down the aisle of an airborne DC-3 was a challenge in and of itself, and required some training to achieve with panache.

Marian's pilot's license gave her an edge over the majority of her classmates in the eyes of her instructors in any event, but her vivacity and personal charisma made her something of a classroom star. She was enormously popular with the other girls as well as her teachers, and graduated with the highest possible marks.

Her first flight was an overnighter to Chicago. She'd heard cautionary tales of the practical jokes regularly played on new girls, and kept a wary eye on the rest of the flight crew. Fortunately, Captain Fogelman, the pilot, treated her with kindness and courtesy, which meant none of the rest of the crew thought to make her first flight anything other than it should be.

Weather grounded them in Chicago for two days, during which Fogelman, his co-pilot, and two other Capital Airline crews stuck there made an effort to show "the new girl" the town. Marian spent two fun-filled days seeing the sights and eating at some of the best restaurants in Chicago.

On that flight was also a young Captain of the Infantry, known as Jock to his friends, who asked to see Marian the next time they were both in D.C. She agreed and thought nothing of it until two weeks later. By that time, she'd flown multiple trips—primarily to Chicago and Norfolk—and considered herself a veteran of the line. But she'd spent little enough time in D.C., where she was based, that she still hadn't seen much of it. So when Jock called and asked her out on a sight-seeing trip, she eagerly accepted. The two began seeing each other regularly, though Marian dated other men in D.C. and other cities on her regular flight routes.

She fell out of love with D.C. after a man tried to mug her, grabbing her from behind as she was walking home after a late night landing. Her hot temper saved her. Furious rather than frightened, she drove her elbow into his solar plexus hard enough to double him over and make him lose his grip. She whipped off one of her heavy-heeled "baby doll" shoes that were then the height of fashion and pummeled him savagely, lashing him with every vile insult and expletive she'd ever heard but never before allowed to pass her lips. The man fled, arms wrapped around his head, and Marian chased him for two blocks, whapping him as often as she could get within reach and cursing him every step of the way. He was a big man, and finally outran his tiny, terrible pursuer.

Learning of the incident, her brother bought her a .32 revolver for protection. It was a hammerless antique made in the late 1800s and had a trigger-pull so stiff that she found it impossible to hit anything more than a few feet away. She rarely carried it and was never attacked again. But she was quite ready to leave D.C.

Jock's attentions grew more insistent, and he proposed after having known her just under three weeks. He would soon be leaving to return to his duty in Japan for a few months, but then his term in the army would be over. He very much wanted to know that Marian would be waiting for him.

Touched and genuinely flattered, she said, "yes... maybe." After a few more dates, Jock left, and she found she wasn't nearly as certain of herself—or of him.

She'd insisted that she continue to date other men, and Jock reluctantly agreed, though he could not understand why. Marian wouldn't tell him, but it had little to do with her enjoyment of being squired around by a series of handsome young men smitten with her charms.

"The truth of the matter," she later confessed, "was that unless we girls had dinner dates, we didn't eat many dinners. All of us had lived at home and had been working at well-paying jobs before we joined the airline, and we now found that our meager pay simply would not stretch to include food every day of the week."[3] Marian's staple daily diet between dates consisted primarily of two cookies and an orange.

Over the following weeks, the more dates Marian had, the more she realized that she was far from being ready to settle down. The war years had robbed her of the good times a girl her age should have enjoyed, and she wanted to make up for them.

When Jock returned a few weeks later, having been held up in California to await discharge instead of sent on to Japan, she told him that the engagement was a mistake. Jock took it as well as he could, and after trying to persuade her to change her mind, settled for her promise that if she was ever in Norfolk for any length of time, where he was bound and where his parents lived, she would call him.

Two weeks later, Capital called her at three o'clock in the afternoon and informed her that she was being transferred to Norfolk indefinitely. She needed to be on the six o'clock evening flight. After a mad scramble, she made the flight and arrived in Norfolk with all her worldly belongings in two suitcases, happy to be out of D.C. but having no idea where she was going to live.

The airline put her up in a hotel for the night, and then she was sent on a series of trips; when she finally returned to Norfolk, she remembered her promise to Jock and called him. He promptly set her up with a female friend named Vida who needed a roommate. Vida and she took an instant liking to one another, and Marian pulled her suitcases out of storage and moved in that day.

Delighted to have that problem solved, she cheerfully accepted Jock's invitation to come to his parents' place for dinner and to "meet the folks."

Jock's parents were as nice as he was, and she enjoyed the company as much as she did the home-cooked meal. A young lady boarder named Lucy joined them for dinner, and Marian soon realized that Lucy was exactly right for Jock. The girl clearly adored him; she hung on his every word, though in typical male fashion he remained oblivious. His heart, still very much set on Marian, lay on his sleeve for all to see, but she knew with absolute certainty that she would never feel more for him than friendship. Healing the cracks she'd put in that openly offered heart would be ideal and would alleviate the lingering guilt she felt over the whole affair.

Her inner cupid awoke. Bringing Lucy and Jock together would solve everyone's problems all the way around, but how to go about it?

Over the next few weeks, during which she and Jock continued dating when she was in town, she started casually inviting Lucy to join them for picnics, parties, and other group gatherings. Lucy started being included on dinner dates, movies, and theater trips. Marian found reasons to leave Lucy alone with Jock while she slipped away for longer and longer periods.

Finally, Jock realized what Marian had known from the start. He proposed to Lucy, and Marian delightedly celebrated with the happy couple.

Her brother Bun, now going by "P.D." to the rest of the world, was flying for a freight line out of Oakland, California, and they met up in Chicago from time-to-time. After having grown up together, P.D. and Babe were finally getting to know one another as adults, and found they could be, not just brother and sister, but friends. She wrote, "The two of us were seeing more of each other than we had throughout the years of the war, and both of us enjoyed every minute of those meetings."

She almost always got a chance to see her parents and the long-suffering Lady Esther, if she spent more than a day in Pittsburgh or Washington D.C. Between visits, she wrote or called home regularly; even if she'd been the sort to suffer homesickness, she lacked the opportunity. Capital Airlines kept her busy, and life in the skies kept her happy. What more could a girl want?

Through one of her dates, she re-connected with Meck, who was now flying for TWA. The two finally got together in New York and spent two glorious days catching up, gossiping endlessly and regaling one another with tales of their adventures. When they once again parted ways, it was with many hugs, tears, and promises to "do this more often." Each went off to once again take to the air in their particular piece of the sky.

Marian loved her job, but after talking to Meck, she began to yearn to see places beyond the east coast routes covered by Capital. Many of the men she dated were from overseas or worked for other airlines that flew there. What would it be like to fly trips to London, Paris, Buenos Aires, and other locations more exotic than Norfolk or Knoxville? She knew her parents were still opposed to the very thought of her flying overseas, so she decided to wait for another year before trying her luck with another airline. Fate intervened before the year was up.

Stranded again by bad weather in Chicago, Marian accepted a dinner invitation from the flight's captain.

She knew that he and the Chief Hostess had been seeing each other regularly for months but thought nothing of it. After all, it was just dinner and a few laughs with pleasant company. What harm could that do?

Standards of propriety for unmarried women had relaxed considerably during WWII, but well-brought-up young ladies were still expected to be virgins on their wedding days. However secretly hopeful, men didn't automatically expect every evening's excursion with a girl to end in the sack. Marian had seen first-hand the consequences some of her friends suffered when they "slipped." Sharp cookie that she was, she understood the value of toeing the societal line. She loved life and enjoyed male company, but she did not consider herself a flirt. She sincerely believed that men just responded to her own natural friendliness and genuine interest in people.

So she was shocked when the Chief Hostess called her into the office on the return trip to D.C. and furiously accused Marian of "trying to steal her man." Marian thought the charge ridiculous and tried to reassure her at first, but more damage had been done to the romance than she knew. Her quick temper got the better of her, and she returned fire with both barrels.

Within moments, Marian was out of a job.

Devastated, she didn't immediately look for another Hostess position; what if the same thing happened again? Besides, Capital's Chief Hostess had friends throughout the airline industry. She refused to believe that her career was finished, but it might be better to wait until things died down a little.

She reluctantly took a job back in D.C. developing photos for the Photographic Development Company. It paid better than being an Air Hostess, and at least she could schedule regular visits to her family and spend time with her beloved Lady Esther. It was only temporary, she told herself. It had to be. She couldn't bear having her wings clipped. 1947 ended with Marian settled in a rented room and waiting for her chance to get back into the sky.

Near the end of 1947, her brother interviewed for a pilot's position with a small outfit called Alaska Airlines. Due to an unfortunate overlap between the ending of his old job and the new offer, he had to wait for another opening to come along. When a second chance came in the spring of 1948, he snapped it up and was officially hired. Thinking of Marian's plight, he promptly went to their Chief Stewardess—Alaska Airlines preferred that title to "Hostess"—who went by the unlikely sobriquet of Mimpy Crabtree and talked to her about his little sister. Alaska Airlines was chronically short-handed, most experienced stewardesses preferring the larger, more established and better-known airlines. Surely they'd be interested.

They were. P.D. left the office and, since he didn't have Marian's address, wrote to their mother, wanting to know if Marian wanted to fly for Alaska. Immediately upon receiving her mother's letter with her brother's news, Marian shot a telegram off to Mimpy. Mimpy promptly hired her sight unseen based on P.D.'s recommendation. It was by then late April or early May. She was to report on July first to the home office in Anchorage, Alaska.

Giddy with excitement, Marian quit her job and packed her bags. She made a final visit to Beaver Falls to spend some quality time with her folks and Lady Esther, and to get a few more hours in the air under her belt in a rental plane. Toward the end of June, she said goodbye to her parents, gave Lady Esther a final kiss on the nose, and made the journey to Paine Airfield in Everett, Washington to catch her flight to Anchorage.

Snohomish County had just re-claimed the airport from the military, and the airfield was still crowded with military aircraft and equipment, the wreckage of buildings being torn down, and the material and

equipment intended for new structures. The anticipated Alaska Airlines hanger was nothing but a flat ex-
panse of concrete surrounded by piles of lumber. Even
the passengers sometimes had trouble finding the
right planes for their destinations.

Marian expected to ride jump-seat, but apparently
no one had said anything to the Alaska Airlines employees in the tiny terminal. Not knowing what else to
do with her, they told her to wait with the passengers
and board when they did. She finally boarded the
plane only to find there were no vacant seats, and explained her dilemma to the stewardess. The girl bright-
ened with relief.

"Finally!" the girl exclaimed. "We've been expecting
you. We thought you were missing the flight." The
helpful stewardess took her to the cockpit, knocked,
and pushed it open. "Here she is. They made her wait
with the passengers by mistake."

The co-pilot—a handsome, dark-haired young man—
turned around, stared just a little too long and then
only smiled. The captain, busy with something at the
controls, finished what he was doing and finally
turned. "Ah! Glad you made it."

"How do you do," Marian said, her voice pitched to
carry above the roar of the engines. "I'm so sorry I'm
late. They told me to sit with the passengers."

The captain made up for his co-pilot's gaucheness
by reaching out to shake her hand. "No harm done," he
said. "Welcome aboard, Miss Liscomb. Have a seat." He
indicated the jump seat at the back of the cramped
cockpit. "I'm Captain Larry Flahart, and this is my co-
pilot, Warren Metzger. We don't have a navigator on
this trip, lucky you, so there's plenty of room."

She settled in and the plane took off. Gradually the
atmosphere in the cockpit relaxed, and she struck up a
conversation with Captain Flahart and his co-pilot,
whom Marian finally decided was simply shy. Some
men were like that.

By the time they finally landed in Anchorage, the three were on easy terms. Flahart commented that he looked forward to flying with her and seemed to mean it.

As they were disembarking, Warren cleared his throat. "Say, would you like to join me for a cup of coffee?"

Marian hated coffee; she was strictly a tea drinker. She hadn't even found out where she was going to be staying, yet. Going out with this young man was the last thing on her agenda at the moment. She smiled. "No, thank you. Are you stationed up here?"

"No, I'm based in Seattle. Everett, actually."

"Oh. I'll be living mainly here, I'm told. It was nice meeting you. I'm sure we'll run into each other on another flight."

1. Pages of Time: 1922 A Nostalgia News Report, KardLets from Pages of Time, Millersville, TN.
2. 1922 Remember When...A Nostalgic Look Back in Time, SeekPublishing, Millersville, TN.
3. These and other quotes are taken from Marian's unfinished autobiography.

CHAPTER THREE: BIRTH OF A NATION

The nation of Israel did not spring into the world whole and complete like Pallas Athena from the brow of Zeus. When the last of the semi-autonomous kingdoms that were all that remained of a once-powerful nation were finally crushed beneath the might of Rome, the people scattered throughout the known world in a seemingly endless tide of migration known as the Diaspora. A few remained behind in the land of their origin, but they had become a minority in an increasingly diverse and ever-changing population.

United by religion, cultural heritage, literature, and the consciousness of being outcasts—as well as dietary laws restricting social contact with non-Jews even where such interaction was legally permitted—the far-flung Jewish community settled in every corner of the globe, becoming something of an international commercial class in a world largely divided into aristocracy, peasantry, and clergy.[1]

Jewish communities around the world were variously welcomed and despised as anti-Semitic feelings ebbed and flowed through the centuries. But overall, civilization progressed, and the Age of Enlightenment brought with it a level of acceptance toward the Jews previously unknown throughout most of Europe. In many countries, Jews ceased to think of themselves as Jews first and considered themselves citizens of their countries, equal to their Christian and secular brethren.

But with the rise of the Industrial Revolution came a re-birth of anti-Semitism in many European countries. Once again, the scattered children of Israel began to dream of a homeland, a place where they could be free to flourish without envy and live in peace in a land with others of their own culture.[2]

As Zionism grew and solidified into a political force to be reckoned with, many lands were proposed as potential sites for a new Jewish homeland. Cyprus and Uganda were proposed at one point and, much later, the territory of Alaska, but none had the powerful grip on the collective Jewish psyche as the land they still remembered in blessing ("Next year in Jerusalem!"), poem ("By the waters of Babylon, we lay down and wept for thee, Zion") and prayer. The land of their origin; known at various times as Judah, Judea, Zion, Israel, Syria Palaestina, Outremer, the Levant, and more recently as simply Palestine.

Beginning in the late 1800s, diplomatic efforts to win international recognition for a Jewish homeland were reinforced by waves of Jewish immigrants who returned to the land of their ancestors, determined to re-create their homeland.

Over the centuries of the Diaspora, Jews had mastered many crafts, trades, and skills. Alas, farming was not among them, and the land once known as the Land of Israel was largely over-grazed and overburdened desert interspersed by malaria-ridden swamps. Few of the early Zionist immigrants had any idea how to work the land to which they had returned with such high hopes. The majority of them either gave up and returned to Europe or died of hunger, thirst, or malaria, or hired Arab laborers to do the tasks for which they had neither training nor inclination.[3]

The settlers who followed them were better educated and better prepared. Gradually, using the most advanced farming, irrigation, and soil-restoration techniques, they began to work magic on the exhausted land. They drained swamps, enriched the soil, planted trees, and returned many vanished native species to the long-barren hills and mountains. For the first time in centuries, the fabled cedars grew along the hills, and rich harvests sprang from increasingly fertile fields. Slowly, the Holy Land came back to life, becoming at last the land of milk and honey that had once been prophesied.

The Arab Palestinians, many of them also immigrants, owned little of the land; they were mostly tenant farmers working acreage owned primarily by wealthy, absentee Jordanian landlords. At first, the Arab and Jewish settlers worked side-by-side in relative harmony, and the Arab Palestinians benefited from the Jews' industry and modern farming methods.

But as the 19th Century passed into the 20th, and Anti-Semitism made more and more European cities uncomfortable or even dangerous for Jews, more Jewish families finally accepted the challenge of the ancient toast "Next Year in Jerusalem" and emigrated to the new Israel. More came each year, the influx swelling from a trickle to a flood. The Arab Palestinians grew less welcoming and finally openly hostile to the newcomers. Conflicts became open violence and then armed battles.

While most of the Jewish immigrants purchased or leased the land they wished to settle, fanatical Zionists had no compunction about driving their non-Jewish neighbors out by force. Tales of open warfare and atrocities on both sides spread throughout the Arab lands and into Europe.

When the British wrested control of the area from the crumbling Ottoman Empire during World War I, they had no idea of what to do with it or the increasingly vocal and mutually antagonistic Jews and Arabs inhabiting the area. The famous explorer, political officer, writer, and all-around Renaissance woman Gertrude Bell, who had been instrumental in establishing the countries of Transjordan and Iraq, and who had the ears of a multitude of Arab leaders as well as British, used her tremendous influence to swing sympathies toward the Arab inhabitants of Palestine.[4] Political powerhouse Winston Churchill championed the Jewish cause, and so did the immensely wealthy Jewish financier, Walter Rothschild, the 2nd Baron Rothschild. Britain's government became hopelessly divided between the two camps.

In a vain attempt to mollify one group while not alienating the other, Britain drafted the Balfour Declaration,[5] which, like most other documents written by diplomats, satisfied neither side. The Balfour Declaration was in fact so vague that it—and Great Britain's constant re-interpretation of it, alternately favoring first one side and then the other—eventually led to open hostility toward Britain from Jews and Arabs alike.

The rise of Nazism in Germany and Stalin's increasingly brutal and oppressive rule in the new Soviet Union drove frantic waves of Jewish immigrants to flee for their lives into an area already rife with violence. Desperate to head off open warfare, England made one last attempt to reconcile the two nationalisms—Arab and Jewish—with the Peel Commission Report, recommending the partition of Palestine into a small Jewish and a much larger Arab state. The Jewish community accepted it with great reluctance, seeing no alternative. The Palestinian Arabs, however, rejected it resoundingly with a savage campaign of arson, bombings, and murders aimed at the Jews and the British alike.

With a European war already on her doorstep, Britain threw her hands in the air and responded with the White Paper. Issued in 1939, at the same time

Neville Chamberlain was blithely handing Czechoslovakia to Adolf Hitler, the White Paper negated the Balfour Declaration. This restricted Jewish immigration just when the Jews of Europe were in most desperate need of it, and provided for the creation of an Arab Palestinian state within ten years.

David Ben-Gurion, head of the Jewish Agency in Palestine, publicly pledged that the Palestinian Jewish community would "help the British in their war against Hitler as if there were no White Paper, [and] resist the White Paper as if there were no war."[5] What this meant in practice was that the various Jewish paramilitary organizations made it their business to drive the British out of Palestine by force.

By the end of World War II, Great Britain was punch drunk, tottering, and bankrupt. In no condition to pacify or control an increasingly violent and hostile force of Jewish terrorists in Palestine, she shrugged her once mighty shoulders and, with a gusty sigh of relief, handed the whole problem over to the newly formed United Nations. That august body appointed the United Nations Special Committee on Palestine, which on August 31, 1947, recommended an unwieldy and insanely complicated system of partition into two separate states—one Jewish and one Arabic.

Again, the Jewish Palestinians, this time represented by the Zionist General Council, reluctantly accepted partition. The Arab League opposed it with characteristic vehemence.

Though he later spoke of his sincere hope for "equal citizenship for Jews in Arab Palestine," Abdul Rahman Hassan Azzam, more often known as Azzam Pasha, then Secretary-General of the Arab League, was quoted in an Egyptian newspaper as saying, "Personally, I hope the Jews do not force us into this war, because it would be a war of extermination and momentous massacre which will be spoken of like the Mongolian massacre and the Crusades."[6,7] His dire prediction was immediately misquoted as a direct threat and has been cited ever since as the ultimate illustration of Arabic genocidal fury. Considering the response of the various Arab nations, Azzam Pasha's words might just as easily have been literal. War broke out between Palestinian Arabs and Jews, as armies from the Arab League, consisting primarily of the surrounding Arab states of Syria, Lebanon, Iraq, Jordan (still called Transjordan on most maps of the region), and Egypt prepared to invade.

Not all the Arab nations were eager to ride to battle.

Legend says that when the Queen of Sheba left the kingdom of Judah and the arms of King Solomon, a single tribe of Jews followed her back to her kingdom and were thereafter lost to history. The Kingdom of Sheba, too, faded and was forgotten, swallowed up in the tides of war, migrations, famines, floods, and the slow, relentless changes carved on the land itself by the hand of time. Modern scholars debate where Sheba actually lay, but many believe it may have existed somewhere within the boundaries of the region now known as Yemen.[8]

Though one of the most ancient centers of civilization in all of the Near East, by the mid-twentieth century Yemen was all but forgotten. A land of mystery to most of the world, its culture and most of its people were firmly mired in the middle ages. Constant intertribal conflict, invasions from Persia, Egypt, and Portugal, decades of misrule and exploitation by the Ottoman Empire, and finally the loss of its southern coast to Great Britain in 1839, left its boundaries in some doubt outside of the ancient capital city of Sana'a.

The British East India Company landed Royal Marines at the ancient port city of Aden in what was then Yemen with the stated intent of wiping out a supposedly thriving community of pirates that had been plaguing British shipping to India and which called Aden home.[9] That accomplished, the Crown wasted no time expanding into the surrounding territory and establishing informal "protection arrangements" with nine tribes that had traditionally held the areas immediately surrounding the port city. In exchange for British "protection," which they had little choice but to accept, the various tribal leaders agreed not to enter into treaties with, or cede territory to, any other foreign power.[10]

From there, Great Britain expanded its influence to the west and east along the coast of the Arabian Sea, though after thirty-five years of testing the tolerance of the Ottoman Empire that then held it, England tacitly agreed that its influence stopped at the border of Yemen.

Establishing a legal system based on secular law rather than Sharia—which made the Protectorate entirely unique in the region—Great Britain divided what became known as the Protectorate into municipalities. They established appropriate governing bodies for each of them, instituted mandatory education for boys and girls, and settled into a more-or-less comfortable living arrangement with the various Arab and Jewish tribes within its province. The port of Aden's importance increased exponentially with the opening of the Suez Canal in 1869. Merchants and business opportunists from nearly every corner of the globe flocked to the Protectorate. Aden became something of an international city.

The winds of Zionism, which the atrocities of Hitler and Stalin had whipped into an irresistible political force storming throughout the rest of the world, had only lightly blown across Yemen's landscape prior to 1947, but Yahya bin Muhammad Hamid ad-Din, the powerful Imam of North Yemen, had proved an immovable object. Occupied initially with driving out the Ottoman Turks, and later with keeping his country insulated from corrupting influences of the outside world and suppressing the fledgling Free Yemeni Movement, he had little interest in the Yemenite Jews who had lived as *dhimmīs*[11] among his people for centuries.

Though for reasons explainable only by the weird quirks of human psychology, he was considered by his Jewish subjects to be a fair and honorable leader, his own decrees of previous decades had, in fact, increased the restrictions under which they lived.[12] Yemenite Jews were required to stand up in front of Moslems and to treat them with "honor and respect" at all times, the interpretation of which was entirely up to the individual Moslem. They must pass a Moslem only on the left side, and accidentally touching a Moslem in passing was forbidden, punishable by means as unpredictable as they were draconian. Nor could any Jew plead in court against a Moslem for any reason.

Jews were forbidden to raise their voices in front of Moslems, even when praying in the Synagogue, or to be seen studying where a Moslem might see them. They could not build their houses higher than those of their Moslem neighbors, engage in any of the traditional trades and occupations of Moslems or ride horses. They had to dismount from a donkey if passing an Arab in order not to be able to look down upon him.

A Jew was also forbidden to laugh or make remarks at the sight of a naked Moslem. One can only imagine under what circumstances such a sighting might come about, and how easy the temptation would be to overcome.

Beginning around 1929, they were also forbidden to emigrate to Palestine.[13] Imam Yahya was naturally sympathetic to the Palestinian Arab cause and somewhat influenced by his friendly relationship with Italy. But more, watching the growing violence as Jewish immigrants fought for sanctuary in Palestine, Muslim Palestinians fought to keep them out, and the British fought to honor impossible promises made to all sides, the Imam hoped to keep the rising tide of bloodshed from lapping against his shores. Or at least to keep from fanning the flames of war. While he made no real attempt to prevent those who gained certificates for immigration from the Jewish Agency from leaving for Palestine on the ships provided for that purpose, he did not lift his ban.

Yemen was not involved in World War II, but the war strangled trade and supply lines into the country. A devastating drought during the early 1940s brought outright famine to many of its poorer districts. The Jewish population, already at the bottom of the economic scale, was hit hardest. Hoping for passage to Palestine, and if not, better conditions in Aden under the offices of the British Protectorate (or at least aid from the more prosperous Jewish community living there), hundreds of Jews abandoned their homes. In defiance of the Imam's ban, they stole through the night across the borders of the Protectorate and into the city of Aden.

Most were doomed to disappointment, and the streets of Aden became filled with homeless vagabonds without jobs, food, or any way to care for themselves. As one Yemenite wrote, "If there are seven stages of hell, then Aden is the sixth."[14]

An outbreak of typhus in 1944, brought to Aden by largely Jewish refugees fleeing the disease raging in the outer reaches of Yemen, swept through the Protectorate, killing hundreds—among them the Acting Manager of the Jewish Agency in Aden.[15] Desperate to control the spread of the disease, the British rounded up many of the refugees and quarantined them in an old prisoner-of-war camp outside the city of Fayoush.[16] Once the plague was contained, the camp proved inadequate to house the ever-increasing numbers of refugees. The death toll was nothing short of appalling; infant mortality reached 90%[17] at one point.

In 1946, the British agreed to open another former prison camp to house the growing number of refugees.

Hashed, originally established during World War II for Italian prisoners of war taken in Somaliland, consisted of a fenced enclosure divided into two parts by barbed wire. The former administration building, a medical facility, and a building formerly used for "recreational services" took up one side; in the other was nothing but open desert.[18] There was no electricity and the British forbade the building of permanent structures, but it was larger than Fayoush and at least nominally better than the streets of Aden.

As many Jews as could be found were rounded up from the streets of Aden and neighboring districts and taken there. Working around the restrictions imposed by the British, the Yemenites built reed shacks or shack-and-tent combinations in which to live, but conditions were appalling even by the standards of refugee camps around the world. An American doctor, Olga Feinberg, after visiting Aden and observing a level of misery that horrified her, offered her services. She was made Camp Director but given neither the funding nor the authority to overcome the problems she faced. The improvements she did manage to impose were quickly negated by the continuous influx of more refugees.[19]

A small, modern appliance making its way into Yemen tipped the balance further: the radio. The Yemeni Arabs, formerly quite tolerant of their Jewish neighbors, heard, many for the first time, the news bulletins coming out of Palestine and became incensed. It needed only one last spark to explode into open bloodshed.

The 1947 U.N. Partitian Plan forced Imam Yahya to take fresh notice of his Jewish subjects, as Muslim rioters in Aden devastated Jewish homes and businesses and killed at least eighty-two people, both Arab and Jew. He had little time to do anything about it, however. His assassination early in 1948 embroiled his son, Ahmad bin Yahya, in a struggle for power with one of Imam Yahya's former generals, Sayyid Abdullah al-Wazir, and set the stage for a major upheaval. Civil war erupted; the bloody chaos raged across the Yemen, with the Jews frequent victims of both sides.

Desperate to escape the conflict, Jews across the country abandoned everything and fled to the Protectorate by any means possible, hoping for some measure of safety. The flood of invaders inflamed the Adenite Arabs no less than their Yemeni brethren. Aden, too, exploded into violence.

The British hastily abandoned their imposed limit of 2,000 persons permitted to live at Hashed and shoveled every Yemenite Jew they could collect into the camp. Within its guarded confines, the Yemenites were safe from Arab aggression, but Hashed now held more than twice the number it was built and equipped to handle. Conditions within the camp, already poor, became nearly intolerable.

The new Imam watched the steady flight of Jews from his lands with mixed emotions. While Ahmad shared his father's belief that Yemen should remain isolated from the rest of the world, he was canny enough to see the problems inherent in trying to hold thousands of his subjects against their wills. Famine still raged over his lands and the removal of thousands of hungry mouths could only help relieve the situation. Several thousand Jews had now made the long and difficult trek to Aden and thence to Israel on their own, and while he made scant effort to either impede or aid them, he knew that this constituted the merest tip of the iceberg, so to speak. He had little faith that his aggressive northern neighbor, Saudi Arabia, or Egypt, on the other side of the Red Sea, would respect Yemen's borders if the cries for Jewish blood continued to grow louder. Or if they suspected Ahmad himself of harboring Jewish sympathies, as they might if he were to provide open assistance of any kind to the Jews fleeing Yemen.

But Ahmad had a dream. A dream in which the British were forced to surrender their hold on Aden and the nine tribal territories of the Protectorate. The ancient kingdom of Yemen would then be restored to its original size and splendor, creating, at last, a unified nation. Forcing the government of Aden to shoulder the crippling burden of so many sick, starving people and, in doing so, become the focus of the anger and outrage of the members of the Arab League, could only weaken Great Britain's grasp on their colony.

And so, despite the united hostility of his neighbors toward the new Jewish state, Ahmad did nothing to halt the migration. He instead let it be known that all Yemenite Jews wishing to emigrate to Israel must leave any unsold property to him, to be held in trust against their return. The announcement discouraged very few.

The American Jewish Joint Distribution Committee (JDC), established in the United States after World War I, had been spearheading relief efforts for displaced Jews around the world by World War II. When Palestine gave birth to Israel, the organization's primary focus became getting those the war had made homeless into the new Jewish nation.

For many of the organization's members, it was a personal mission. In an almost unique partnership with the new government of Israel, the JDC marshaled its forces to attack the staggering number of difficulties, obstacles, legal entanglements, international laws, political booby-traps, financial burdens and logistical nightmares presented in bringing home the wandering children of Israel. Their representative in the Middle East was an American-born Lawyer living in Tel Aviv named Harry Vitalis.

Vitalis and his wife, Rose, were passionately dedicated to what they saw as a sacred calling: making the new nation a safe and welcome haven for the displaced Jews of the world. Vitalis was hardly alone in noticing the plight of the Jewish population in Yemen, but he was certainly one of the most vocal and active in trying to make them a priority for Israel as well as the JDC. He campaigned tirelessly to have a larger proportion of immigration certificates allotted to Yemenites, while even the JDC was more focused on the plight of European Jewish survivors of WWII.

To better position himself to focus on this one particular issue, he took the post of JDC representative in Tel Aviv. With Joseph Simon as his counterpart in Aden, he applied every possible means of persuasion to the authorities in Israel, the U.N., the Protectorate in Aden, and Great Britain in trying to get them to agree to allow refugees in Hashed to finally reach their long-desired goal. He even campaigned to approach and gain the Imam's compliance in allowing his subjects to emigrate from Yemen directly to Eretz Israel.

The British, caught between a rock and a hard place, argued amongst themselves and wavered between repatriating the refugees to the Yemen and helping move them on to Israel. Neither solution was a good one from Britain's point of view. But to keep them in Aden was intolerable for humanitarian reasons as well as economic, political, and reasons of public health. Neither had England any wish to offend the new Imam of Yemen, whose tolerance for British rule in the Protectorate was notoriously thin.

Sir Reginald Champion, the Governor of Aden, was in the unenviable position of being forced to make decisions that might well touch off another war on one hand, or condemn thousands of people to endless, intolerable imprisonment or genocide on the other. Understandably enough, he was ready to consider almost any proposal that offered an honorable way out.

Perhaps that is why he was receptive when Vitalis and the JDC, hoping to cajole him into releasing the refugees, presented what Vitalis was certain was an acceptable suggestion, a beginning, a foot in the door: to allow the creation, in Aden, of a staging area from whence Yemenite Jews wishing to emigrate could be taken to Palestine. Israeli doctors, nurses, and other personnel would operate it and look after the refugees under the supervision of British officials. The JDC would obtain the necessary certificates from Israel and provide the financing.

Champion considered the consequences and hesitantly conceded that it might be possible. But he countered with more conditions, in which there was no room at all for compromise. If air transportation was needed, the RAF Air Officer Commanding had to agree to the use of RAF Khormaksar, the airfield at Aden, which was still engaged in active military operations due to the escalating conflict in Palestine and on almost continual High Alert. Additionally, the Chief of Police had to agree to arrange protection for the operation on the ground. Finally and most importantly, the entire operation had to remain top secret, most especially from the surrounding nations of the Arab League.[19,20]

The first condition was no problem; Hashed already fit the bill. Palestinian Jews and other volunteers from around the world, working primarily through the JDC, were available to provide aid. The AOC and Chief of Police were quick to agree; the Chief of Police, convinced of a violent Arab reaction, advised extreme haste and the addition of Arab observers to avoid perceived slights and other diplomatic difficulties. However, ships were impractical under the circumstances, which left air transport as the only option.

There remained only to find suitable airplanes with pilots willing to take the enormous risks such an enterprise entailed. Vitalis sent word to the JDC headquarters immediately, before anyone could change their minds.

Eddie Warburg, the co-chairman of the JDC, and his friend and frequent collaborator, wealthy philanthropist Marshall Field III, pondered the situation only briefly. The JDC was already deeply involved in rescuing Jewish refugees from around the world and trying to arrange safe haven for them anywhere that would take them. Out of all the transportation services they'd employed, one had come through and gotten the job done every time, despite sometimes nearly overwhelming bureaucratic entanglements, vast distances, frighteningly short time frames, and other difficulties.

That one service was a tiny, virtually unknown airline that operated a small fleet, primarily out of the largely unknown U.S. Territory north of Canada, the land once known as "Seward's Folly." It called itself Alaska Airlines.

1. Phillip Marguilies, "Foreword" and "Introduction to Disputed Ground" *Turning Points in Word History: The Creation of Israel,* ed. Phillip Marguilies, San Francisco, Greenhaven Press, 2005, p9-27.
2. Abba Eban, "Modern Anti-Semitism in Europe," *Turning Points in World History: The Creation of Israel,* p31-39.
3. Amos Elon, "Jewish Pioneers in Palestine," *Turning Points in World History: The Creation of Israel,* p53-65.
4. Georgina Howell, *Gertrude Bell: Queen of the Desert, Shaper of Nations,* New York: Farrar, Strauss, and Giroux, 2007.
5. Naomi Shepherd, "The Genesis of the Balfour Declaration" *Turning Points in World History: The Creation of Israel,* p66-76.

    *There are several variations of this quote. Another famous version is: "We must support the army as though there were no White Paper, and fight the White Paper as though there were no war." Statement (12 September 1939), quoted in Teveth, p717, Shabtai (1987), Ben-Gurion: The Burning Ground, 1886-1948.
6. "A War of Extermination," *Akhbar al-Yom,* October 11, 1947.

7. Tom Segev, "The makings of history / The blind misleading the blind." *Haaretz,* Oct 21, 2011.
8. http://en.wikipedia.org/wiki/Sheba, and multiple sources.
9. https://en.wikipedia.org/wiki/History_of_Yemen# Modern_history
10. https://en.wikipedia.org/wiki/Aden_Protectorate.
11. Dhimmī: *Arabic.* A historical term referring to non-Muslim citizens of an Islamic state. The word literally means "protected person." http://en.wikipedia.org/wiki/Dhimmi.
12. Tudor Parfitt, *The Road to Redemption – The Jews of the Yemen 1900-1950,* Brill, 1996, p41.
13. Shlomo Barer, *The Magic Carpet,* Harper & Brothers, New York, 1952, p158.
14. Parfitt, *The Road to Redemption,* p146.
15. Parfitt, *The Road to Redemption,* p149.
16. Parfitt, *The Road to Redemption,* p150.
17. Parfitt, *The Road to Redemption,* p151.
18. Barer, *The Magic Carpet,* p143-144.
19. Barer, *The Magic Carpet,* p159-160
20. Parfitt, *The Road to Redemption,* p183-186.

1. From L to R: Glen, Teddy, and Warren, around 1927 (Metzger collection).

2. The Gang in 1928. Typically, Warren wears his aviator helmet and carries a friend (Metzger collection).

3. 1938: Walking 10 feet off the ground after his first solo (Metzger collection).

4. The cuckoo in the Metzger nest. From L to R: Earl, Lew, Warren, Elsie, Glen (Metzger collection).

5. Bun and Babe Liscomb, around 1923 (Metzger collection).

6. The Cottage in Beaver Falls (Metzger collection).

7. From L to R: Marian, Paul E., and Mary Liscomb,
1938 (Metzger collection).

8. Warren in uniform, 1942 (Metzger collection).

Merry Xmas and a Happy new Year

Lady Esther, Marian & Frost King

9. Marian's 1942 Christmas card featured Lady and Rusty (Metzger collection).

10. Marian on Lady Esther, a winning team. This photo and an interview with Marian appeared in a local paper (Metzger collection).

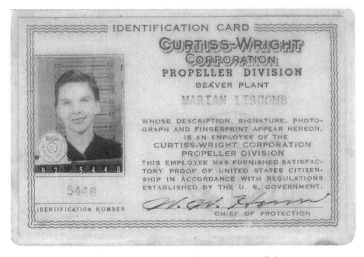

11. Marian's Curtis Wright I.D. card (Metzger collection).

12. First training flight in San Antonio with buddy J.J. Lamb. Inscription reads: "Aviation Cadet Lamb spun in March 28, 1942" (Metzger collection).

13. The wreck, 1942 (Metzger collection).

14. First visit home after the wreck, 1943.
Warren didn't go home until he could walk
unaided (Metzger collection).

15. Passport photo, 1945. Ever the optimist, Marian got a passport before she was even accepted by Capital Airlines, hoping for overseas flights (Metzger collection).

16. Marian's Capital Airlines I.D. photo, which she hated (Metzger collection).

17. Marian's second I.D. photo; Capital Airlines refused to let her use it (Metzger collection).

18. Alaska Airline's newest hire: Warren in 1948 (Metzger collection).

19. Marian in the galley of a DC-4 in one of her first flights, probably her first publicity shot for Alaska Airlines (courtesy Alaska Airlines).

20. Alaska Airlines crew dealing with a typical cargo flight on St. Lawrence Island, late 1940's (Metzger collection).

21. "The Clickest Chick at Alaska Airlines,"
1949 (Metzger collection).

22. Another publicity shot featuring Marian,
around 1949-1950 (Metzger collection).

CHAPTER FOUR: JIMMY WOOTEN AND ALASKA AIRLINES

From its founding in 1932 as Star Airlines by a couple of famous (or infamous, as the case may be) bush pilots, the re-named Alaska Airlines struggled to survive. Starting out as a one-plane operation, it had almost died a dozen times. Each time, a merger with another minuscule bush airline, a lucky charter, or some fortuitous circumstance kept it in the air.

Eventually, the little company that would one day become Alaska Airlines acquired planes capable of ferrying freight and passengers—who had to be nearly as intrepid and fearless as the pilots—all over the territory, up and down the Alaska panhandle and even sometimes to Seattle or Portland.

Alaskans had embraced aviation long before most folks in the continental U.S. thought of it as more than an interesting novelty. Alaska went straight from the dog sled to the airplane without a pause, and Alaskans quickly turned to the sky for transportation, communication, and supplies. Since the vast Alaska Territory consisted largely of frozen wasteland or boggy wilderness, depending on the season, no one had ever managed to construct a road of any distance capable of supporting vehicular traffic. While the good old dogsled retained its usefulness well into the first half of the twentieth century, the more remote settlements and villages relied on airplanes for almost everything. They were more than convenient; they were, in many cases, essential for survival.

But conditions in the Alaska Territory were rugged at the best of times, and the overall population small. Generating enough income to support itself was the primary hurdle every Alaskan air service had to face. Most never made it.

Alaska Airlines proved the exception. From its very beginnings, the primary thing that kept it aloft was its employees. The men and women who flew the planes, kept them functioning without adequate replacement parts long past their required maintenance and over-haul dates, found, booked, and loaded passengers and cargo, kept the books, manned the desks, answered the phones, held creditors at bay, and took care of passengers and crew alike were fanatically loyal to one another and to "their" airline. When a part was needed and couldn't be purchased, mechanics or pi-lots made trades or played poker with buddies at other airlines to get one. They scrounged through wreckage, dove through dumpsters or, if all else failed, reverse-engineered the necessary piece and built it in someone's garage on personal time. Sick or injured crewmen-or-women got driven home, and whoever was at hand, regardless of job title, stepped up to the plate and took over. Pilots turned wrenches and mechanics flew planes when necessary. Anyone who needed a helping hand got it, usually unasked, from other employees, from money, to food, to will-ing hands and strong shoulders. They worked, played, hunted, fished, partied, fought, and, in some cases, lived together, supporting each other in and out of the office.

Like a company of soldiers who'd been through the wars, they'd been through the mill together. They'd built the company up, made sacrifices, and carried the airline on their shoulders in the face of every obstacle. Some had started with the airline when it was one plane and a handful of aviation pioneers; others had come aboard with mergers or joined because this was Alaska's own airline, conceived, owned, and built by Alaskans. They had no desire to work anywhere else.

Even during the WWII years, when the airline was snapped up by an "Outside" owner who cared nothing for the airline's future,[1] the employees grimly soldiered on, determined not to allow anyone or anything to take their airline down.

It was the various officers' greatest wish to someday have a solid, well-paying, scheduled route to Seattle (or anywhere in "the Lower 48") but despite one or two "almosts," that wish remained a frustrating dream until mid-1947.

Enter James "Jimmy" Wooten.

Wooten came to Alaska Airlines directly from American Airlines, where he'd been head of the Contract Air Cargo Division. He'd created and built the division and, by all accounts, made it highly successful. However, something—most likely his sometimes questionable business practices and admitted tendency to heavily abuse internal politics—ended both the division and his employment with American.

Before the dust had time to settle, he landed the job as President and CEO of Alaska Airlines. He quickly shed the cloud under which he'd left American, and for good measure took several pilots and executives with him to his new employer.

He started at Alaska in June of 1947 and immediately saw a golden opportunity spread before him. With the end of the war, the government was left with an enormous surplus of planes, some of them barely used, that could be purchased for a quarter of the price of a new one. At the same time, in an effort to stimulate the economy and keep the wartime boom going that had finally ended the Great Depression, the Civil Aeronautics Board (CAB)[2] relaxed many of the standing regulations over air freight services.

The result was that anyone who could scrape money together for a down-payment was buying a DC-3 and starting up an airline somewhere. Previously dominated by the giants like Pan Am, the big, blue frontier overhead was suddenly wide open. Ambitious pilots and aviation buffs took to the skies with a vengeance.

Jimmy Wooten contacted C.R. Smith, the Chairman of American Airlines, and reminded him the company now had two DC-4s that, with the demise of his Air Cargo Division, were in mothballs. Despite their acrimonious parting, he talked Smith into selling the planes to him. According to Wooten, the conversation went something like:

Wooten: "C.R., I don't have any money. I'll have to pay you by the month."
Smith: "I'll sell them to you with nothing down. But if you can't make the payments, let me know. Don't leave those ships stranded halfway around the world."
Wooten: "If I can't pay for them, I'll land 'em right in your lap, C.R."
Smith: "And try to get your payments in on time. Our treasurer thinks you're a double-dyed bastard."[3]

Wooten had the planes repainted with the Alaska Airlines' logo: a blue circle around the curved horizon of the earth, Alaska prominent in white, with the northern star burning overhead in a red sky, and added them to the airlines' small stable.

Then, armed with a business acumen that was nothing short of genius, an array of wild west tactics and sleight-of-hand tricks, a talent for bending rules without—quite—breaking them, and the sort of personal charisma that not infrequently convinced usually sensible people to do things of which they would never normally conceive, he flew around the world wheeling and dealing.

His usual brand of diplomacy was to bring along a case or two of Johnny Walker or Jim Beam, several cartons of cigarettes, a box or two of Cuban cigars, and a roll of cash that could choke a horse. For the most part, it did the job, and he was adept at knowing various officials' favorite brands and weaknesses.

In six months, he took Alaska Airlines from struggling to hold onto a handful of contracts within the Alaska territory to becoming the world's single largest non-scheduled carrier.

Alaska pilots, already adept at seat-of-the-pants flying, making do with inadequately maintained planes, and constant last-minute schedule changes, learned to live out of their flight bags. Like sea captains of old setting sail for the horizon, they never knew whether they'd be home in three days, three weeks, or three months.

Warren Metzger, transferred to the flight line in the summer of 1948, once had to cancel a doctor's appointment in Everett because he found himself in Amsterdam the day before, after what was supposed to be a straight run to Anchorage. He ended up making stops across most of Western Europe before he saw Everett again.

Larry Flahart, then the Chief Pilot, left for Tokyo on what he thought was a weekend run. He ended up flying to Hong Kong and from there to London, Rome, Venezuela, New York, and Seattle before finally returning weeks later to Anchorage and his very upset wife.[4]

Another pilot, Clarke Cole, circumnavigated the globe for a month. He began with ferrying supplies from Anchorage to Tokyo and ended in ferrying a load of guinea pigs from Massachusetts to Tokyo, having been to Thailand, Ceylon, Israel, Paris, Ireland, and Newfoundland, among other ports of call in between.[5]

Finding himself in Australia some two months after leaving home, co-pilot Bill Lester told an Australian newspaper reporter, "Someday we're going to find Seattle again, and see our homes in the U.S." He was only half joking; the crew he was with ended up spending three months flying together across half the globe.[6]

Wooten didn't achieve his astounding success without opposition. Pan American World Airways, owned by the politically powerful and savvy Juan Trippe, and Northwest Airlines, Pan Am's strongest competitor in the northern United States and upper pacific coast, protested vociferously at Alaska Airline's temerity in invading what they considered to be their territory. Northwest Airlines virtually owned the Seattle to Anchorage run, and Alaska Airlines had begun to make serious inroads on their profit margin. Pan Am, at that time America's primary international airline, was already feeling the pinch of other airlines such as TWA and Braniff nipping at their heels and wanted to squash this newest upstart before it became a real threat. Howling like wounded wolves, they inundated the CAB with demands that Alaska Airlines be slapped back into place.

Wooten was not particularly alarmed. As far as he was concerned, the regulations concerning scheduled vs. non-scheduled carriers were downright immoral and un-American, existing only in order to grant bigwigs like Trippe a virtual monopoly over air travel of any kind and keep competitors out of the sky. They deserved to be bent, twisted, and otherwise gotten around in whatever way proved necessary in order to get the job done. As a life-long Democrat, he was generally pro-government and thoroughly enjoyed playing politics. However, he understood that if you let the government get a foot in the door, pretty soon it took over your whole house, and he preferred to play by his own rules.

He was convinced he had the upper hand in any legal contest. He counted Jim Landis, a CAB Chairman, and Oswald Ryan, another CAB member, as personal friends. Both had strongly urged him to accept the job in Alaska and work his magic on the territory's troubled supply lines to the United States, granting an exemption to allow his new airline to transport emergency food, medical, and—most importantly from many Alaskans' point of view—alcohol supplies from Seattle to Alaska during a maritime worker's strike.[7]

Moreover, both had promised him they'd support another exemption so that Alaska Airlines could continue to operate on a non-scheduled basis between Alaska and Boeing field in Everett, Washington. Wooten was prepared to argue—and had done so more than once—that the overseas contracts Alaska Airlines took constituted the "casual, occasional, and infrequent service" allowed for non-scheduled carriers; perfectly legal and above-board. Which gave Alaska a perfect right to snap up contracts the larger, scheduled carriers such as Pan Am refused. Or would have refused, if they'd known about them.

To top it all off, he claimed a long-standing friendship with President Harry S. Truman; a photo of the two of them together graced the wall of his New York office. With all that political firepower at his command, how much trouble could he get into?

Never one to take the slow, safe route, he charged full steam ahead. "I went all out, operating four or five trips a day if we could get that much business, or two or three if we didn't, from Seattle to Anchorage," he recalled later. He did make the formal application and asked for the exemption, but he carried on with business as usual without waiting for approval.[3]

The little airline's enemies geared up for war. Pan Am, Northwest and Pacific Northern Airlines[8]—another small Alaskan airline started by a former bush pilot named Art Woodley—spearheaded several lawsuits against Alaska Airlines with the full support of the CAB. The attack was intended, not only to keep them from establishing a foothold in the Lower 48, but aimed at curtailing the growing number of overseas contracts. In September, 1948, the Alaska Third Division Court went so far as to grant a permanent injunction, a Cease and Desist order, restraining Alaska Airlines from—among other things—operating overseas except in the case of the aforementioned "casual, occasional, and infrequent service."[9]

Wooten filed a counter-suit through the Alaska Federal Court, presided over by another old friend and crony, Judge Tony Dimond, in which he asked for an injunction against the CAB, setting aside the Cease and Desist Order. Dimond cheerfully granted the injunction. Wooten dusted his hands and continued booking flights whenever and wherever he could, leaving the aeronautical giants and their political allies fuming. Not willing to take a slap in the face by a bunch of pipsqueak upstarts in what wasn't even a real state yet, the CAB came roaring back, urged on by Pan Am and the other offended airlines.

The whole shebang went to trial without Wooten's participation; his attention was focused on what was rapidly becoming a world-wide circus of unscheduled freight runs, airlifts, charters, and rescue missions happening simultaneously.

He evidently paid the various legal entanglements little heed while buzzing around the world putting out fires and starting new ones. He'd made a career out of cheerfully thumbing his nose at the CAB and getting away with it. This time, he was certain, would be no different.

Even with half-a-dozen firms, airlines, and Federal agencies after him, Wooten had no qualms about using his political connections to not only help him keep

Alaska Airlines out of the hole but to create new charters he could nab. In November of 1948, Alaska Airlines won a contract to ferry food and medical supplies to overseas military bases for use in the Berlin Airlift. And, conversely, to ferry everything from military personnel and equipment to several thousand German war brides out. Wooten not only set the whole thing up right under half-a-dozen larger airlines' noses, he did it despite having earned the undying animosity of General Lucius Clay[10]—both due, he later asserted, to having ignored Clay's direct orders and earned General Eisenhower's gratitude by rescuing Caaci, one of the General's beloved Scotties, along with several thousand other dogs belonging to recently discharged G.I.s.

Whether it's true or not is open to debate, but Wooten later claimed that without his efforts, the German war brides Alaska Airlines transported to the States on the return trips would never have been able to enter the U.S. The McCarren act, set to go into effect on January 1st, 1949, would have prevented some 40,000 German women who had married American G.I.s in the wake of World War II from joining their husbands in the United States after December 31, 1949. To get them into the U.S. before the deadline required fast action, but that was something at which Wooten excelled.

"I lobbied that whole bill through Congress," he admitted. "Then I went over to Europe and organized 16,000 of them, ready to go when the bill passed. And when the bill passed we hauled them in quickly." The victory was short-lived. "And then Pan American and TWA screamed like a stuck pig and they got the rest of them."[3]

Among the jobs he contracted for Alaska Airlines from the time he first took over the reins in 1947 were several for the American Jewish Joint Distribution Committee (JDC), transporting displaced Jews from all over the world to Alaska, South Africa, and even

Australia at a handsome profit. It meant a lot of people over a lot of distances, but it was guaranteed money in the bank if he could pull it off.

Since the war, groups of Jews had found themselves stranded everywhere around the world. With the U.S. restricting the number of Jewish immigrants, most of those remaining were clamoring to get to the newly-created state of Israel, even if only long enough to get Israeli passports that would let them go somewhere else. While the United Nations and the rest of the world haggled over what to do about the Jewish refugee problem, the refugees themselves, many of them survivors of Hitler's and Stalin's atrocities, re-mained trapped in camps and ghettos in whatever safe harbors they had managed to reach. It was a tragic and untenable situation, compounding the suffering so many had already endured.

Wooten didn't care about the politics; that was for other heads to worry about. He was too busy looking for ways to get more planes and more people into the air, and push Alaska Airlines from the tail of the pack to a more comfortable, tenable, and profitable position somewhere in the middle.

He was not a commercial pilot himself and, even by his own account, an indifferent flyer. Possibly he suf-fered from more than a touch of jealousy toward those who thought of planes as extensions of their bodies, their souls manifest in aluminum and steel shells. When deep in his cups and far from the ears of the pi-lots who flew under him, he sometimes allowed his sour grapes to show. "Never was a pilot; to be a good pilot you have to be a high-grade moron; you had to think of nothing but flying, drinking, and pussy. I had too many things on my mind for that," he said during one interview.[3]

But he did know his aircraft. Alaska Airlines had only two DC-4s when Wooten first took over the reins, and while he quickly set about acquiring more, he wasn't about to waste the talents of the other planes in the airline's diverse and somewhat idiosyncratic fleet.[11] The overworked C-46s the airline primarily used hadn't the range for many of the trips he had in mind. They'd have to be modified. He ordered extra fuel tanks added to two of them,[12] running down the middle of the big birds' fuselage. Once covered with plywood and carpeting, the tanks would be undetectable to passengers, with an interior like that of any other C-46. To increase the passenger loads, the seats were removed and replaced by benches along the walls, so the interiors were laid out more like the troop carriers they'd started life as.

Through Jim Landis, his primary ally in the CAB, he learned that the CAB had gotten wind of the project and intended to reject his plans. The only way to circumvent the anticipated rejection would be to have a certified Aeronautical Engineer run a full stress analysis on the proposed modifications.

Wooten hired Warren Metzger in January of 1948 to approve the modifications and perform the stress analysis on the C-46s. After studying the problem, the young Aeronautical Engineer knew that the planes would lose none of their flight capabilities; his only reservation was a nagging concern about the distances they might be asked to fly. The C-46 had a given flight range of over 3,000 miles; on paper, the aircraft was certainly capable of carrying the extra fuel tanks plus a reasonable payload that far, given perfect wind and weather conditions.

As a pilot, however, Warren knew that counting on perfect conditions was a possible recipe for disaster. He had nagging questions and concerns about just what sort of mission the modified aircraft and its crews would be asked to fly. At the speed the plane flew, a 3000 mile range meant 10 to 12 hours in the air—a lot to ask of men and machines. A host of logistical problems were plain to the young engineer; he wondered if they were as obvious to his new employer. What route, exactly, would they be flying? Would regular maintenance be available? Would they be carrying standard loads? Would there be places to land and refuel if needed?

Wooten, already busily expending time, energy, and money to ensure that these difficulties would be overcome and uninterested in "what ifs," assured him that everything was in hand. Warren accepted his assurances, and his personal reservations did not go into the report; he knew which side his bread was buttered on. In flight tests, the modified C-46s responded beautifully; even the CAB inspectors were impressed. Alaska Airlines was ready to take on the world.

Wherever his planes and pilots went, Wooten usually went along, ready to use his unconventional brand of diplomacy to get the refugees who were his passengers out of any sticky situations. On one such flight, with a load of Jewish refugees out of China aboard a DC-4, he and Captain Bob Maguire, who had followed him from American Airlines and whom he considered his best pilot as well as a close personal friend, landed at Bangkok. There, they discovered they were going to have to make the following landing at Karachi, in Pakistan—at that time, prior to its division, perhaps the largest Muslim nation in the world.

Naturally, they had no landing rights. So, naturally, they landed at Karachi anyway, and Wooten set out to obtain rights after the fact, armed with his signature cases of whiskey, cigarettes, and cash.

Fortunately, he just happened to know the airport director, a former British Colonel now serving in the Pakistani army. Wooten had the Colonel take him to lunch and sat down to bargain.[3]

"We spend two and a half hours at lunch," Wooten later related. "Meantime all these Jews are sitting in this airplane and it was 115 degrees and they were really suffering. So we came back around 2:30, and I gave him a case of Johnny Walker Black that was always his favorite and he said, 'Oh my God, thanks" And I gave him a case of Camel cigarettes and told him 'here, these were always your favorite cigarettes' and he said thanks, and then I handed him $1000 in twenties and told him 'here's a thousand dollars for you,' and he said, 'Oh, no, I can't do that.'

"So I said to him, 'tell you what; I'll take off right after you receive the flag.' He said, 'But my relief is the Prime Minister's nephew, and he's your friend. You don't want to do that to him.' So I said, 'I'll tell you what I'll do. I'll give the same thing to him. Whiskey, cigarettes, $1000, and I'll take off this wing. I'll put the cowling back on this airplane after you leave me, and you can tell him that we're running it up to maintenance to see if it checks out all right. And as you go over to accept the flag, as soon as you snap him to attention to receive your relief, I'll start taxiing, and I'll take off, and you guys can argue for the next two years whether I took off on your shift or his shift.'"

The plan worked beautifully, though the temperature had reached 120 degrees by the time the badly overloaded plane took off, with no safe landing possible for roughly 2300 miles. "We were an hour and a half before we could get 500 feet above the sea, we had such a load on in the heat. After an hour and a half or so, we got so we were able to get up to three-four thousand feet and were able to get better. We landed at Aden with less than 150 gallons. That isn't much fuel. But we didn't have many alternatives. There was nothing but Muslims in between."

But the job paid handsomely; well worth the risks, in his opinion. So when Eddie Warburg and Marshall Field III met him in Paris with a new proposition from the JDC, he was all ears.

Initially, they spoke to him only of around 1,000 to 1,500 orphaned Yemenite Jewish children stranded in Aden who needed to be taken to Israel before they were either given to the Arabs to be raised as Muslims or killed. Warburg related a story of how an old Jewish doctor—a colonel in the army back from India—had seen them there and forced the governor to give them an abandoned prison camp for a temporary refuge, but they had to be taken from there to Israel. A Jew could not come through the Suez Canal, and there were no ships available that could possibly take them around the Horn, because all ships were under allocation for another year and a half. They estimated a 2,200 mile haul to Tel Aviv by air. Could Alaska Airlines do it?[3]

This was right up Jimmy Wooten's alley; since the war's end, any explosive, dangerous situation revolving around orphans or refugees was potentially lucrative to anyone bold enough to seize the opportunity, and he had an uncanny ability to turn opportunity into ready cash.

One small drawback: the JDC was officially a charity, which meant funding wasn't always immediately available for things like airline charters. This approach went nowhere with Wooten; planes didn't fly on good intentions. They assured him they could get the money, as they had before. Payment would be waiting for Alaska Airlines at the American Jewish Joint Distribution offices in Paris.

Wooten juggled some numbers, calculating planes, distances, risks, and possible rewards, and put in a bid. To no one's surprise, the JDC awarded the contract to Alaska Airlines.

For some reason, probably due to some bureaucratic mix-up or to eliminate a red tape snarl, Wooten had to re-submit a brand new stress-analysis on the modified C-46s and ordered Warren Metzger to do it again. This time, it reaped an unexpected benefit; Wooten discovered that 1) Warren had a current commercial pilot's license, and 2) he'd been a test pilot for the Air Corps. Feeling like he'd struck gold, Wooten promoted Warren to the flight line, and this time had him do the test flights himself. Thrilled to be flying again, Warren leaped at the chance and never looked back. The C-46s were again approved.[13]

It took time to work out all details of the airlift. Before long, the contract and its associated red tape wound around and through several other organizations associated with the JDC, including the United Jewish Appeal (UJA) and the Jewish American Federation (JAFCO), all of whom had differing opinions about the terms and conditions. The entire operation soon fell under the auspices of the U.N., the U.S. State Department and the Jewish Agency in Israel. This was a lot of bosses for one contractor, none of whom agreed on the conditions or areas of oversight for the proposed contract, and all of whom wanted it kept Top Secret.

Somewhere along the line, the mission was given the code name "Operation On Wings of Eagles," but the Israeli authorities dubbed it "Operation Magic Carpet," and the name stuck. It worked as well as any other name for the purpose, though Wooten himself never used it. Negotiations concluded, he signed a final contract for $100 per passenger and two DC-4s and two C-46s, with the first haul to be made in December of 1948.[3]

Despite growing threats of legal problems from competitors, the CAB and others, Wooten rolled up his sleeves and set out to find ways of increasing the airline's profit margin. Since his contract as President and CEO gave him a healthy percentage right off the top of Alaska Airlines' gross earnings, he had a personal stake in making sure every plane spent as little time on the ground as possible.

Within weeks, Wooten became aware that the airlift was almost certainly not going to consist of merely a few orphaned children. While in Tel Aviv ironing out logistical details, he learned that far more refugees than expected were pouring into Aden. The Hashed[14] refugee camp had already grossly exceeded its maximum capacity. The Israeli authorities feared that, if the population wasn't soon thinned by relocation, another disease outbreak like the typhus plague of 1944 might very well do the job. The JDC, the U.N., Israel, and even the U.S. State Department made weekly inquiries as to the status of the operation. They sent Wooten everything from gentle hints to frantic pleas to stern warnings for the start date to be moved up.

He set his sights on October 1st and scrambled to have things ready in time.

It was no easy job to move the target date ahead by two months. For one thing, the Yemenites weren't the only group of refugees he'd arranged for the airline to transport. At least 500 refugees from Germany and Russia, living in a ghetto in Shanghai, were now threatened by Mao's Communist forces and needed to be gotten out immediately. Rumor had it that those numbers were swelling as more refugees fled to Shanghai from other Chinese cities. Alaska Airlines still had half-a-dozen other charters going on around the world at the same time, for which planes and pilots were just as necessary. Not to mention the airline's regularly scheduled runs within the Alaska territory. It was a lot to coordinate, but if anyone was up to the challenge, it was Jim Wooten.

He initially solicited the assistance of Harry Vitalis, the JDC representative living in Tel Aviv, in ironing out some of the details, such as finding housing in Tel Aviv for his crew during the operation and locating and obtaining adequate sources of aviation fuel. He and Vitalis discussed the problems at length, and Wooten left believing the JDC would handle that end of things[15]. With that load off his plate, he worked his logistical magic to arrange for the DC-4s to pick up the refugees in Shanghai while the C-46s started on the much larger population waiting in Aden. A deal was a deal, and by now a lot of people were counting on Alaska Airlines. His reputation and his airline's were on the line. It was up to him to make it happen.

He set his legal team to unravel the tangle of suits and counter-suits swelling ever larger at his back and went back to work. He had a rescue operation to oversee and an extremely complex time-table to completely re-arrange. No bureaucratic nonsense was going to stand in the way of him and Alaska Airlines succeeding in their mission.

He reckoned without Raymond Willett Marshall, the highly unpopular owner and Chairman of the Board of Alaska Airlines. Who was, as it happened, violently opposed to the whole idea.

Marshall, by all accounts, never brought a dime into the company and had little interest in it beyond using it for a ready cash cow.[16] Notoriously tight-fisted, he scrounged every penny from Alaska Airlines, keeping it so cash-poor that it had developed a reputation for not paying its bills. Many places would not accept the company's credit cards. Pilots frequently had to buy fuel out of their own pockets. They were always reimbursed, but the embarrassment was a constant and entirely unnecessary aggravation. Paychecks almost invariably bounced the first time around, so those who couldn't get to the bank before the company's funds vanished had to wait until the company executives could beg the money out of Marshall or scrounge it from somewhere else.

Marshall owned several companies and used them to make money off one another in ways both inventive and shameless enough to awe the great robber barons of yore. He regularly had Utilities Equipment Company, one of his other holdings, purchase used machine parts, most of them either already worn out or outright factory rejects, which he would turn around and force Alaska Airlines to buy at a healthy mark-up. Aside from being left with no workable parts for needed maintenance on its planes, the airline had to find a way to dispose of the useless parts on its own dime.

Warren Metzger watched tons of worn-out scrap parts being buried at the end of a runway. "Half the backfill at Merrill field (a municipal airfield in Anchorage) is spare parts from Alaska Airlines, because we'd get them and they'd be useless, but we'd paid for them, so we just gave them away or used them for backfill." He shook his head at the memory. "Makes me wonder what archaeologists would think if they dug that place up in a thousand years."

When Marshall had hired Wooten, he'd done so thinking he'd found a kindred soul, a go-getter who didn't let little things like scruples get in the way of a fast buck. He soon realized he'd taken a tiger by the tail.

Yes, Wooten loved money and was very good at making it. And like Marshall, he gave little heed to such minor issues as long-range planning, maintenance, or company morale. But unlike Marshall, money was mostly a way to keep score for Wooten. The game itself was what mattered: seeing opportunities where others saw only problems, outwitting opposition, making things happen, using his brains, his know-how, his skills, his planes, and his pilots to do what no one else seemed able to manage. By the time Marshall found out what Wooten had gotten his company into with Operation Magic Carpet, the two were already almost constantly at loggerheads.

Despite the number of lucrative and highly successful charters Wooten had brought in, Marshall was sure Wooten was setting up Alaska Airlines to be cheated out of all the money this time, and that they'd never get paid. He mistrusted almost everyone on general principle, and the JDC—or any other Jewish organization—in particular.[3] And he didn't care who knew it. When the first C-46 landed at Teterboro in New Jersey in early October on its way to Aden, Marshall was on the runway to prevent it from taking off again.

Wooten had remained in Alaska to finish working out logistics. Marshall called him to tell him what he'd done, and that he had called an emergency meeting of the Board of Directors. "You'll be here for it," Marshall said, "or you won't be at Alaska anymore."[3]

Wooten caught the next plane to New York. Upon arrival, he found himself hauled before the board, where he was given the ultimatum: cancel the charter or be fired.

Wooten had been clever with the terms of his contract with Alaska Airlines; certain he had the legal leverage to overturn any objections, he was ready to call what he thought was Marshall's bluff. Instead, he found himself faced with an ugly surprise: through Marshall's wife, his wife's relatives, his secretary, several of his other companies, and under his own name, Marshall held over fifty percent of the company; an overwhelming controlling interest. He really did own the airline, and he really did have ultimate control, no matter what any of his employees' contracts said. His word was law.

But Wooten wasn't ready to give up yet. "I made an impassioned plea for permission to go ahead with it," he said. "And Marshall finally said that if I thought so much of the idea, I could do it myself. I said I would be happy to, but I didn't want any conflict of interest charges filed by Marshall or any other stockholder." Marshall promised to make that a matter of record at the board meeting but, naturally, didn't.

Wooten rolled up his sleeves and got down to bargaining. He worked out a lease with Marshall for planes, crews, and equipment. Marshall demanded a $50,000 advance. Wooten didn't have that kind of money, and Marshall knew it. "You have fifteen days to come up with it," he told Wooten, "or the deal is off and we drop the charter."[3]

Wooten wasn't about to let it go now. He went to a friend, Boris Jaffe, a partner to one of Wooten's occasional business partners, Ruben Feldman Zimmerman. Boris Jaffe had a New York travel agency called

Consolidated Tours. He and his company agreed to back Wooten with cash and credit for gas in return for being appointed agents for all the Jewish immigration business Wooten kicked up. Jaffe made a hell of a bargain for Consolidated Tours, as it turned out; the appointment became highly lucrative. But at the time, what mattered was that the deal gave Wooten the leverage he needed.

The next day he was back in Marshall's office with cash in hand. He counted it out, and Marshall, only slightly mollified by the money, stuffed it into a safe. "Fine," he growled. "This mess is all yours. Get the hell out of here."[3]

Wooten headed back to the lone C-46 waiting on the runway, climbed aboard, and gave Bob Maguire the okay to take off. In moments, they were on their way to Israel.

1. Raymond Willett Marshall, a wealthy and prominent New York businessman, owned Alaska Airlines and dictated most company decisions from about 1942 until he was forced out in 1957. He continued to hold partial interest in the airline until 1961.
2. The CAB and its sister agency, the Civil Aeronautics Administration, were the forerunners of the FAA. In 1940, President Roosevelt split the CAA into two agencies, the Civil Aeronautics Administration, which went back to the Department of Commerce, and the Civil Aeronautics Board (CAB). The offshoot of the original CAA retained responsibility for ATC, airman and aircraft certification, safety enforcement, and airway development. CAB responsibilities included safety rulemaking, accident investigation, and economic regulation of the airlines.
3. Archie Satterfield; interview with James Wooten, 1979.

4. Archie Satterfield, *The Alaska Airlines Story,* Alaska Northwest Publishing Company, 1982, p96.
5. Satterfield; interview with Clarke Cole, 1970.
6. "Tramp of skies just drops in," The Sunday Mail, Brisbane, Australia, March 27, 1949.
7. According to former Alaska Airlines Director of Purchasing, Van Ostrander, Wooten considered the demand for "emergency" shipments of alcoholic beverages ridiculous, and refused to ship them.
8. Pacific Northern Airlines was another small Alaskan airline started by a former bush pilot named Art Woodley. What had started as a personal rivalry became a feud between Woodley and Alaska Airlines that lasted until Woodley's death.
9. Civil Aeronautics Board Aviation Cases, Report 43-54, Pacific Northern Airlines v. Alaska Airlines, September 17, 1948, p14,711-14,724.
10. General Lucius DuBignon Clay, commander of U.S. forces in Europe and U.S. military governor in Germany from 1945 to 1949, and the primary orchestrator of the Berlin Airlift.
11. According to the 1948 and 1949 Annual Reports, the company owned everything from a Cessna single-engine bush plane on floats and several Bell Helicopters to six C-46 Commandos, several DC-3s and at least five DC-4s. Other aircraft listed include a SeaBee, a Pilgrim, 4 Norsemen, at least one Grumman Widgeon, and a Consolidated Vultee.
12. The number of tanks added is unclear and may have varied from plane to plane. Bob Platt, a mechanic for Alaska Airlines, remembers 3 tanks; other pilots or mechanics remember one or two. Warren Metzger, who did the original stress analysis on the modified C-46s, claimed 4 tanks were added.
13. Metzger was hired by Alaska Airlines as an Aeronautical Engineer specifically to perform stress

analysis on C-46s modified for long-distance human transport in January of 1948; his later understanding was that they were specifically for the airlift later known as Operation Magic Carpet. However, Jim Wooten remembers the stress analysis having to be done in mid-summer of 1948, which prompted Metzger's transfer to the flight line as a pilot. This is my best guess as to what might have happened.

14. The original camp was called "Hashed." It was demolished in April of 1949 and replaced with another, which prompted a re-naming: "Geulah Beth," which means "redemption." It was still more commonly known as "Hashed" or "New Hashed." Photographs taken at the time also list the camp name as "Hashid."

15. The JDC was occupied running a massive, highly complicated, world-wide rescue operation; it might have been expecting too much to have Harry Vitalis or Joseph Simon, the JDC representative in Aden, both of whom were heavily involved in these undertakings, be responsible for making living and other arrangements for the airline and its crew. But Wooten and Bob Maguire were certainly under the impression that such had been promised.

16. Satterfield, *The Alaska Airlines Story.* Also, several unpublished interviews; no one seems to have a good word to say about Marshall.

CHAPTER FIVE: MARIAN AND WARREN AND ED

Marian thought little about the handsome young co-pilot she'd met on her way to Anchorage during her first few days as a stewardess for Alaska Airlines. She was far too wrapped up in finding a place to live and learning about her new duties and her new employer. It didn't take her long to discover that Alaska Airlines and the men and women who worked for it were a breed apart.

While most of the pilots were World War II veterans, many were also experienced bush pilots with hair-raising tales of flying in the howling wilderness. The mechanics to a man were engineering wizards, con-stantly challenged to keep the overworked fleet in the air with little more than duck tape and coat hangers,[1] and always finding resourceful and ingenious ways to meet that challenge. The stewardesses were a fearless group of highly capable women with a spirit of adven-ture stronger than any Marian had ever known. Many could turn a wrench or fly a plane at need and did so at the drop of a hat.

Marian was finally in her element.

Working for Alaska Airlines presented challenges she'd never previously imagined. On one flight, she might be asked to help wrangle a herd of reindeer on board or keep crated sled dogs from howling. The next, she might have to help an Inuit bride give birth or control a planeload of drunken miners or fishermen who hadn't seen a woman in months. "Those were the flights the girls all said you made with a baseball bat in one hand and a fire extinguisher in the other," she later recalled.

She fell passionately in love with the wild beauty of Alaska, its savagely rugged terrain passing beneath her, the astounding array of wildlife, and the pioneering "can-do" attitude of the people who chose to live there. She even found herself missing it during her fleeting times in Seattle; homesick in a way she'd never been for Pennsylvania.

She limited her dating mostly to Air Force servicemen based at Elmendorf, the Air Force base just outside of Anchorage. A little to her own surprise, she found herself falling for one of them. The young Air Force pilot, Ed Childs, talked her into saying "yes" to his marriage proposal.

Ed wasn't handsome, but he was a sweet guy with a great sense of humor, and she enjoyed his company. Life in Alaska was hard enough without living alone. Maybe it was time. But with no specific date set, she again insisted on being able to continue dating others.

She did occasionally go out with pilots from other airlines but avoided dating other Alaska Airlines employees, despite being voted "The Clickest Chick at Alaska Airlines"[2] and receiving a constant flood of offers and invitations from her fellow crewmembers. Once bitten, twice shy. She would not again make the mistake of risking her job over misplaced jealousy.

That didn't mean she made no friends at the airline. Alaska Airlines was small enough that all the employees knew one another, and most were good friends. Many had served together during the war, their spouses were all friends, their children all went to school together, and everyone enjoyed socializing with one another, even in their off-hours. The company Christmas parties held at the Idle Hour Roadhouse Inn on Lake Spenard were legendary; after hearing some of the stories, Marian could hardly wait for the next one.

This clannish attitude did not necessarily extend to management. Alaska Airline employees of all levels were united in their loathing and mistrust of the airline's absentee owner, R.W. Marshall, the New York businessman who had acquired controlling interest in the airline some five years previously and was widely regarded as "crooked as a dog's hind leg." Marian quickly came to agree with her fellow employees that every major problem the airline faced could be traced directly back to Marshall's indifference and insistence on making a fast buck at the expense of anything and everything else.

Many were almost equally distrustful of the new President he'd hired away from American Airlines the previous summer, Jim Wooten. Marian met Wooten on only a handful of occasions. She felt the powerful pull of his charm but never warmed to him. Her immediate gut reaction was that he was "too slick by half."

When in Seattle, her social life was severely curtailed. She stayed with her brother, P.D., whose wife, Betty, was back in Pennsylvania with her parents, as she was expecting their second child and the pregnancy was a difficult one. Betty was a diabetic, and the prognoses for a successful pregnancy and childbirth were grim; their first child, a boy they'd named Paul Darragh II and who went by Darry, had been premature and a close call. P.D. lived in a constant state of nerve-wracked misery, alleviated only by Babe's presence. She longed to bring Lady Esther out to join her in Washington, to keep her own spirits up, but the cost of shipping the mare cross-country daunted her. Marian's naturally optimistic nature was strained to its limits.

P.D. had one other close friend; Marian was pleasantly surprised to learn it was the same young man who had asked her out for coffee on her flight north. Warren Metzger was also stationed in Seattle—or rather in Everett, which was a few miles north, near the airfield Alaska Airlines now called home. The three started going out together whenever Marian was in town. "The Three Musketeers," she dubbed them, enjoying the lively banter and uproarious humor they inspired in one another. She also enjoyed the easy camaraderie, the chance to be "just pals" with a man without the strain of fending off unwanted attention. Warren seemed completely unaffected by the feminine charm that drew other men helplessly into Marian's orbit.

Which, she sometimes had to admit to herself, was just the tiniest bit annoying. Not that she had any intention of trying to change that, of course. She liked Warren a good deal, but why rock the boat? She was already engaged to Ed. Warren had an on-again-off-again relationship with a girl named Kay, and Marian wasn't entirely sure how serious it was on either side. And after all, under the circumstances there was small chance for romance to blossom.

One lovely October day when she was in town, one of those brisk, Indian summer days when the clouds part and rain-soaked Western Washington displays its most glorious face to the world, Warren called. "It's too nice to stay inside. I thought you'd like to see some of the rest of the country around here," he said. "Want to take a drive?"

Why not? P.D. was flying a trip, and Marian was alone and bored. She and Warren took off in his car, a 1946 Hudson Hornet he'd bought used from another pilot. They ended up near Port Townsend on the Olympic peninsula.

She didn't know exactly where they were when the view of the ocean against the sky and the distant San Juan Islands was too lovely to drive past. They pulled over to watch the sea. Having grown up well removed from the ocean, both found the restless waves and their raw, natural power awe-inspiring.

They talked for a while, though she never remembered later what about. Warren was always easy to talk to, the conversation unforced and natural, and their minds often roamed along similar tracks.

She tried to pry a bit into his relationship with the mysterious Kay, about whom she knew almost nothing, but Warren was less than forthcoming. Unknown to her, he had been questioning his feelings for Kay almost from the day he'd met Marian, and he had come to the conclusion that it was time for them to finally part ways. He asked Marian about Ed, and she found herself just as reluctant to discuss her relationship with her fiancé.

It all happened suddenly and, like so many matters of the heart, seemed perfectly natural at the time. On an impulse she could never later analyze or explain, she leaned over and kissed him on the corner of the mouth. "He was very shy," she remembered later. "But that's when he gave up." His reaction left her in no doubt of his feelings for her. What surprised her was the strength of her own response.

This wasn't supposed to be the way things happened. She'd always been the one calling the shots in her relationships. She loved Ed. She wasn't about to cheat on him. Warren was already involved with someone else as well, and she was no poacher. She pulled away, a little shaken.

Both tried to make a joke of it, but the laughter was forced. Their easy camaraderie had vanished; something new filled the space between them. Warren cleared his throat, started the engine, and they spoke little on the return trip to Everett.

After a week or two, Marian was able to think more objectively about that had happened and decided it meant nothing. Both of them were away from their steady relationships too often; that was all. Warren made every effort to put their relationship back on their old footing, and she decided to put the momentary lapse in both their judgments behind her.

She continued to see Warren whenever she landed in Seattle, but Ed when she was in Anchorage. The situation was troubling but less awkward than it might have been. Ed frequently flew missions that took him to far corners of the earth, but then, so did Warren.

And finally, so did she. Marian jumped at the chance to work charter trips that took her all over the world. Despite the extra long hours and the often utter lack of preparation, she delighted in finally getting to see new places and distant shores. Stranded in Tokyo for almost three weeks, she spent the time picking up small Japanese knickknacks and antiques. Many people impoverished by the war were selling family heirlooms to make ends meet. She learned how to say, "please," "thank you", and "excuse me" in Japanese. She learned how to wear a sari in Bombay. She went dancing in Buenos Ares, prowled art galleries in Paris, bought a gorgeous plaid shawl for her mother in Scotland and a tweed hat for her father in London. She saw Paris, Rome, Amsterdam, Hong Kong, and Rio de Janeiro. She tried new foods and explored places that had been only pictures in magazines to her before.

It also meant she actually spent relatively little time with either of her beaus, especially since she continued to date other men.

In November, Marian was assigned to assist on the flights for the Berlin Airlift, though rarely with Warren. Planeload after planeload of German war brides and their babies were heading for a new life in the U.S. to meet an immigration quota, and they needed a woman's touch.

Three years after the war's end, most of those young women were just emerging from the far side of hell. Their plight and the steadfast courage with which they seemed to deal with it touched Marian's soft heart. She did her best to ease their fears and make the long, exhausting flights more endurable. She helped some with their English, imparted nuggets of American customs and a bit of what the girls could expect in their new homeland. She talked some out of their airsickness and cleaned up vomit when that didn't work.

She'd expected to have to help with the babies, too, but to her surprise, almost all the children slept throughout the trips. She'd flown with enough squalling infants over the years to wonder how this miracle occurred. She finally asked one of the girls and learned the secret: a shot of schnapps in each bottle of milk. That particular pearl of wisdom was, she mused, one she would probably never use but worth remembering, just in case.

The situation changed again in late November. With P.D. busy with the airlift, she and Warren had taken advantage of a rare day off for another casual day of driving around the countryside and talking. This time, Warren wasn't his usual, cheerful self. He was troubled, withdrawn, and seemed unwilling to discuss whatever was the matter. After a late meal in a local diner, he dropped her off and left for home, as he had a flight in the morning. She was more of a night owl, and decided to read for a bit before turning in.

Perhaps half an hour later, there was a knock on the door. It was Warren. He wasted no time. "I broke things off with Kay last month. I can't keep doing this, Marian. It's not right. Make a choice. Either you give Ed back his ring, or we have to stop seeing each other. That's just the way it is."

She needed time to think. She sent Warren home and tried to pick up her book again, but the pages were a meaningless blur. Somewhere inside, she'd known this day was coming. She paced the floor, made herself a screwdriver—she rarely drank, but this seemed like an occasion for it—and thought about Warren. And Ed. And how much she couldn't bear the thought of hurting either one. What would life be like without Ed in it?

Or...life without Warren?

The words came into her mind from somewhere, almost as if whispered into her ear. "I can't lose this one."

Ed Childs took the news hard, though he said he had half expected it to happen. He asked to write her, and told her if she ever changed her mind, he would be waiting. A letter written in December of that year to her is signed, "I love you very much, please call me, Eddie." He was later killed in the Korean War, still unmarried.

Marian never spoke about Warren's reaction. But on November 22, 1948, he made a notation in his pilot's log book: "MFL breaks engagement!!"

December was winding down to a close when she landed in New York and found a note waiting for her from the Head Stewardess. Curious, she called in. Mimpy answered the phone. "Hi, hon. Get yourself to Seattle; you're going from there to Hong Kong."

She thought she was accustomed to her airline's oddball assignments but still had to ask, "Hong Kong?"

The phone line crackled, and she lost part of Mimpy's answer. Something about refugees. Refugees coming in from Shanghai; they were to meet them in Hong Kong and take them on to Tel Aviv. "There's a big pay bump for this one, Marian," said Mimpy. "Say you'll do it."

Marian had never turned down an assignment and didn't intend to start now, but the comment made her pause. She had been at the airline for half a year, far less than some of the other girls who had seniority over her. "I'm just wondering, why me?"

"You still have your pilot's license, don't you?"

On record, Marian was still a licensed pilot, though she'd flown seldom in the past few years.

They want extra pilots aboard for this one. It wasn't the first time her license had played a role in her airline career, but now it gave her pause. Whatever this mission was, if they wanted spare pilots aboard the planes and were offering hazard pay, it was clearly a dangerous mission. Mimpy wasn't even making an effort to disguise the fact.

Marian knew of the war in China, where Mao's Communist forces were beating back Chiang Kai-shek, step-by-step. Millions of people were caught in the crossfire.

She was being asked to fly into a war zone.

The thought should have frightened her. Instead, as she hung up the phone, the familiar tingle of excitement banished the exhaustion of her grueling trip from Germany. Here were refugees, people who desperately needed help. Here was history in the making. Here was something no one else was going to see.

And she was going to be right in the thick of it.

.   .   .

Warren had a suspicion—not quite strong enough to be called a hope—of what was coming when Wooten called him into his New York office late in December of 1948.

He'd been hearing rumors for weeks about a major contract Wooten had wrangled to ferry Jewish refugees to the newly-declared state of Israel, though Wooten was being tight-mouthed with the details. For months now, the airline had been hauling Jewish refugees from places all over the world to destinations as diverse as Australia and Alaska as well as Israel, but this sounded like something different—something bigger.

Wooten's office came as a bit of a surprise. Alaska Airlines—or, rather, Jimmy Wooten; no one was quite sure if they were his, personally—had offices in Scotland, New York, London, Chicago, Germany, Seattle, and Anchorage, that Warren knew of. He expected something grander than the simple room with a desk, chair, and a few mementos of Wooten's political connections. Wooten often boasted of his friendship with Harry Truman, and later boasted just as often of how he convinced Eisenhower to run for president, even though it cost him his friendship with Truman.

Few outside of the territory of Alaska had heard of the faltering and debt-ridden airline. Since Wooten had taken over the helm a year-and-a-half ago, Alaska Airlines had become the largest unscheduled carrier in aviation, flying everything from Swedish fishermen, cattle, and airplane parts to cars, livestock, and grain all over the world.

Since Warren had been transferred to the flight line six months earlier, he'd become one of the airline's busiest pilots. He never knew, when he took off from Anchorage, Fairbanks, or Everett whether he'd be home in a day or so or weeks later, having meanwhile ferried gold miners to San Francisco, rice to embattled Chinese troops in Taiwan, race horses from Ireland to Cuba, or used airplane parts to Buenos Aires.

Though only the military flew into and out of Berlin itself during the Berlin Airlift, Alaska Airlines carried out many of the flights from New York to Dresden, Frankfurt, Munich, and other secondary staging points, ferrying food, military personnel and, once, several thousand dogs belonging to newly-discharged G.I.s back in the U.S., including one of Eisenhower's famous —and famously spoiled—Scottie dogs. December was spent delivering planeloads of war brides and their babies to their new homes in the U.S., trying to beat the McCarren Act's December 31st deadline.

Naturally, Warren was flying the Berlin Airlift as well, though mostly as a co-pilot in the DC-4s. He had already logged almost two hundred hours flying back and forth across the Atlantic. Federal regulations at the time allowed a pilot a maximum of one hundred fifty hours, but the limit was suspended in the cases of "emergency situations"—and the month was far from over.

It was a typical December day in New York: dark gray skies, streets blanketed with snow already developing an icy crust and a dirty tinge that made the streets disappear into the air when one could look down their crowded lengths, and a bitter, piercing cold that no ordinary winter wool coat could keep at bay. The office was, at least, heated, and for that Warren was grateful. As a newly-minted Alaskan and a native of Canada, he was well acquainted with winter weather with the bit in its teeth, but he was just as glad to escape it, if only for a few moments.

Wooten loved the sound of his own voice and sounded a bit like John Wayne, if John Wayne had been a used car salesman in Chicago. He could spend hours spinning yarns to beguile the credulous or unwary, but rather to Warren's surprise, he got to the point fairly quickly. "You know those C-46s we sent to Aden?"[3]

Warren was, of course, very familiar with the two planes mentioned; both were cargo carriers he'd been hired to help modify for long distance passenger hauling. He'd now researched and authored twice an official report for a very suspicious and mildly hostile Civil Aeronautics Board, and he'd flown at least one testflight in them. While Wooten and everyone else in the airline's upper echelon who might be in the know were keeping the details pretty close to their chests, Warren had heard rumors about the planes' whereabouts.

Wooten asked him, "How'd you like to fly some trips with them?"

"Where?"

"Israel. We're transporting a bunch of Jewish orphans from Yemen to Tel Aviv."

"Israel?"

"It's tragic." Wooten paused, tapping his pen on the desk; he was always fidgeting with something. Had he been a smoker, he would have gone through at least a pack a day. "Yeah, all these kids, their parents have been butchered by the Arabs since Israel declared itself, so they're in a camp in Aden. It's a mess. They say these orphans are going to be adopted and turned into Muslims, but the Jews won't stand for that, and the Governor of Aden wants the kids out of there so they don't get invaded by Arabs trying to kill Jews or by Jews trying to get to the kids."

The scenario sounded less-than-probable to Warren, but he wasn't going to argue about it, and if it was true...his heart gave a sympathetic twist. He had a soft spot for kids and found the tales of hardships suffered by children around the world in the aftermath of World War II wrenching.

He'd never known any Jews growing up—they were scarce on the ground in Lethbridge—and he had never developed any particular antipathy toward them, or indeed, any opinion one way or the other. He'd been around the world enough times to know that, deep down, people were just people. To him, the Mennonites who had built a community just two miles south of his father's farm seemed far more alien and incomprehensible.

But since the new nation of Israel had declared itself mere months ago, rumors, opinions, and pro-and-anti hysteria had been rife in the press. He was pretty sure no one knew the real story, or no one had reported it yet. And of course, he knew that the surrounding Arab nations had universally sworn to eradicate the feisty little country before it was even dry behind the ears. Like most Americans, his sympathies naturally went to the underdog.

"Don't know for sure how many trips," said Wooten. "You'll fly as Captain, of course."

That meant a promotion and a pay bump—both equally welcome—but Warren couldn't help questioning his good fortune. "Why aren't we using the DC-4s?"

He was only rated as co-pilot on the DC-4, but the company had recently acquired several of them. They were better suited to the task than the C-46s, even with the modifications. He had assumed that the reason for the purchases was probably to replace the C-46s for this particular job.

Wooten waved away the question. "They're over there, too. But this is what we did all that work on the '46s for. You're the one who proved they could do the job."

"That they could handle the extra loads and cargo weight, yes, certainly. The range might be a concern, though. Are there enough—"

Again Wooten waved away the objection, this time with a touch of his customary impatience. "What do you think I've been doing, sitting on my ass? I've worked everything out. You'll have fuel where you need it. Look, we can go over all this later, but I'm busy right now, and you've got a flight to catch. Do you want this or not?"[3]

There had never truly been any question. Following orders without question was a habit drilled into military pilots and remained a hard one to break afterward. And you didn't say "no" to a job; not if you wanted to keep it. Besides, it would give him a chance to see for himself what was going on over there—the real story the press wasn't telling.

And what an adventure he'd have to tell his own children, some day!

"Yes, sir. Be glad to."

"Good." Wooten flipped his pen over, laid it down and picked it up again. "You're leaving New Year's Day."[3]

1. Literally. One retired mechanic described to this author how he was taught to weld cracks in DC-3 exhaust tubes using coat hangers. The character of Scotty from the original Star Trek series must have been based on Alaska Airlines mechanics.

2. "Clickest Chick" means "most photographed." Marian was often used as a model in promotional photos.
3. Author; interview with Warren Metzger, 2008.

INTERLUDE: THE WAR BELOW

The war between Israel and most of the surrounding Arab nations, called "The Israel War of Independence" by Israel and a number of other less flattering names by the Arab nations, could be said to have actually begun long before Israel declared herself an independent state on May 14, 1948. Riots, bombings, skirmishes, murders, and other acts of violence had erupted as early as the 1930s, escalated into open battles in late 1947.

By the time the nation of Israel was born, true warfare between various groups of Arabs and Israeli forces had been going on for more than half a year.

Contrary to popular belief, Arab and Israeli forces were fairly equal numerically. Many of the Arabs—especially the Egyptians—were crack troops trained by German officers and often led by British. As desert warriors worthy of their ancient heritage, they fought like tigers, but the Arab League forces lacked a unified leadership.

King Abdullah of Jordan (still often referred to as "Transjordan" at that time) had been willing in the early days to co-exist with the new Jewish state. He had been gradually coerced into supporting the war

but remained uncommitted, vacillating among different goals. His heart wasn't in it, and the other leaders
within the Arab League, sensing this, mistrusted him.
King Farouk of Egypt not only wanted to usurp leadership, he wanted to claim southern Palestine for his own.
Syria committed troops but had few battle-tested officers. Lebanon sent a token force and stayed out of the
inner-League quarrels. Safwat, the Iraqi military leader,
was constantly frustrated with the Arab League's inabil-
ity to stick to any single plan of attack.[1]

The Israelis, on the other hand, were fighting for their
very existence. Each man carried the lives of his parents, brothers and sisters, wives and daughters on his
shoulders every time he went into battle. Each woman
knew she fought for her home, husband, and children.
It made them more than human on the field of battle.
They did not fight like tigers; they fought like gods.

The war was interrupted by numerous truces of
sadly short duration. The first truce was declared on
June 11, 1948, and by the time it was over in early July,
the Israelis had established an air force, a navy, and a
tank battalion; the latter courtesy of two sympathetic
British soldiers who stole a pair of Cromwell tanks
from an arms depot at the port in Haifa and delivered
them directly to the Israeli Defense Forces (IDF).[2]

A second truce, declared in mid-July, ended on October 15, 1948[2], when the Egyptians, in defiance of the
truce, stopped Jewish convoys from passing through
their lines. The convoy was actually bait in a cleverly
offered trap, which the Egyptians swallowed. The IDF
immediately launched Operation Yoav—"Fist," though it
was also sometimes known as "Ten Plagues"—targeting
areas all along the Egyptian front. The Israelis purpose-
fully attacked at numerous points in order to ultimately capture Beersheba.

Operation Yoav was meant to open a corridor to the
Negev, cut the Egyptian lines of communications along
the coast and on the Beersheba-Hebron-Jerusalem

road, isolate and defeat the Egyptian forces, and ultimately to drive them out of the country. The Israeli Air Force (IAF), already becoming a formidable presence, disabled Egyptian air bases and kept the Arab planes out of the skies. Israeli ground troops mined railways, bombed roads, and engaged Palestinian and Egyptian forces throughout the southwest and all along the borders of the Negev...directly beneath the air corridor between the Bay of Aqaba and Tel Aviv.

After fierce fighting, the IDF drove back the enemy troops and opened the road to the Negev. From there, they moved to capture Beersheba. The Egyptian garrison finally broke and by 9:00 that morning, Beersheba, capital of the Negev, had surrendered to Israeli forces. The Arab inhabitants fled before the Israelis entered the town.[3]

Throughout October and into December, along the coast to the south and west of Jerusalem, to the east of the Gaza, all over Palestine and Israel, military brigades met and fought with the savagery only hereditary enemies can achieve.

To simultaneously launch a civilian rescue operation in large, highly visible, unarmed and slow-moving aircraft that of necessity had to fly directly over the worst areas of conflict was, perhaps, an act of madness.

1. Derek J. Penslar, "The First Arab-Israeli War: 1947-1948", *Turning Points in World History: The Creation of Israel*, p117-125.
2. "1948 Arab-Israeli War", http://en.wikipedia.org/-wiki/1948_Arab%E2%80%93Israeli_War.
3. "Timeline: Israel War of Independence", http://-zionism-israel.com/his/Israel_war_independence_1948_timeline.htm.

CHAPTER SIX:
THE FIRST LAUNCH

I n his efforts to move up the start date for the refugee flights out of Aden, Wooten created something that the military euphemistically sums up with the acronym "SNAFU." The planes and pilots he'd intended to use somehow ended up on opposite ends of the earth on different missions when it came time to send the first of his fleet eastward. One lonely C-46— not even one of the modified ones—and a C-54 Skymaster, the military equivalent of a DC-4, were all he could muster to Aden in October of 1948 to get things started.[1]

The Skymaster was available solely because it had been sidelined in Anchorage with engine trouble. It was supposed to seat thirty passengers. With the armrests ripped out it could carry a lot more. It would do. Wooten ordered it repaired and put back into service.

Parts had to be scrounged from another airline, and the mechanics couldn't guarantee it. Like most of the Alaska fleet, the ship had what a modern airline would refer to as "an extensive DMI (Deferred Maintenance Items) list" and was badly overdue for a complete overhaul. Shortly after Bob Maguire landed the C-46 at Lydda,[2] he turned around and headed back to the

States to ferry the old bird over himself.[3] He loaded the plane with supplies, more Alaska Airlines personnel, and set out for Israel.

Bob Platt, a mechanic who had only recently come to work at Alaska Airlines, accepted the assignment for the sake of the promised bonus. He was newly married and figured he'd need the money, so he hopped aboard after settling his new wife at her parent's house in Montana, thinking he'd be gone for a few weeks. He was rudely disabused of the notion when the plane reached New York. "When we landed in New York, one of the secretaries asked if any of us had brought their wives. That was the first inkling we had that it wasn't going to be a short stay," he said later. "We didn't even know we *could* bring our wives."[4]

The weary Skymaster started protesting almost as soon as they cleared the runway. Approaching Newfoundland, the newly repaired engine died, but conditions at Gander didn't allow them to land there. They turned around and headed back to Nova Scotia, where on approach a fierce downdraft tried to hammer their plane into the ground. Maguire caught it and brought the crippled bird in. They were able to borrow parts from a KLM crew and then took off for Lagos.

A little over halfway there, another engine started coughing and lurching. Maguire had to nurse it the rest of the way in. On landing, they talked the Portuguese military into giving them space in a hanger, and to cement the new friendship, proceeded to go on a massive drunk with them. "I woke up in Casablanca with a bottle of wine clutched under one arm," Platt recalled. "I still keep in touch with a sergeant from the Portuguese army."

They were running out of gas when they reached Nicosia, Cyprus, and landed despite having no clearance. After several very tense hours, Maguire got the clearance, and as soon as the plane was fed, they headed on across the Mediterranean to Israel.

"Suddenly, a P-51 whizzed past us on one side, then one on the other side, both whipped around and hung right on our wingtips and herded us down the neutral corridor to our base,"[5] said Platt. "We learned after we landed that the P-51s were scrambled to shoot us down."

It was the first close call of the mission, and it wouldn't be the last.

Once put into service, the C-54 lived up to its initial promise by breaking down on every single run. While this was hardly unusual—during the entire duration of the operation, virtually every airplane required daily, exhaustive maintenance—the C-54 proved the most problematic of the planes Alaska Airlines sent over. It was eventually relegated mainly to fuel runs, which left Maguire and another pilot, By Sharp, to rotate shifts in the C-46. Captain Hershal Patton was on his way to Amsterdam to start runs from Europe and Asia with a DC-4, but another DC-4 was still weeks away from being available.

Maguire intended to fly the first few loads out of Aden[5] on the C-46. When he and Wooten arrived in Tel Aviv, they found many carefully arranged preparations had come unraveled. The JDC had been completely unaware that they were supposed to have taken care of a lot of the preparations for the planes and crew. Harry Vitalis was unavailable when Wooten tried to call him. After being bounced from one minor official to another, Wooten came to the conclusion that no one else had any idea the JDC had been expected or even asked to make arrangements for housing, maintenance bays, fuel, and equipment.[6] No one had even finalized any of the provisions he and Maguire had initially lined up.

As Chief Pilot and General Manager for the Operation, Maguire needed to stay on the ground and apply his attention to problem-solving. Wooten had planned to accompany the first flight; he always tried to be the first into a new situation to grease any wheels—or palms—and make sure any potential road-bumps were smoothed out. But the tangle of red tape between the British authorities in Aden, the U.N., and the JDC had created a snarl that had to be unknotted first. He headed for Paris to straighten things out at that end. By Sharp, at the helm of one lonely C-46, was not going to be able to do the job by himself.

If the operation were to get anywhere, they needed an additional C-46 and another C-46 pilot. After going through the roster, Wooten decided to call in Clarke Cole, solely because he liked "that cocky little bastard."[6]

Only twenty-three in 1948, Cole was the youngest Captain in the airline and possibly in the U.S. He'd completed his pilot training in the Air Corps just in time for WWII to be over and went straight into commercial aviation. Though a native of Oregon, he was flying as a bush pilot out of Cordova, Alaska, working for the legendary Merle "Mudhole" Smith, when Jim Wooten met him and offered him a job at Alaska Airlines in 1947.

Like most fighter pilots, Cole was a bit on the short side and slim, and by all accounts, he retained his "fighter jock" temperament as well. He kept himself in excellent physical condition and meticulously well-groomed; "dapper" was how others described him. He was also gregarious, good-looking, had a ready smile, and a blazing hot temper. His fellow pilots liked Cole, but even they sometimes had trouble swallowing his out-sized ego.

Cole liked Jim Wooten well enough, but he didn't always see eye-to-eye with his charismatic boss. For one thing, Wooten's compulsive need to manipulate people and circumstances to fit his schemes grated on Cole's nerves. For another, Cole was a straight-shooter and didn't appreciate Wooten's ongoing shell games and prestidigitation where money was concerned. When Cole could, he did his best to out-maneuver his sometimes slippery boss.

Wooten's contract gave him a guaranteed fat cut off the top of all profits in addition to his salary, which, given R.W. Marshall's insistence on receiving all other monies directly, meant too often not a penny actually made it back to the airline's coffers. On more than one occasion, when Cole was paid in cash by a charter client,[7] he hid the money in the hollow bottom of his flight kit and smuggled it back to Alaska Airlines headquarters. There, Hank Bierds and Elsie Brislawn, respectively the over-burdened Purchasing Manager and Office Manager (and frequently de facto financial managers), used it to meet payroll and pay bills.[7] The maneuver earned all of them Marshall's wrath, but Wooten usually ignored it, more amused than angered by his employees' cunning. It was no skin off his nose, as he got paid regardless, and he appreciated someone who could beat him at his own game.

What Cole did enjoy was that Wooten knew how to keep life exciting, a sentiment shared by Warren and many of the pilots. "He kept the adrenalin going at about the right speed," Captain John Thompson once dryly commented. Flying under his command was always an adventure, and Cole expected this latest enterprise to be one of the biggest.

Wooten sent for Cole and told him to bring one of the modified C-46s, as soon as it came in, and meet him at Consolidated Tours, 7 Boulevard Capacines, in Paris. He wired a set of typed instructions that Cole was to follow to the letter, taken straight from the contract with the JDC. Cole was delighted to accept what sounded to him like a plum assignment he could rub Warren Metzger's nose in.

Warren and Cole had forged a friendship early on, which had even withstood the younger man's pursuit of Marian Liscomb and the sneaking and envious suspicion he harbored that she might prefer Warren. The cheerful "Three Musketeers" act she and Warren were putting on with P.D. Liscomb wasn't Cole's style, and he suspected it wasn't Warren's either.

She'd laughingly refused his invitations to dinners, films, or other outings, but he hadn't given up on somehow getting the upper hand over Warren and talking her into going out with him. She didn't have many flights with him, but she didn't have that many with Warren either. There was still a chance, if he could do something that would really impress her.

By the time the C-46 he was supposed to fly got back to Anchorage, and the necessary plane-swapping had been arranged, Cole was running behind schedule. His instructions said that Alaska Airlines had already been cleared to land at Gander, Meeks Field, Prestwick, Paris, Marseilles, and Cyprus (Wooten was still working on obtaining clearance at Rome). He decided that rather than cross the north Atlantic to Iceland, he would follow the more favorable winds to the Azores. With a navigator, a couple of radio operators, and his co-pilot, he took off, navigating by dead reckoning. After refueling at Santa Maria, he headed for Paris.[8]

On arrival, he found a message at the hotel telling him to meet Wooten at the Folies Bergère rather than the business offices of Consolidated Tours. Cole had no objection to holding a business meeting at the Folies; he'd flown into Paris on previous occasions, but only to fly right back out again, and had always been eager to see more. Since, as it turned out, none of the others had ever been to Paris either, he hauled the rest of his crew along.

Over a round of drinks between acts, Wooten regaled them with a blow-by-blow account of his battles with the U.N. and the JDC. He passed on to Cole a fresh set of instructions for the operation, making it clear that Maguire was in charge until Wooten's return.

Technically, a navigator was required by law on any overseas flights. But since the C-46 had no master dome or the radio altimeter a navigator would require for use on an overseas flight, the navigator he'd brought with him wasn't really needed. Cole, knowing how tight funding was, pointed this out, and Wooten agreed; the man could stay in Paris until he could catch a ride back home.

Just as business seemed to be winding up, and Cole and his crew prepared to sit back and enjoy the evening, Wooten dropped the last bombshell on them. They had to load all the supplies he'd collected onto the plane that night, and the crew would have to stand guard over it. "Here we were in Paris for the first time, and all these stories we'd heard about the French girls," Cole lamented, "and Wooten tells us we're spending it loading the plane and guarding it."

He protested the unfairness of it, and Wooten relented a tad; only one crewman would have to stand guard. Cole pushed harder: how could he ask one of his crew to stay out there all night, while the rest enjoyed themselves? Wooten, however, remained firm. The plane was going to be stuffed full of valuable cargo, and no way was he going to allow it to sit there unguarded all night.

The navigator, somewhat ungratefully, refused the assignment; after all, he was officially off-duty. Cole reluctantly caved in. "So I had the two radio operators sleep in the airplane all night, while the rest of us went in to the Folies Bergère," he said later. The order caused a bit of ill feeling. The hapless radio operators apparently never forgave either the navigator or Cole.[8]

Slightly hung-over the next day, Cole and his crew— minus the navigator—took off for Athens and stayed overnight there. "Our maps were few and far between in 1948, shortly after the war," he remembered, "and I navigated by my fourth-grade geography as I remembered it."

Feeling considerably better early the next morning, he prepared to leave for Tel Aviv only to be stopped by customs agents. "Because we had an extra fuel tank[9] in the center of the fuselage and covered it with plywood and had all the blankets and spare parts piled over it, the customs looked under there and automatically thought we were smuggling guns and ammunition," Cole recalled. "I finally ended up getting in a cab and going out to see the American Ambassador and appealing to him for help."

The Ambassador spent the rest of the morning and well into the afternoon making phone calls. He finally got the customs office to release plane and cargo. By that time, it was close to 3:00 in the afternoon, and Cole feared he couldn't make Tel Aviv before nightfall. Wooten had warned him in no uncertain terms of the dangers of flying into Israeli airspace after dark. But it seemed like a bad idea to stick around in Athens and risk another clash with the by-now thoroughly riled local authorities. Cole decided to make a run for it.

Nearing Cyprus, he gave a position report and received an unwelcome response: an order to land there for the night. He decided against compliance. "I'd been told whatever I did not to fly into Nicosia, because they're on the side of the Egyptians and they'll confiscate the airplane and everything else," he said later. "So I just pushed her up to climb power and got my airspeed up a little bit and made Tel Aviv at real dusk."

No sooner had he entered Israeli airspace when a couple of fighter planes appeared alongside him. After a few tense moments, he realized they intended to escort him the rest of the way and relaxed somewhat. The party landed in Tel Aviv a short while later.

He and his crew were met by a small man who turned out to be a professor of Hebrew. The professor took them to their hotel and spent the next couple of hours telling the men the history of the country, and what this exodus meant to the people of Israel. He also told them not to land at Cairo, or their passports would be taken and they would be shot. Or worse, he implied, pointing at his groin and tongue. Cole left wondering exactly what he'd signed himself up for. Maybe Warren had the better deal after all.

The next day he met with Maguire, who was in town trying to find a house for his wife and three children that he brought with him, blithely believing they had a place to live. He was less than happy about the situation. As a result, the briefing he gave Cole was even more terse than was his wont, though he did pass on a bevy of warnings and instructions that made the whole assignment sound downright grim.

Finally, thoroughly disgruntled, Cole and his crew took off for Aden later that day and landed just as dusk fell, planning to depart again at first light.

There was only one hotel in Aden available for European guests, the Crescent. Rooms had supposedly been arranged some time before. However, when Cole and his crew got there, the promised rooms were already occupied. He called Maguire and a three-way argument with the management ensued; Cole was furious and the management apologetic, but there was nothing to be done.

Finally, the hotel agreed to rent them beds on the open roof—a tent could be erected over them as soon as one could be located—for a much-reduced rate. Knowing it was the best they were going to get, Maguire agreed. Cole fumed but saw no alternative.

He arrived less than well-rested at Hashed the next morning for his first load of passengers. He was met by a sturdily-built, uniformed woman with a stubborn jaw, who looked like a German *hausfrau*, who he learned was the doctor actually in charge of the camp.[10] With her was a man in British uniform shorts whose role was unclear to Cole, but who was evidently assisting the doctor.[11]

They gave him a quick briefing as to some of the difficulties and offered to show him around the camp, an offer he declined. The place was crowded and dirty, and he'd seen enough squalor around the world to have lost any voyeuristic desire to see more.

When configured as a passenger vessel, the C-46 was designed to carry 45 to 48 adults. The modified C-46, which had benches along the side of the fuselage to carry riders in troop-fashion, could fit at least half again as many. The first several loads were supposed to be children half the size of the adults. The Yemenites were a small people, made more so by prolonged malnutrition. The average adult male in the camp at that time stood no more than five feet tall and weighed perhaps 85 pounds soaking wet; the women, considerably less. The children seemed like living dolls—miniaturized humans out of a fairy story.

Cole was more interested in the task at hand than the people he would be flying, but he couldn't help studying them now and again out of curiosity. They just as obviously returned the same toward the American stranger in their midst. They were dark-complexioned, their features unlike any other Jews Cole had ever seen, with large, deep brown or night-black eyes that seemed to see more than what lay around them. "Like people going through a dream awake," as another pilot once described them.[12]

The men wore their hair short, for the most part, though long curls framed their bearded faces. The women were unveiled, in the Jewish fashion, and he thought them lovely, though hardship weathered their high-cheekboned faces at an early age.

The man in shorts wanted to include a few of the adults who were ready for travel. He asked Cole if he could cram at least double the limit on board, but Cole balked. They argued, and Cole finally decided he could push the load up to as many as 70—mixing children and adults—without endangering either passenger safety or the plane's capacity.

The children were so small they could fit three and sometimes four to a normal seat; on the benches, they could be stacked like books on a shelf. Who knew how many might fit? Many passengers would be without seat-belts, which was illegal, but there was no one around to report it. The closest CAB official was in Cairo, and he was certainly not in a position to find out.

When it came time to get the passengers and the two volunteer Israeli caretakers aboard, Cole encountered a heretofore unforeseen obstruction.

Many of the Yemenite Jews had lived in isolated communities for centuries, where they survived much as their ancestors had. Those who had come from one of the cities or larger towns had lived in houses similar to their Arab neighbors, others had never dwelt in anything other than tents or even caves. Few save those who had lived in Aden or Sana'a, the capital, were more than vaguely familiar with the trappings of modern life; most had never heard a radio, seen electric lighting, water running from a tap, or an airplane, save perhaps as a roaring shape far overhead.

After trekking hundreds of miles, in some cases, and enduring exposure, starvation, predatory attacks by bandits and various Arab tribes whose territory they crossed, and untold numbers of other hardships, their capacity to absorb new experiences had been strained to the breaking point. The adults could not be persuaded to board the airplane. The children, raised to obedience, could have been compelled but were clearly terrified. The volunteers were afraid of endangering their often fragile health by simply carrying them aboard by force.

When it became clear that no one was going anywhere that day, Cole and the rest of the Alaska crew discussed ideas and options. Not knowing what else to do, they asked the two Israeli volunteers for advice. The volunteers suggested talking to one of the Yemenite Rabbis. They offered to interpret and helped track one down.

Through the interpreters, the Rabbi told them he had already been working on the problem by reminding his people of two pertinent biblical passages, which he believed prophesized the airlift. He quoted first from Exodus 19:4:

"You yourselves have seen what I did to Egypt, and how I bore you on wings of eagles, and brought you to Myself."

He followed with a quote from the Book of Isaiah 40:31:

"But those who hope in the Lord will renew their strength. They will soar on wings like eagles; they will run and not grow weary, they will walk and not be faint."

The same passages had inspired the operation's original name: On Wings of Eagles. Now, like a light dawning, it inspired a fresh idea in the Alaska Airlines crew.

After some scrounging around, someone managed to locate some model paint. A couple of the more artistically inclined crewmen climbed up and painted an American eagle with outstretched wings over the passenger door of the plane. It was the wrong kind of paint and would not survive the scouring, sand-laden winds for long, but it did the job.[13]

The next morning, seeing the ancient prophecy fulfilled before their eyes, the Yemenites lost their fear. The adults made the laborious climb up the unfamiliar ladder; the children scurried aboard with wide, shining eyes.

It was not possible to fly from Aden directly to the airfield at Lydda in Israel; in between was nothing but territory filled with armed Arabs, every one of them looking for an excuse to fire on aircraft going to and from Israel. Cole had to fly directly over the Red Sea then veer north and up the Gulf of Aqaba, keeping to "neutral" airspace—which existed more in theory than fact—and stay out of range of all air bases and known anti-aircraft emplacements.

Israel had only one set of radar equipment, which could only provide a single corridor of identification. Cole's instructions called for him to fly a narrow route between Transjordan and Egypt.[14] To enter Israeli airspace by any other route meant getting fired upon by the Israeli anti-aircraft weapons, or worse, the newly-formed, very precise, vigilant and already fearsome Israeli Air Force.

The IAF was manned almost entirely by World War II veteran combat pilots, the *machal* (or *mahal*). As volunteers from many countries fighting for Israel and devoted to the cause of establishing her as a sovereign nation, most of them held a deep-seated conviction that it was the right thing to do. They were, to a man, quite ready and able to give their last drop of blood to defend the Holy Land. Flying mostly surplus P-38s, they had already proven themselves even more ready and able to make their foes do the bleeding. Cole couldn't risk coming into their sights.

But there was also a war below along almost the entire length of the corridor to Tel Aviv. He didn't know what kind of weapons were in play, but given the amount of German and British activity in the area during WWII, he suspected everything from German 88 anti-aircraft guns to tanks. He hoped they'd stay too busy to look up.

It was still early in the morning when he taxied the C-46 down the runway and headed into the skies, wondering what awaited them along the route.

As the sun rose, the air temperature rose with it, and turbulence jolted the aircraft more and more often. Dust filled the air, obscuring landmarks and making the engines cough and lurch. Cole took the plane higher, trying to get above the dust. He had his co-pilot keep his eyes glued to the instrument panel, and hoped he was still on course.

Perhaps three or four hours into the flight, someone knocked on the cockpit door. The very young stewardess came in. "I'm sorry, but I can't stand it," she said, nearly in tears. She didn't have to say what; the awful stench wafting through the door did that for her.

The co-pilot clapped his hand over his nose and mouth. "What the hell—?"

Cole turned the controls over to him and went back to look. "It was god-awful," he said later. There were simply too many refugees for the volunteers at Hashed to ensure they all bathed. So many of them crammed into such a small space would have made for a thick atmosphere in any case. But most of them now suffered from air sickness as well. Neither the stewardess nor the volunteers were quick enough to reach all of them with air sickness bags or get across the concept of how to use them. The passengers vomited straight onto the gas tanks, where it oozed down into the heated undercarriage and spread the stench of baking puke throughout the craft.

Neither were any of them familiar with the idea of modern plumbing. Try as they might, the beleaguered stewardess and volunteers were unable to stop them from urinating and worse in the back of the plane.

Cole stepped back into the cockpit and closed the door. "Just stay up here," he told the stewardess. "Nothing you can do for them back there, anyway. Leave it to the volunteers."

The glittering waters of the Red Sea were gradually replaced by those of the Bay of Aqaba. Soon the narrow margin of safety offered by "neutral" waters vanished. He wondered about the war being fought all along the route under him. He could hardly avoid seeing parts of the action; puffs of smoke, black lines of scurrying figures that sometimes dissolved into individual men. He wished he could head for a higher elevation, but he hadn't been this way before and needed to eyeball the terrain to stay on course. He shrugged and left it in God's hands, worrying instead about nursing his plane through the clouds of choking dust.

God and fortune favored him; nine hours after takeoff, with barely enough fuel left to keep the engines running, he landed safely near Tel Aviv at Lydda airfield. Waiting there was a huge crowd singing to welcome the new arrivals to their long-lost home.

As the Yemenites left the plane, some of them dropped to the ground and kissed it. For a moment, Cole thought they were just grateful to have survived the flight. Then he recognized the gesture for it was: an act of worship. These people were setting foot on land that had been a sacred myth and beloved legend to them for more than two thousand years. He was seeing something unique in all of history, something that would live forever. "That was the start of Exodus," he said later. And he had made the very first flight.[15]

Maybe he hadn't gotten to shoot down any Germans or Japanese, but he'd scored a much bigger victory in the air. It was something he would take pride in for the rest of his life.

It may have occurred to him that it might impress the hell out of Marian Liscomb, too.

.   .   .

Jim Wooten arrived in Tel Aviv a day or two after the first flight, intent on overcoming the hurdles springing up on all sides. He left the housing problem for Maguire to handle, and set himself to deal with issues such as refueling the planes and where to station his personnel.

Aircraft fuel was almost entirely unobtainable in Tel Aviv, much to his surprise and dismay; he had been assured that it would be forthcoming. He was directed instead to RAF Khormaksar, the British base in Aden. After the fourth flight, the British officials flatly refused to re-fuel the Alaska Airlines planes, citing a fuel shortage.[16] Another answer had to be found. And more money to pay for another answer.

Fuel was occasionally available in Asmara, Eritrea, which was within easy flight range and not at war with either Israel or the Arab nations. But the airfield at the city was used seldom since the end of WWII and didn't maintain aviation fuel often enough or in sufficient quantities to be relied upon. Still, with the airport at Tel Aviv under constant threat of bombing, it made sense to move their base of operations there. Wooten made the suggestion to Maguire; the fuel problem could be dealt with by creating a fuel depot at Asmara. Maguire got to work on it.

Another RAF base at Nicosia in Cyprus agreed to provide fuel, but it meant Alaska Airlines had to transport it back to Aden and Asmara. This meant creating a fuel depot at Aden as well.

Finding solutions to the fuel problem was proving expensive. Frustrated but determined, Wooten had Cole take him back to Paris to collect Alaska Airline's first payment from the JDC's auxiliary office in order to finance the search for fuel.

When they arrived, Wooten was presented with a check for half the expected amount. He exploded; what the hell was this? The officials argued that the aircraft had so far been hauling almost exclusively children, which should be half-fare.[17]

Livid with rage, Wooten stormed out; he was still cursing the air blue when Cole joined him at their hotel. They retired to the bar and started drinking heavily. Wooten didn't usually discuss details of his schemes with Cole, but this time his buttons had been pushed and his dander was up; he talked more freely than was his wont. Cole listened and learned a lot of things Wooten probably hadn't intended to reveal.

Wooten was in a bind. While his personal gains from the enterprise wouldn't be affected, the money lost to the terms of his lease agreement with Marshall on top of the loss of revenue from hauling children meant the airline was operating in the red. No way was he willing to crawl back and admit Marshall might have been right.

Besides, he was fighting for Alaska Airlines' place in the skies, citing the emergency status of the rescue and relief operation as his reason for flying where his airline had no official business being. There was no way around it. Alaska Airlines was on the spot, and that meant he was, too. They'd just have to work out how to fit more people onto the planes.

The next day, he called Maguire. "Cancel flights for the next couple of weeks. We're taking the planes back to Anchorage."

Maguire knew better than to argue. As soon as the two DC-4s touched down at Lydda, he told them to head back to Alaska. He followed shortly with the previously unmodified C-46.

Wooten called in a meeting with Maguire and the best of the Alaska Airlines' engineers. It was Maguire who came up with the plan to double their passenger load: the seats on the DC-4s could be replaced with wooden benches, not lengthwise, as the C-46s had been done, but across the width of the plane.[18]

The solution wasn't without a certain amount of difficulty. Like all aircraft, the DC-4 and C-46 had balance points. Wooten compared them to big teeter-totters, for loads had to be carefully placed to allow the craft to take off and land safely, let alone offer a reasonably smooth and controlled flight.

Maguire knew his aircraft and the engineers knew their jobs. They ripped out all seats and replaced them with wooden benches set precisely where the ship could most easily carry the weight. Comfort was of negligible importance at this point, and they figured the Yemenites were used to roughing it anyway. They were required to provide seat-belts of some sort, so one of the engineers strung rope across the length of each bench. Good enough.

Sand and dust had all but ruined the delicate instruments and landing gear; clearly, the amount and frequency of lubrication had to be increased as well. So in addition to the extra fuel tanks, they needed a way to transport extra oil. Whether it was Wooten's idea or not is unknown, but he took credit for discovering how to fit a sixty-to-eighty-gallon tank inside the nosecone without disturbing the plane's delicate balance, though his engineers made it happen. "There was plenty of space, but when the wheel got up there, it had a chance of flapping, and the flap on the wheel might go as high as 6 inches. You know, the terrible vibration when it got up there, it just rolled around," Wooten recalled. "So to make sure we had clearance, we put a bunch of clay up there. And hardened the clay. And then went out on the runway to see what happened, see what our clearances were. And then we came back, cut the clay out, and used it as a form to make the tank. Then we built the tank and put it in there, and we put the transfer pump up in the cockpit. We could transfer from that to anything to regular oil tanks."

Wooten was proud of his development, but it did cause problems. "It was a tremendous amount of weight at a very critical point, because we got two pounds in the rear for every one pound we had up there under our teeter-totter."

Time was running out; the refitting was done in record time, but it was still nearing mid-December; almost six weeks since he'd pulled the planes out of Aden. He decided against having Warren Metzger perform another stress analysis. He already knew the thing worked and just had to get the CAB to give it the okay. He submitted the refitting directly for approval.

The CAB promptly refused it. "This plane is incapable of landing safely," insisted one snooty inspector.

Wooten called their bluff. "We told them (CAB) to come out and see it," he said later, "and the inspector was so pissed off when he was trying to prove that we didn't have proper stress that he put so much stress on a chain that it snapped off and broke his arm."

Repairs were hastily made, and with Wooten and his maintenance manager, Freddie Perino, aboard and Maguire at the controls, the modified DC-4 took off from the Anchorage Airport for the final flight test. "We did all kinds of tricks with it, and we landed and took off and landed three times," he later recalled. "The military and everybody was watching us, because this was something fantastic."

Having proved his point, Wooten didn't waste time, and his ready temper got the better of him. "We landed and loaded the ship with spare engines and parts and took off for Aden. Took off that same afternoon, and we didn't have the final (CAB) approval on it, but we'd gone through the tests with them and I said, 'screw them, I'm going over to Aden and if they want to go over to Aden and holler, let 'em come... I'm not going to wait around for approval.' Well that was unheard of then, that you did something without waiting for their approval. And they all threatened dire consequences on that, but I didn't care."

The decision would cost him dearly later, but Operation Magic Carpet was once again open for business.

1.   Based on Clarke Cole's recollections and some references by other pilots. No specific records seem to exist.
2.   Lydda became known as Lod after Israel declared its independence, but was still listed as Lydda on maps and pilot charts. The Lydda airfield was later renamed "Ben-Gurion Airport."

3. This is a "best guess" on my part; there are several contradictory accounts about how which planes got over there and when. I am relying on mechanic Bob Platt's recollections here.

4. Satterfield; interview with Bob Platt, 1979.

5. RAF Khormaksar was the Royal Air Force station in Aden.

6. Satterfield notes, source unknown.

7. Satterfield; interviews with Clarke Cole, 1970, and Henry "Hank" Bierds, 1979. Passengers paying in cash happened more frequently than one might think. Swedish, Italian, and Chinese commercial fishermen, for instance, always paid for their chartered flights in cash when flying to Alaska for the lucrative fishing season. Bierds and Brislawn kept the money hidden in the office freezer and referred to it as the company's "frozen assets."

8. Satterfield; interview with Clarke Cole, 1970.

9. Again, there is some disagreement in the records as to the number of extra tanks added during the modifications. The most likely number is 4 tanks.

10. Cole did not remember her name, only that she was a woman doctor, so I am assuming it was, in fact, the remarkable Dr. Olga Feinberg. Several other female doctors worked at Hashed at one time or another, but I know of no others who were appointed Director.

11. There are several references to this man among the pilot interviews, but not his identity, or if he was British or Israeli. Cole thought he was Dr. Feinberg's assistant; Warren Metzger thought he was a British officer from Aden. It may be different people, but if so, they all seem to have worn British shorts, and spoke with a British accent.

12. Barer, *The Magic Carpet*, p220; Hank Mulleneaux, who often flew with Bob Maguire and later become Chief Pilot for Near East Air Transport.

13. There are numerous references to and stories about the eagle painted on the planes made by several pilots; the painting is also referred to in newspaper articles at the time. However, no photos seem to exist that show it. I am assuming that either it was on the door itself instead of over it, or it wore off.

14. According to the flight instructions included in the contract between Alaska Airlines and the JDC, Item #5 reads: "A 'Corridor' must be flown between Transjordan and Egypt. Stay southwest of AHMAN as the British restrict any flights."

15. Mechanic Bob Platt believed that Bob Maguire made the first flight of Operation Magic Carpet. Maguire himself never made that claim. While Cole was known to be boastful at times (a character flaw not shared by Maguire), for lack of definite proof to the contrary I'm going with Clarke Cole's version. No one seems to have recorded a date anywhere, only that it was in late in October of 1948.

16. Satterfield, *The Alaska Airlines Story*.

17. Satterfield; interview with James Wooten, 1979.

18. Wooten credits himself with the engineering designs. However, Bob Platt and others say Bob Maguire came up with the concept and worked out the designs with the help of two of Alaska's top engineers. This is not the only instance where Wooten takes credit for someone else's innovations. However, there's no doubt he did create many "firsts" in aviation, including design work on various aircraft; he may actually have come up with the extra oil tank design himself.

CHAPTER SEVEN: THE PROMISED LAND

Robert Francis Maguire, Jr.—"Bob" to everyone at Alaska Airlines—had accepted with alacrity when Jim Wooten asked him to act as Chief Pilot and General Manager of the newly-dubbed Operation Magic Carpet. It was Maguire who ended up making most of the arrangements, though he left the politicking to Wooten, who was quick to take credit for most of the operation. "I had worked with Jim and had business experience that the other pilots didn't," Maguire later explained. "The combination of business and flying experience was the reason I was asked to start Operation Magic Carpet."[1]

Leon Uris supposedly based the characters of Stretch Thompson and Tex MacWilliams in his epic novel "Exodus" on Wooten and Maguire. In the latter case at least, there was little resemblance between fiction and fact. While Maguire could live up to the stereotypical, high-flying, wildman-of-the-skies image near and dear to the hearts of the young pilots of the era when he chose, he was far from the drunken, profane sky-tramp of the novel. Most of those who knew Maguire remember him as a quiet man with a deadpan sense of humor, who didn't suffer fools lightly. He was also a man whose passionate love of flying never overcame his innate professionalism.

Unlike his voluble friend Wooten, Maguire was never one to use two words when one would do. He wasn't given to talking about himself much, either. Few knew that his father, Robert Francis Sr., had been a judge at the Nuremberg War-Crimes trials in the late 1940s. Some of his pilot friends knew he began flying as a teenager and then with the Army Air Corps in World War II, but few knew he'd enlisted in a silent but towering rage the day after Pearl Harbor. Only a handful knew he was accounted a crack shot and carried a .32 at all times during the entire Operation Magic Carpet. And only years later did anyone learn that, before Operation Magic Carpet was over, David Ben Gurion bestowed upon Maguire the nickname "The Irish Moses" for his almost superhuman efforts on behalf of the airlift.[2]

Maguire returned to Tel Aviv for Operation Magic Carpet's official re-launch in mid-December of 1948 in the newly re-fitted aircraft expecting, once again, to fly the first several trips himself. Many of the other Alaska Airlines pilots and crew were occupied with the Berlin airlift and would remain so until the end of December. Wooten was in the process of hiring several new pilots and other crew members for this undertaking, but Maguire hadn't yet even met them all, let alone had the chance to take their measure. He wanted pilots and crews he knew he could trust, and he himself was foremost on that list.

Clark Cole had helped Maguire make some of the arrangements for fuel, crew living quarters, and airplane maintenance that had been overlooked by Vitalis, as well as flown two of the first four flights in mid-October. Cole and Wooten were butting heads more and more often, and Maguire knew Wooten would want to check and re-check everything that had been done. In any case, the flights had ceased while the planes returned to Anchorage for re-fitting, and the JDC and its affiliates scrambled to find more funding, food, and medical supplies.

Back in October, Maguire had looked into moving the base of operations out of Tel Aviv. Since then, the situation had worsened; the airfield at Lydda had been bombed once in December, and more attacks were expected.

Using Aden for a base was out of the question. Wooten's suggestion of Asmara, in Eritrea, was a sound one that solved a lot of problems but added considerably to the mileage of each trip and created a need for another fuel depot. It also necessitated three revolving sets of ground crews.

Mechanic Bob Platt later remembered the headaches all too well. "The Arabs threatened to burn our aircraft on the ground at Aden, so we had to move our operation up to Asmara, Eritrea. We had one engineer in Aden, one in Asmara, and one in Tel Aviv so we could rotate from place to place and nobody would be stuck in the same town very long."

The biggest problem by way and afar was that fuel availability was even more limited than Maguire and Wooten had first thought. The British officials at RAF Khormaksar, the base in Aden, had been very helpful initially. Cole, Sharp, and Maguire had been able to re-fuel their planes there on a number of occasions back in October. But the last time Maguire had flown in, they'd refused to refuel the plane, citing a shortage. "Sorry, we can't provide fuel for non-military planes; we've only enough to fuel our own." [3]

Maguire later heard a rumor that the base commander had received orders from Whitehall to cease openly providing any aid except for exit visas for the departing Yemenites; evidently, Arab pressure within the U.N. had proved too overwhelming. While the

British continued to be helpful behind the scenes, they had to "play dumb" publically. Obtaining extra fuel to supply non-military aircraft for the airlift was, apparently, offering too much open assistance.

Alaska Airlines had counted on getting fuel from the base; with that avenue gone, other options had to be found. The RAF base at Nicosia in Cyprus agreed to provide aviation fuel, and fuel was occasionally available in Asmara, as well. But it meant Alaska Airlines had to maintain their own depots in Aden and Asmara and transport the fuel themselves from Cyprus in extra tanks inside the C-46 and fifty-gallon drums that filled the aisles. Another logistical nightmare.

In order to minimize wear and tear on planes, crew, and passengers, Maguire scheduled arrivals at Aden before nightfall. Aden had no runway lights, and after several close calls, Clarke Cole and By Sharp refused to land there after dark. They then departed at first light, or as close to it as possible, before the wind woke and filled the air with choking, engine-shredding clouds of dust, that during the heat of the day sometimes reached an altitude of 8,000 feet. He established who would be working with whom and where, created the flight schedules, encountered and overcame several problems, and knew there would be more to come.

On December 15, 1948,[4] Maguire took off for Aden for the first load of the second chapter of Operation Magic Carpet. Wooten came along specifically to take care of a lot of the footwork, but Maguire knew it would all be his headache before long; Wooten had an entire airline to run and couldn't stick around for the duration of the project. Still, Maguire had confidence in his own ability to get a handle on what was needed in order to bring the operation to a successful conclusion.

Like Warren Metzger, Maguire had been a test pilot during WWII and flown in the Pacific theater, so he was familiar with the devastation of war zones. The conditions he found at Hashed, when he touched down near the refugee camp in one of the C-46s, still took him by surprise.

When he'd first laid eyes on the camp back in October, he'd found the section reserved for the refugees to be no more than "a stretch of dirty ground with a few straw huts where babies were born and the sick were attended to."[5] While on the Administration side the structures left over from its first incarnation still stood, nothing much seemed to have been added. He'd expected a few more buildings by now, such as holding areas, a better hospital, and basic facilities for handling the influx of refugees. After all, the JDC's Israeli contacts in Aden had at least six months to prepare for the exodus. The changes and doubtful improvements were so minor it was easy to overlook them.

Maguire hoped it was not an omen of things to come.

Something few outside his family knew was that he had a personal as well as a professional stake in the outcome of the mission. He had already flown several of the refugee flights to and from other parts of the world—including Shanghai—and had seen firsthand the magnitude of the problem. He had met and spoken to countless refugees flown under his care and had gone from seeing the flights as just another job to a mission of mercy.

He had a sense that, somewhere, a giant clock was ticking: the displaced Jews had to be gotten to Israel as fast as possible, before they were swallowed by a combination of the world's war-weary indifference and growing Arab aggression. A devout Episcopalian in his private life—again, something few knew—he believed that God had put him in this time and place for a reason. It was his duty as a human being and a Christian to help these people any way that he could.

With the modifications, the C-46 could now seat up to 70 adult Yemenites, but the first several loads were, once again, supposed to be all children. On that first run, they ended up loading a total of 104 children, the oldest of them eleven years old, all of them tiny by American standards.

Bob Maguire took off for the nine-hour, second inaugural flight to Tel Aviv on December 16, 1948. Operation Magic Carpet had officially begun.[6]

Jim Wooten sat in the navigator's seat for take-off and then went back for a quick check of the cabin. He accepted Maguire's judgment, trusting to his pilot's flying skills, and decided to concentrate his own efforts on keeping the children from being frightened by the experience. He was sure he'd have his hands full; as if the sensations of flying weren't scary enough, he fully expected to be fired upon by the Egyptian troops, at the very least.

Though the plane had been thoroughly disinfected back in Anchorage, the odors of its previous journeys lingered in the air; diminished, but not eliminated. Not the most comfortable ride for a veteran, let alone a bunch of kids who'd never even seen an airplane until recently. He made a quick pass through the cabin before the smell drove him forward again.

A short time later, the Israeli volunteers, both of them nurses who spoke English, made their way to the cockpit and asked to speak to him. They were relatively young women; he judged the elder as no more than in her mid-thirties, and the other perhaps a decade younger. The elder one addressed him with polite firmness. "If you would be so kind, please let us know as soon as we reach Israel."[7]

"Do you mean Israeli air space?" Technically, Israel would be under them from the time they left the Bay of Aqaba.

She shook her head. "No. When we have truly reached the land of Israel."

It seemed a small thing. Wooten smiled. "Certainly. Be glad to. You just sit tight, and I'll let you know as soon as we're about to start our final approach for a landing."

When the plane passed over the Bay of Aqaba and started up the Negev, he opened the door and signaled the senior of the two nurses; forewarned, after all, was forearmed. He started to pat her arm, remembered that as a gentile and a man who was not related to her he was not allowed to touch her, and settled for a reassuring smile. "Now, we'll probably get fired on in this trip," he told her. "You go back and tell them all to be quiet and that God is with us, and we'll get through."

The nurse was still shy of middle-age, but her face bore marks of harsh experience that made her look older. Her eyes, though, held remarkable calm, a certainty usually seen only in the very old. She simply nodded. "We know that. God is with us, and we will get through."

Wooten was not a religious man; he had said what he had only to reassure her. "But by God," he said years later, "after you'd listened to her, you had to have faith in the statement."

Over Beersheba, they encountered a fierce east wind that veered them too far over territory held by the Egyptians. Below them were 2500 Egyptian troops —"Gyppos" was the pejorative term—manned by German officers from the Afrikka Corps. More importantly, they were armed with German 88 anti-aircraft guns that had a 40,000 foot range. Perhaps hoping for a lucky shot, they began firing as soon as the plane passed within twelve miles of them. "They started throwing lead at us," Wooten recalled. "But fortunately we were slightly out of range when the first burst came, and by diving we were able to stay out of range."[7]

The nurses led the children in prayer until the uneven boom and crash of the shells fell behind.

If Wooten was worried, Maguire was almost enjoying himself. He later admitted to appreciating the show. "I had a grandstand seat over the battle front, and it was a wonderful feeling to know that we were bringing them in all the time the battles went on."[8]

They reached Tel Aviv safely at last; Maguire brought the plane down for a perfect landing and taxied to the end of the runway. And then, a thing happened that Wooten never forgot and shook him to the core.

The children rose to full attention and burst out in the "HaTikva," the National Anthem of Israel. The sound reverberated through the aircraft and filled the cockpit. Wooten's throat tightened up. "One hundred and four kiddies. And the oldest one was eleven years of age, but by God every one of them was singing. They had arrived at the Promised Land."

The moment was a game changer in Wooten's eyes. "I never had anything wring my heart quite so badly or severely," he admitted later.[7]

For the first time, a new idea took shape in his mind; a concept he could not quite put a name to. Operation Magic Carpet stopped being just about the money, or the politics, or getting the best of Marshall, or anything else. It also became about getting these people safely home.

The children were unloaded and taken into a newly-constructed compound for medical attention, food, and new clothes from the bizarre mish-mash of donated garb collected, for the most part, in the U.S. As soon as the last one disembarked, Wooten sank down on the bottom step of the ladder leading to the door of the plane.

Bob Maguire sat next to him and waited. He'd known Wooten long enough to tell when something was eating him.

The compound was fenced to keep the refugees from wandering off into Tel Aviv and disappearing before they could be processed and assimilated into their new society. A few previous arrivals squatted near the fence and stared at the plane and the two men sitting on the ladder beneath its open door. They'd greeted the arrival of the children with great excitement and waited patiently for the chance to express their gratitude to the American crewmen who had brought them. They smiled and even waved when Wooten or Maguire looked their way.

After a few minutes, Wooten waved back, which encouraged the watchers to greater effort; some shouted words in their unknown language. The meaning might have been obscure, but the intent came through loud and clear.

Wooten spoke without ceasing to smile and wave at the Yemenites behind the fence. "Y'know, Bob, when I started this, they were all just so many dollars a head to me."

Maguire said nothing and waited until Wooten spoke again. "Marshall and that lease are gonna kill us. I've got to find another answer." He cleared his throat. "We've got to make this work, Bob. These people—" he waved again, garnering more broad smiles and a fresh crop of flying palms "—they need to be here. They need us."

Again, Maguire waited. None of this was news to him. He had already committed himself, body and soul, to this endeavor. He liked Wooten but knew all too well his friend's more mercenary attitude. This was new, uncharted territory for Jimmy Wooten. Maguire gave him the chance to explore it.

Finally, Wooten burst out, "Dammit, we're not letting these poor bastards down. I'm gonna make this happen if it kills me."

Bob Maguire nodded. "Goddamned right."[9]

.   .   .

Wooten had come up with the concept of forming his own transport charter airline when Marshall had forced him into the lease. He was, after all, still the president of Alaska Airlines; it made better sense to form a corporation, at least on paper, that could lease the planes and crew needed for the job from Alaska. But up to now, it had remained a dummy corporation, one of several he already owned. Wooten decided to turn it into the real deal. As a separate entity, his new airline could acquire the equipment needed without being answerable to Marshall.

Moreover, it irked him to be making piles of money on Marshall's behalf when Marshall had done everything in his power to prevent it, getting in his way and interfering on every level. It was maddening. Why not ditch that crippling lease and keep the profits for himself and those who justly deserved them?

And then there was the annoying reality of the ever-growing pile of lawsuits and injunctions being filed against Alaska Airlines and, in some cases, James Wooten personally. If he made Bob Maguire the president and put the whole works in his name, then no matter what happened to Alaska Airlines, R.W. Marshall, and Jim Wooten, the airlift charter business was safe.

Maguire agreed. When the time came, he would resign from Alaska Airlines and become the new president and CEO of Near East Air Transport. Both agreed to keep NEAT a total secret, even from the other pilots. Gossip reaching the wrong ears could shoot them down before they even got started.

Wooten left to put things in motion. Bob Maguire went back to flying planes. And they waited for what would happen next.

1. "Challenges and Inspirations," *Magic Carpet Pilots*, http://www.alaskaair.com/content/about-us/history/carpet-pilots.aspx.
2. "Robert F. Maguire Jr., 94: Helped Airlift Thousands of Jews to Israel", Dennis McLellan, *LA Times*, June 17, 2005
3. Paraphrased quote, as remembered by Clarke Cole, 1970.
4. Parfitt, *The Road to Redemption*, p185-187.

5. Barer, The Magic Carpet, p9.
6. This would later be recorded as the official beginning of the entire operation. Other sources cite the beginning of Operation Magic Carpet as June of 1949, when Alaska Airlines signed a second contract to continue the airlift.
7. Oral account given during a speech Wooten gave before the JDC some years later.
8. Barer, *The Magic Carpet*, p10.
9. Satterfield notes, source unknown.

INTERLUDE:
SANCTUARY

E ven as the IDF launched Operation Yoav, on October 15, 1948, Operation Magic Carpet was nearly
stopped before it began.

The Immigration Department of the Israel Government informed the JDC that they would accept into Israel 3,500 Yemenite Jews instead of the 2,000 they had
previously specified. At first, this news came as a relief;
already, nearly 4,000 filled Hashed's boundaries and
strained the JDC's resources.[1]

But then Sir Reginald Champion, the Governor of
Aden, reversed his earlier support for the operation, in-
forming Harry Vitalis that it would be impossible to
carry on with the project "at the present time."[2] He could
not imagine how such a massive undertaking could be
kept secret, especially since the planes would be forced
to fly directly over the battlefields more often than not.
Almost certainly, he feared an eruption of fresh violence
within Aden itself. Riots incited by the news coming out
of Palestine and Israel had already killed dozens of Jews
and Arabs alike, destroyed entire city blocks and, with
the British forces now severely undermanned, he had no
way to contain it if it happened again.

Vitalis, equally worried about what would happen if the population of Hashed continued to grow and by the fact that these people had nowhere to go, urged him to reconsider. As a compromise, he proposed the immediate emigration of about 1,700 children fourteen years or under and about 150 widows. Champion relented and gave the okay for the project to proceed under a few added conditions. Only women, orphans, and men of non-military age would be allowed to leave, and Israel had to provide four children's nurses and two representatives from Youth Aliyah to accompany the children.[2]

The Jewish Agency at first opposed the splitting of families. When it became clear that the choice was to either allow some family members to go and forbid others, or that no one would be going anywhere, they relented.

Vitalis sent the new contract terms to Jim Wooten and prepared himself for the next crisis.

After Operation Yoav, the Egyptian Army had tried to stabilize a defensive line between its two arms of controlled territory in the Negev, along the Beersheba-Gaza road to hold onto the western and southern Negev Desert. Instead, on December 5, IDF cut through Beersheba to hit the Egyptian Army's rear flank, catching them totally by surprise. The IDF captured three major Egyptian positions without major combat or casualties, and the next day added a fourth.

The Egyptians dug in and fought tooth and nail, holding the fifth position, while a minefield on a sixth position stopped the Israeli troops in their tracks.

Encouraged, Egypt launched a counter-attack, but lost five of its twelve attacking tanks in the effort. The IAF spotted a weakness in their formation and radioed ground command. The IDF pounced and chased the Egyptians westward. A hundred Egyptian soldiers were killed; the Israelis had two wounded and zero killed.

During another operation happening simultaneously,

the IDF managed to take Iraq el Manshiyeh (now Kiriat Gat) for a time. But guards mistook an Egyptian counter attack for friendly forces and allowed them to advance, trapping a large number of Israeli fighters. 87 Israelis perished, including defenders of a religious platoon.[3]

In retaliation, other IDF troops advanced into Egypt.

On December 28, Nokrashy Pasha, the Egyptian Prime Minister, was assassinated. Egypt reeled but came back with a roar, determined to wreak vengeance.

As Israel mounted their incursion into the Sinai, the RAF began flying regular reconnaissance missions over Israel and the Sinai. RAF aircraft took off from Egyptian airbases and sometimes flew alongside Royal Egyptian Air Force planes. High-flying British aircraft frequently flew over Haifa and Ramat David Airbase; the Israelis called them "shuftykeit."[4]

On November 20, 1948, an unarmed RAF photo-reconnaissance De Havilland Mosquito flying over the Galilee towards Hatzor Airbase was shot down by an IAF P-51 Mustang flown by American *machal* pilot Wayne Peake. He opened fire and took out the port engine. The aircraft exploded and crashed off Ashdod. Both pilots were killed.[5]

Late in the morning of January 7, 1949, four British Spitfire FR18s on another reconnaissance mission flew over an Israeli convoy that had been attacked by five Egyptian Spitfires a few minutes earlier. The pilots had spotted smoking vehicles and were drawn to the scene out of curiosity. Two of the planes dove down to take pictures of the convoy, while the remaining two covered them from above.

Israeli soldiers on the ground, mistaking the planes for another Egyptian air attack, grabbed their machine guns and opened fire. One plane was shot down; the other took a hit but pulled up and out of range.

Two patrolling IAF Spitfires, flown by none other than Slick Goodlin and another *machal* pilot, a Canadian named John McElroy[5], dove down to attack the three "enemy" fighters. All three RAF planes were shot down, and one pilot was killed.[6]

There is considerable discrepancy in the reports of what happened next. Some say the British sent a Mosquito and two Tempests to look for the missing Spitfires later that day; others that it was four RAF Spitfires escorted by fifteen Tempests that went searching for the lost planes. Regardless, they were attacked by four IAF Spitfires.

The Tempests could not jettison their external fuel tanks, and some had non-operational guns. The Israeli flyers, led by Ezer Weizman[7], shot down two of the Tempests and two British pilots died before the Israeli pilots realized their error and disengaged.

Furious, Britain and the U.S. forced Israel to withdraw on January 7, 1949.[8] The RAF prepared to bomb IAF airfields and attack any IAF aircraft they caught in the air. British troops in the Middle East were placed on high alert with all leave canceled, and British citizens were advised to leave Israel. Even the Royal Navy went on high alert.

Most of the IAF pilots at Hatzor Airbase, where several of the attacking planes were based, had flown with or alongside the RAF during World War II. They were sure the RAF would not take the loss of five aircraft and two pilots lying down and expected a retaliatory strike at dawn the next day. Few had the heart to go up against their former allies. Some decided not to offer any resistance and left the base.

A few, however, strapped themselves into their cockpits at dawn and watched the sky.

The injured RAF squadrons bayed at the leash in vain, and cooler heads prevailed; British commanders refused to authorize any retaliatory strikes.[5]

The next day, British pilots were told they could shoot down any Israeli aircraft caught in Egyptian or Jordanian airspace but to avoid Israel's borders. The British Foreign Office also slapped the Israeli Government with a demand for compensation over the loss of personnel and equipment.

Throughout January of 1949, the skies above Israel and along her borders were a deadly hunting ground.

1. Parfitt, *The Road to Redemption*, p181.
2. Parfitt, *The Road to Redemption*, p183-185.
3. Herzog, Chaim and Gazit, Shomo; *The Arab-Israeli Wars: War and Peace in the Middle East*, Vintage, rev. 2005, p. 97.
4. "Spyflight."
5. John McElroy was another friend of Warren Metzger's from the Canadian Air Force.
6. Israel: The Birth of a Nation (History Channel).
7. Ezer Weizman was the Commander of the Israeli Air Force and Minister of Defense. He later became the seventh President of Israel, first elected in 1993 and re-elected in 1998.
8. "1948 Arab-Israeli War," http://en.wikipedia.org/wiki/1948_Arab%E2%80%93Israeli_War.

CHAPTER EIGHT:
WARREN ARRIVES

Warren Metzger arrived at the Lydda airfield near Tel Aviv on January 3rd, 1949, flying as co-pilot beside Captain Floyd Wacha in a newly-modified DC-4. Its plush seats were replaced with wooden benches and rope. Fortunately, the plane carried only the crew, extra personnel, a load of parts, and other supplies bound for Asmara.

The airport had recently been bombed by Egyptians, but Warren noticed no obvious damage. The few other airplanes sat on the tarmac in the sun, waiting for freight, passengers, or perhaps just permission to go elsewhere. He saw no others with the tell-tale logo on its flank of a snow-covered Alaska beneath the North Star or the broad-lettered "Alaska Airlines" along the sides. There were supposed to be two Alaska Airlines C-46s there somewhere and a second DC-4 as well, but there was no sign of them at Lydda. Warren assumed they were off flying missions, but that didn't jive with the timetable as he understood it.

They weren't due to fly on to Asmara until the following morning. Once the plane was settled for the night, Warren, Wacha, and the others crossed the tarmac into the small, rectangular building with its single, central tower that comprised the terminal.

Clearing the various checks the Israelis had in place for them took less time than he had expected; the Israelis were taking no chances, but at the airport at least, they seemed to be efficient. A short while later, the American crewmen were left standing in the middle of a largely empty terminal, wondering where to go from there.

Someone was supposed to be there to meet them, but Warren saw no one he knew. Carrying their bags and followed by the others, he and Wacha exited the terminal on the other side and took their first look around at the Holy Land.

Warren hoped he'd have an opportunity to explore Tel Aviv at some point during the mission. Compared to Alaska or New York, the weather was balmy, the temperature somewhere in the mid-fifties, and a few clouds scudded past in an otherwise bright blue sky. The airport itself was distinctly sparse; built on the southern outskirts of the city by the British in 1936, it hadn't changed much since.

Lydda airfield was ideally situated on a small plateau above the Lydda valley. The city center of Tel Aviv, which had started life as a modern suburb of the ancient port town of Jaffa and had since engulfed it, was more than ten miles away. In the immediate vicinity of the airfield and spread out through the valley below, however, what remained of the town of Lydda offered some interesting sights.

Beside piles of shattered concrete and bullet-pocked walls, souvenirs of the violent take-over six months earlier from the Arab Palestinians, sat clean, modern storefronts with colorful awnings and gleaming glass. Shaded by waving palm trees, sleek Mercedes-Benz and Citroën sedans parked between worn military vehicles, while donkey-drawn carts wove among bicycles and strolling pedestrians. Men in well-cut three-piece suits crossed the streets with robed tribesmen who could have stepped into Jerusalem a thousand years before and gone unnoticed. Well-dressed young people planted shrubs and flowering plants along the swept streets, while others shoveled up piles of rubble from bombed-out houses.

Looking out over the valley, Warren could see the tall minaret of the Great Mosque and the rounded domes and stone walls of buildings that had probably been old before Christopher Columbus had set sail from Spain. He wished he could go explore them.[1]

Hearing someone call his and Wacha's names, he turned and saw Clarke Cole, waving from beside a car that had seen hard service since well before the war. Warren knew Cole had already flown several trips in the region, some of them with Wooten aboard. He wondered how that had gone. Cole and Wooten had already butted heads multiple times that he knew of since Warren had joined the Airline. But it was good to see a friendly face in a strange land.

Cole greeted the crew with his characteristic broad smile. "Welcome to Tel Aviv. Hope you brought your waders, because the bullshit is hip deep around here."[2]

Cole had been in Tel Aviv for nearly four months, the first several weeks of which were spent almost entirely on his own. He was delighted to have the other pilots and crew join the fun or share the misery. Warren and three others piled into the car with Cole, the rest following in a jeep driven by a young woman Warren didn't know. On the trip into town, Cole regaled them with tales of airline hardships already faced in trying to carry out this mission.

The primary issue was again fuel; it was proving impossible to obtain a steady supply. The pilots were now going to have to fly to Nicosia, the Royal Air Force Base in Cyprus, in order to refuel. Cole had heard a rumor that "the Brits are catching flak for helping out the Jews. So the local commanders are being told to back off."

When Warren asked where the planes were, Cole barked out a short, sharp laugh. As usual, he explained, the planes were out looking for fuel. Probably up at Cyprus, but they could be anywhere. He entertained them with the saga of the ongoing fuel shortage and the string of bureaucratic snafus that kept it going. The C-46s were consistently overloaded and half the time coasting into Tel Aviv on fumes, and all the additional miles didn't help. Cole had sent one wire after another to headquarters, telling them that he needed a DC-4 to do the job, but so far, no dice.

The fact that he wasn't yet certified to fly the DC-4 didn't bother him; like most of the other pilots, he could fly anything but hadn't yet been checked out by the Check Pilot or a designated senior pilot. As with most issues with Alaska Airlines, it was a matter of money. The twin-engine C-46s were more challenging to fly, but DC-4s were a 4-engine plane, so the pilots got paid more, and the airline wasn't in a huge hurry to "bump up" anybody it didn't have to.[2]

Maguire had established fuel depots at Aden and Asmara, but that meant flying extra trips just to bring in the fuel to keep them stocked. Cole and the other C-46 pilot, By Sharp, now steadfastly refused to fly into Aden at night, as the runway had no lights. "Pappa Wooten" had threatened to send both of them home, but Cole laughed off the notion. It would never happen. Wooten needed pilots too badly on this venture.

Nor was the fuel problem the only hiccup. Promised lodgings in Aden for the crew had not been forthcoming, and the crew either slept in their planes or under open sky atop the only available hotel. The eternal and all-pervasive dust chewed hell out of the planes' engines and instruments. The mechanics were working almost around the clock and still couldn't keep up with repairs. Alaska Airlines had negotiated a deal with KLM to handle their maintenance[3], but the nearest hanger, in Rome, was usually backlogged.

There were problems with the refugees, too. Many having finally reached the refugee camp were technically forbidden to board the planes by the terms of the agreement between the JDC and Aden. While most of the Yemenite Jews were craftsmen and artisans, primarily silver and metal smiths by tradition who were forbidden to own weapons, a few were hereditary warriors and swordsmen who had refused to surrender their traditional arms. The Imam of Yemen had expressed the fear that these and any other military-aged men would only go to swell the ranks of the Israeli army. Rather than risk the Imam's wrath and perhaps goad him into taking action against the exodus, the JDC enforced the ban.

When possible, exit visas somehow found their way into the hands of any refugee healthy enough to travel. The pilots and the Israelis in charge of the camp looked the other way when it came time to board the planes. Word apparently got out, for officials from Aden had turned up to make sure the terms of the contract were strictly enforced. Families were forcibly divided, and there was nothing the Americans could do about it.

When Warren asked what would happen to the ones left behind, Cole just shrugged. He himself had written a blistering letter to the U.S. Consul, furiously protesting the conditions under which the airline was being asked to fulfill its contract. He had received a four-page reply that boiled down to, "You should have made better preparations. Don't see how you're going to manage. Tough luck."

Cole drove them to their hotel, the Yarden, long enough to drop off their bags and check in. "Don't get used to it," he warned them, "half the time they don't have any rooms and you'll sleep on the roof if you're lucky." He then escorted them along with three other new-arrivals—pilots Lyle Edwards, Bob Morris, and Gene Wheeler[4]—to meet the Israeli authorities who would be their contacts in Tel Aviv. Henry "Hank" Mulleneaux, who had recently begun acting as assistant Chief Pilot to Maguire as the latter took on a more managerial role, was there. So were Harry Vitalis and a thin, weathered Israeli officer who looked as if he were made of hickory and dried leather.

The officer laid down a rumpled and coffee-stained map of the Red Sea and the surrounding countries. It was almost unreadable with lines and circles in red or blue ink. Warren noticed that Israel was still labeled as "Palestine." The very edge of the Mediterranean Sea lay along one side.

In accented English, the officer explained the route Warren and the other pilots were to fly, making new lines on the map as he went. The planes would take off from Asmara to fly directly to Aden, then Tel Aviv and finally Cyprus to refuel before flying back to Asmara.

Mulleneaux pointed to a spot on the other side of the Red Sea. "Here's Asmara, where we're based. We have ground crews in all three locations; we'll be rotating everyone, so no one is stuck in one place for too long." He went on to explain that, because the city of Asmara sat at around 8,000 feet above sea level, the planes couldn't take off from there with full tanks. The fuel needed to get them from Aden to Tel Aviv, and then from Tel Aviv to Cyprus, would be waiting at a depot in Aden.

The Israeli officer and Vitalis both issued stern warnings about landing anywhere in Arab territory. When pressured, Vitalis did point out Port Sudan as a possible emergency landing location. "But only in the event of emergency, and I don't mean if one of your passengers is ill or injured. For one thing, it wouldn't do any good; you wouldn't receive any aid. For another, you would be endangering yourselves and all your passengers."

Navigational aids in that era were negligible at best and, except for a single radar array in Tel Aviv, even fewer and farther between than in most of the world. Alaska Airlines didn't have enough navigators to go around; regulations aside, many flights went out without navigators aboard, even on the airline's regular runs. The crew for each flight would consist of a pilot and co-pilot. A few questions gave Warren the expected answer: pilots would be flying by dead reckoning and the simple, time-honored expedient of looking out the window. The thought was not terribly worrying; they flew all over Alaska that way.

The route outlined to Warren was mostly over the Red Sea and straight up the Gulf of Aqaba, along the border between Egypt and what was then called Transjordan, to reach Israel. Anti-aircraft emplacements left over from World War II still waited along the borders, now manned by Egyptian or Jordanian soldiers who had been trained by German gunners.

Israeli airspace was no safer. No one could predict with certainty when or where battles would take place between Israeli forces and invading enemy troops supplied by Egypt, Jordan, Syria or other members of the Arab League. It was a virtual certainty that the Alaska pilots would be flying directly over every possible conflict. All sides had artillery perfectly capable of removing questionable aircraft from overhead, and no one on the ground was particularly trusting. The officer assured the pilots that the IDF would not fire upon them, if they were identified in time. The warning that accidents could happen went unspoken.

And then there were the enraged Arab tribesmen armed with sniper rifles, who lurked between borders and battles and watched the skies. They invariably assumed—not without justification—that any plane they saw was an enemy plane.

If you are seen, Warren was warned, expect to be shot at. If you fly too low, expect to be shot at. And if you miss the corridor into Israel, expect to be shot at. Though in the latter case, it would be by Israelis, and they'd be in P-38 fighters or possibly the new Avia 9-90s, the Czech version of the Messerschmitt. If you come in unannounced or at an unscheduled time, expect to be shot at by either the Israelis or the RAF.

On the way back to the hotel, Cole expounded in his usual off-hand style: "Movement on the ground means go up or get shot at. Fly too high, miss your landmarks and get shot at. I'll bet you never thought you'd have this much fun when you signed on for this one."

After the sobering introduction to his mission, Warren returned to his hotel and was pleasantly surprised to run into several Israeli Air Force pilots at the bar. He had known a few of them from his Army Air Corps days or the Royal Canadian Air Force. They now flew as *machal*, volunteers fighting for Israel. Some were as dedicated to the cause as any Israeli. Others were mercenary warriors unable to adjust to civilian flight, simply addicted to the thrill of combat flying. In Israel, they could have their fill.

Among them was Chalmers "Slick" Goodlin—best but unfairly remembered as the man who passed up the chance to break the sound barrier in the Bell X-1 fighter plane, an honor that went to Chuck Yeager. Slick had become an acknowledged ace and the chief test pilot for the IAF. Lou Lenart, one of the most celebrated heroes of the Israeli wars, was also present, though he and Warren had not previously met.

Goodlin and Lenart knew about the airlift and were curious. Since Warren hadn't yet made a flight, he could add little to their knowledge, but Cole—who enjoyed nothing more than playing raconteur—filled in the blanks and kept the table entertained over lukewarm beer. He'd also met Goodlin before at that same bar and insisted that the fighter pilot had once almost taken a shot at him, when he'd been coming into Tel Aviv at the tail end of a run.[5]

Goodlin confirmed it. "Good thing I got close enough to read the company logo." He smiled. "Relax. We're

watching for you guys, now. Just make sure you identify yourselves coming in. And try not to come in after
dark."

Cole asked them if they wanted to fly some of the
trips. "We're always looking for good pilots. Just talk to
Maguire or Jimmy Wooten next time he's around."

Goodlin and Lenart avowed that they probably
would, and the impromptu party broke up.

Warren flew with Wacha in the DC-4 to Asmara the
next morning, settling into the surprisingly comfortable
and well-appointed if somewhat overcrowded Albergo
Ciaao Hotel and listening to stories from his fellow
Alaska Airlines employees about the task at hand. Like
himself, most had recently arrived and were preparing
to fly their first loads while still wondering what lay
ahead. Others like Cole, Sharp, and Larry Flahart had already made several flights. They readily regaled the
others with tales of mishaps and near-misses.

Warren had expected to start flying missions right
away; instead, Floyd Wacha took off in the DC-4 for
parts unknown with someone else flying co-pilot.
While Warren had also expected to fly the occasional
trip as co-pilot, Maguire didn't schedule him on the
roster and told him to just be patient.

With no planes at hand, Warren had nothing to do
but explore Asmara, write letters, and nap. He'd long
ago learned to get sleep while the getting was good,
because it often wasn't.

Asmara was not without points of interest. Rebuilt in
the 1930s as a showcase of Italian modernism architecture, it was an undeniably lovely city in areas. The
Viala Roma, or the main boulevard, looked like a park,
lined with flowering trees, statues, and buildings that
took art nouveau to daring new extremes.

But it was still an African city, with a weird and wonderful mix of old world elegance cheek-by-jowl with
the very wild and colorful reminders of the Dark Con-
tinent's tribal heritage. It wasn't unusual to see a camel

recumbent in the parking place next to a gleaming new Rolls Royce, or a line of hot new sports cars parked behind an overloaded donkey cart. Men in three-piece suits straight from Savile Row or Brooks Brothers strolled next to towering tribesmen in flowing robes of brilliant yellow, orange, and red. You could find anything at the marketplace from fresh produce to transistor radios to slaves, or so rumored, though the latter were not openly displayed.

It was here that Mussolini had built his infamous "House of Mirrors"; a private bordello where he kept his own stable of girls from around the world. Most of the interior was completely lined with mirrors, so Il Duce could see his ladies from all sides at any time. Warren, Cole, and a few others looked for it over a period of several days but never found it. Another bordello—reputed to be the "other" House of Mirrors—was located farther south. It turned out to be a false rumor and the building itself was a disappointment, being dilapidated and no longer used for its original purpose.

The city was not without its perils. The native Ethiopians, largely descendants of the Tigrinya and Tigre peoples, were not ready to forgive the Italians. The latter still ran much of the bureaucracy despite making up barely one-third of the population and also despite Eritrea having been taken over by the British in 1941. It was not terribly unusual for an Italian who mistakenly found himself on the streets after dark to be found dead the next morning. "You wanted to be damned sure you said 'hi' to people," remembered pilot Larry Roger. "Nobody else said 'hi' except an American. That would keep you out of trouble."[6]

Warren wasn't terribly concerned about his safety, since the natives were invariably profoundly polite to him and his fellow Alaskans, if still rather distant. But he did rapidly become restless. He was here to do a job, not play tourist. He was running out of ways to amuse himself.

He spent days wandering around the city looking at buildings. He found a postcard with three topless native girls, scrawled on it "The one in the middle is mine," and mailed it to his parents.[7] He watched a couple of films at the town's only movie theater.

And he thought about Marian. Where was she right now? Was she in a hotel somewhere, waiting to catch a flight to somewhere else? At her apartment in Anchorage reading a book?

Between flights for the Berlin airlift, her brother stayed back east, grieving with his wife—their daughter had been stillborn in late November—and Marian stayed with another friend when she was in Seattle, which wasn't often.

They'd hardly seen each other since November. She'd broken off her engagement to Ed, but their own relationship hovered in limbo. Surely she wouldn't have ended things with Warren's rival if she hadn't felt the same way he did. Or at least been heading in that direction.

Most days, Warren was sure she loved him, but sometimes it was hard to feel perfectly confident. She could have her pick of men. She had no particular reason to fall for a slightly gimpy C-46 Captain working for a marginal airline, who had nothing but a used car and a pittance to his name in the bank.

On the morning of January 12th, he sat down to write her a letter, planning to mail it to her care of Alaska Airlines. She'd probably get it sooner that way than if he sent it to her home address. In it, he joked about his far-from-grueling schedule and spoke of the missing airplanes. "Poor old 9158 is grinding back and forth like mad, but I am now a C-46 Captain and the C-46s are up north trying to get gas. I have decided to call myself a Connie[9] captain, it sounds better and can't do any harm since we have no Constellations, either."

He assured her that, "no one has been shot at yet; Sharp claims he was, but no one else in the airplane saw it so I'm inclined to doubt it." He offered her the use of his car back in Anchorage while he was gone, if she needed it, since he had no idea when he would be returning. He asked her sheepishly if he'd been spelling her name incorrectly and, almost as an afterthought, mentioned that the other DC-4 numbered 66756 was due in shortly. "...it was in Hong Kong or Calcutta or some place a couple days ago."

After a pause, he went on: "Hank Mulleneaux just landed and says both C-46s will be in this evening, so tonight will probably find me grinding north with a load of odiferous Jews aboard. They've got poor old 915 smelling something fierce."

He closed with, "I wish by some queer twist of fate you were on 667." Perhaps moved by longing and thinking it could be weeks until he saw her again, or maybe just a little nervous at the thought of who she might be dating in his absence, he signed it, "All My Love." On paper, he could say it without the words clogging in his throat and ruining the moment. If she didn't know already, it was past time she did.

True to his prediction, Warren was given the go; later that night, he landed his C-46 at Hashed, ready to fly his first trip for the operation the next morning. It was his first glimpse of the camp. He did not know it, but Hashed had grown considerably from its initial incarnation. Several makeshift buildings and a number of tents had been added to the original site. He thought it seemed terribly primitive.

Small, slender, dark-skinned people whom he assumed were the Yemenite Jews crowded every space, squatting in the tents and reed shacks and around the evening fires. Despite the darkness, he could tell there were more of them than he had expected, though he'd already heard from other pilots that the number of refugees far exceeded the wildest estimates.

The air was thick with cooking smells and less savory odors indicative of overcrowding and illness. He was surprised at the lack of noise; with so many people squeezed into such a relatively small space, he thought it should have sounded more like a busy street in Tel Aviv. Instead, voices were soft, almost subdued, as if the people waiting in the camp wished to pass unnoticed.

He and Lyle Edwards, his co-pilot for the trip, were met by a thin, weathered woman with the complexion of a well-worked western saddle and a British gentleman whose pipe kept the air around him clear of all flying insects. Warren smoked a pipe on occasion, but whatever the other gentleman was using for tobacco made Warren decide he'd prefer the flies.

He assumed that the gentleman—whose name and rank he could not afterward remember—was the camp commander from the offices of the British Protectorate.[10] The woman was a nurse; just another of the volunteers doing what they could for the refugees and trying their best to facilitate the evacuation. Both were exhausted, overworked, and overburdened in a camp never intended to house so many.

Edwards declined the offer of a brief tour of the compound, but curiosity drove Warren to accept. Even had it been light, there was not much to see: a few buildings, mostly shacks left over from the prisoner of war days and some of them barely fitting the description.

On the other side of the dividing fence, to which the refugees were largely confined, there was even less. Shelter consisted of tents of every size, some no more than canvas roofs supported by poles pounded into the ground with rocks. They filled nearly every foot of space within the fence and stretched away into the blackness.

"Best we can do, you know," the British officer confided, trailing along beside Warren. "The Arabs are killing every Jew they can get their hands on. We had to bring them here just to keep them safe. But we simply weren't prepared for it. And neither, of course, was Israel. Not as if they had a lot to spare, of course. The war and all."[11]

Old men squatted around evening fires, talking in their soft voices, sometimes listening to one another read aloud or just watching the flames. Women cooked or held and rocked their children, their huge dark eyes like pools of night watching the strangers pass by. Warren was surprised to see how tiny they were; none, standing upright, would have reached higher than his chest. Most were still emaciated from their arduous journey and could not have weighed above 80 or 90 pounds, even the men.

Between the tents, those who had no shelter filled the makeshift paths and aisle ways, huddling together in the shadows for warmth with their worn shawls or blankets provided by the camp pulled tight around their shoulders.

The tour did not stray far from the Administration complex, where the hospital, such as it was, and offices were kept. Even so, Warren glimpsed a hint of lives and a culture utterly alien to him. Their clothes in un-familiar colors and patterns were sometimes fes-tooned with beads and trinkets.[12] The music of an unknown language rode the night air. Their dark faces shaped in ways unique to them were certainly nothing like Warren had ever seen, though the centuries of im-mersion in a completely Arabic culture had imbued them with a certain similarity.[12] The black eyes that sometimes met his were as full of curiosity as his.

And yet, beneath their strangeness, these folk were not so different from others he had met in his travels. A smile was a smile and a touch was a touch, as much here as back home in Alberta.

A few of the adults smiled shyly and nodded or re-turned his greeting with one of their own, but for the most part, he might have been passing through a gath-ering of ghosts. Few would meet his eyes; most looked away when he glanced at them.

The children, though, peeped out from behind the shelter of their parents with dark eyes round with wonder. His smile brought answering smiles more often than not. Shy and quickly hidden by a ducked head, flashes of white teeth and sparkling eyes met his with the open curiosity of a heart that had not yet learned fear.

The tour ended, and they rejoined the rest of the party back at what passed for an office. While he'd heard enough stories from his fellow crewmen to know that Wooten's initial estimate of one or two thousand children was completely off-base, just how wrong it might have been came as a slight shock.

"The camp was built to house about 2,000 people. We have nearly 5,000 now, and more come every day," the nurse told the Americans. "Word has passed among the tribes that a King David once again rules in Israel. I've heard tales from some that they saw signs in the sky. So they simply packed up whatever small belongings they were allowed and started walking."[14]

"We're trying to process them as fast as we can and move them along," said the British officer. "But it takes time, you know. It all takes time, and we can't move them until they're well enough to travel."

Neither could guess how many had never made it. A large cemetery outside the camp testified to how difficult the journey had been, and those who made it to the camp brought with them tales of those who had not. "We will never know how many unmarked graves lie along the roads to Aden," said the nurse.

Of those who survived the journey, most arrived starved and ill; malaria and dysentery were the most common ailments, but other sicknesses and parasites were rife. Few had more than the clothes on their backs, and some had not even that remaining to them. Many of the sheiks through whose territory each band of travelers had passed demanded taxes or protection fees for being allowed through unmolested.[15] The toll was sometimes impossible to meet, as the Imam had decreed that the Jews could take with them nothing of value. Even paying the exorbitant taxes had not always saved them from robbers, bands of which infested the mountains.

The only things they had been allowed to keep were their books. Their passionate dedication to their religion and its sacred writings left a deep impression on all the pilots. "All they have in this world are a few pots and pans and a brass water pipe, maybe a stove," remembered Hank Mulleneaux later, "But you'll find every man carrying his Bible, and every other man clinging to a huge holy parchment scroll clasped in front of him."

Hundreds of men and women tottered into camp devoid of food or more than a few rags of clothing, but they bore clutched in their nearly skeletal arms ancient scroll cases containing sacred texts handed down for untold generations. Books were precious to the Yemenites. The men were able to read upside down text as well as they could right side up; there were so few books that they all shared.

Despite generous donations from a number of organizations, the camp never had enough medical supplies, never enough clothes, food, blankets, or beds. Not that those had been a great necessity at first; few of the Yemenites coming from the highlands and backwaters of the Yemen had ever seen a bed and chose to sleep under them, using the sheets for shawls during the day.

Nor had many of them ever witnessed water flowing from a tap. Trying to teach and enforce basic rules of hygiene had proved an ongoing challenge. Isolated in hostile territory as they had been and constantly oppressed by their neighbors, they had become a shy people, unaccustomed to strangeness or strangers. "Stick to themselves," the British officer related. "We had one group come in that wouldn't even allow other Jews into their town. It's been a difficult adjustment for many of them, sad to say."

The nurse concurred but added, "They never complain, even when they're terribly sick or injured. I wish they would, actually. It would make it so much easier to try and help them if only they'd let us know when something is wrong. Only after a great deal of time and effort have we been able to get the women to permit medical examinations or assistance in childbirth."[16]

The British officer finally turned the discussion to the job ahead, asking the Americans what they'd been told about their route. He reaffirmed the warnings they'd received back in Tel Aviv and added a new one. "If you get shot down or have to make an emergency landing," he said directly to Warren, "try to come down in the Red Sea, preferably close to a British ship. Your chances of survival are far better that way. If you land anywhere else in Arab territory, you will all be killed." He paused and then amended his statement. "If the military gets to you first, you and your crew might be safe, possibly. But if civilians get to you, any of the tribesmen..." He made a gesture with his pipe. "You and your passengers are all as good as dead."

Warren had seen so many children in his walk through the camp. They would be his passengers. Despite the recent horrors of World War II, he could not quite believe that anyone could harm them. "Even the little kids?"

The officer sighed wearily. "My dear sir, to an Arab, a 'little kid' is just something that will grow up to be a big Jew. They will kill them all like so many animals."[17]

Warren never forgot those words or the shock he felt. "This affected me a lot," he said later, "because I'd seen all those little kids, maybe four or five years old, with their big ol' brown eyes looking up at you...I just couldn't see how someone could walk up to them and slit their throats, but I guess they could."[18]

.   .   .

In the morning, lines of Yemenite Jews waited under the wings of the plane when Warren and Edwards arrived. The painted eagle over the door, though badly in need of a touch-up, worked its magic, and the people filed quietly aboard.

They used a wooden ramp with shallow steps that had been specially built for them; the steel ladder had proved too difficult for most to master. The crew and two Israeli nurses settled them onto the wooden benches, tied the rope that substituted as a safety belt across their laps. Warren counted around eighty passengers, all those who had their papers in order and were considered ready for travel. A very full load for the C-46.

The sun had hours, yet, to reach its full, punishing heat. The perpetual haze of dust had only begun to make its morning assent when Warren taxied the C-46 onto the runway and took off.

After hearing some of the stories of his fellow pilots, Warren more than half expected to be peppered with bullets from the ground or chased by a P-38, but the flight passed without incident. Smoke from nearby battles appeared now and again, but none of them occurred on the route directly beneath him, and he was perfectly happy to miss the excitement.

Nine hours later, he arrived at Lydda and taxied to a halt, with just enough gas left in the tanks to make it to Cyprus the following morning. Even before the engines had finished cycling down, a rush of volunteers swarmed onto the tarmac, singing and waving signs and banners to welcome his passengers home.

Warren and Edwards waited and watched from the cockpit as the Yemenites were carefully helped off the plane and surrounded by the people waiting for them. Singing, the Israelis led the latest arrivals into another compound christened Ras El Ein, newer and better-equipped than Hashed. There, the pilgrims would be given food, water, and medical care. Their journey to their new lives was not yet over, but at least now they were home.

There was nothing to do now but disembark and leave his poor, overworked airplane in the capable and equally over-worked hands of the ground crew. Mechanic Harold "Hank" McCoy, his sun glasses glinting above his somewhat less-than-pristine white coveralls, waved at them from the ground below, signaling them to come down.

Since there were no problems to hash over, the debrief with McCoy didn't take long, and the cheerful mechanic knew the pilots were tired. The worst, he told them, would be getting the thing cleaned out, but fortunately, there were others to take care of that. "We'll grease everything up and get the dust out," he assured them. "She'll be ready to go again by morning." He jerked his thumb over his shoulder. "There's a girl in a jeep waiting out front of the compound. She'll take you into town." Satisfied, Warren headed off, while Edwards lingered to exchange a few more words with McCoy.

As Warren passed the compound fence, his former passengers startled him with a spontaneous burst of cheers and applause. Their great, dark eyes watched him almost as if he were superhuman.

To his knowledge, he had never been a hero to anyone before and wasn't entirely sure he deserved it now. Nevertheless, he grinned, waved, and hurried past, a little disconcerted.

A small glow of warmth and satisfaction sprang to life beside the embarrassment, shoving it into the background.

He'd always known that his job often made a great difference to a vast number of people who would never even know of his existence or spare him a thought. But for the first time, he could actually see the difference he had made in someone's life, feel their appreciation and gratitude for his efforts.

It was nothing he'd ever expected, but it surely was gratifying.

1. Many of the pilots described Tel Aviv as a modern, beautiful city. However, little of it was visible from the airport. Lydda, or Lod, then in the process of being absorbed into Tel Aviv, was a much older city, dating from Biblical times.
2. Many of the conversations have been pieced together from separate accounts by more than one source. Most of my sources are, of course, Warren Metzger, but these stories were often repeated by other pilots at various times in my presence.
3. Alaska Airlines had an agreement with KLM: ASA would carry mail for KLM into the Indonesian countries where KLM was not permitted, and KLM would, in exchange, lend mechanical assistance when needed at certain hangars.
4. No complete list exists of Alaska Airlines personnel who served on Operation Magic Carpet. The names I've included are those gleaned from multiple interviews, letters, postcards, Archie Satterfield's notes and other sources. I've included a list of all those I could find in the back of this book.
5. Satterfield; Larry Roger interview, 1979.
6. Satterfield; Clarke Cole interview, 1970.
7. Later, this caused his mother—Elsie Metzger—no end of anxiety. After receiving this postcard, she and Lew received nothing else until they received a telegram saying only, "My God I'm married." Elsie later confessed to being intensely relieved when Warren brought home Marian; she'd had "no idea what to expect."
8. One of the DC-4s; the rest of its registration number is lost.
9. Lockheed Constellation.
10. Warren apparently never met Dr. Olga Feinberg, who had been replaced as Director of Hashed around that time by Max Lapides. Warren was uncertain of the gentleman's rank or identity. How-

ever, he always referred to him as "the British officer," so I have done the same.

11. This conversation is an approximation, pieced together from recollections by Warren Metzger
years after the fact.

12. Jews in Yemen traditionally wore dark blue or
black except on holidays, but by the time they
reached Aden, their clothes were often in rags.
They were given whatever clothes were available.
Jews who had lived and worked in Aden or Sana'a
were more prosperous, dressed better, and often
still had their jewelry and other decorations which
were noted for their beauty.

13. According to Tudor Parfitt, the Yemenite Jews are
genetically similar to the Yemeni Arabs but entirely
different from any other Jews. Similarly, the
Yemeni Arabs seem to be different from other
Arabs.

14. Many people assumed that the Yemenite exodus
was inspired by Messiahnistic fervor or heard and
believed it at the time. However, the Yemenites
had a good many very practical reasons for trying
to escape Yemen and get to Israel. For a detailed
account of the sociological trials of the Yemenites,
I recommend Tudor Parfitt's *The Road to Redemption – The Jews of the Yemen 1900-1950*.

15. On the other hand, there is a great deal of testi-
mony to the selfless and very kindly assistance by
several Arab Sheiks and other potentates, who fed,
clothed, and protected Jews traveling through
their lands. Others assisted as best they could with
the organization and carrying out of the operation
from the very start.

16. This is an approximation of the conversation
based on Warren's memories and those of other
pilots who had similar conversations in Hashed.

17. I heard this story many times, growing up. The wording varied; the meaning, and the impact it made upon Warren, did not.
18. From an interview with Warren Metzger on KTUU TV, Anchorage, Alaska, 2007.

CHAPTER NINE: JANUARY, 1949

The next morning, Warren flew again with Edwards as co-pilot to Cyprus and the Royal Air Force base at Nicosia to refuel. The commander there—a polite, even courtly gentleman[1]—was in a position to interpret the directives of Whitehall as he saw fit, and he had access to extra fuel he could therefore sell to Alaska Airlines. With half-filled tanks, Warren flew back to Asmara and began the next round of flights.

The days quickly fell into a routine. He would leave Asmara late in the day to reach Aden at or just after nightfall. The night-time landings didn't trouble him as much as they did Cole and Sharp. Once certain that he was in the right area, he simply circled with landing lights on until he spotted the airfield. In the morning, provided the plane was able, he took off for Tel Aviv, then to Cyprus to refuel, and back to Asmara. He also made a couple of runs hauling fuel to the depots at Asmara and Aden.

There were plenty of times when the plane was not able, however; even in less challenging conditions, the C-46 was a notorious "hanger queen" and needed a lot of nurse-maiding. During WWII, the C-46 Commando bore less-than-flattering nicknames such as "The

Whale," "The Plumber's Nightmare," and even "The Flying Coffin," due to its vast cargo space, the disproportionate amount and difficulty of maintenance it required, and the number of mid-air explosions it suffered. The giant engines—2000 horsepower Pratt & Whitney R-2800 Double Wasps—sucked fuel at a horrific rate, far greater than those of the C-47 and the DC-3 it supplanted, let alone the mighty DC-4 that was to become the most popular cargo and passenger plane of the post-war years. But the C-46 could haul loads into the air that kept other aircraft nailed to the ground. Given an abundance of fuel, it was ideal for long-distance hauling.

From inside the cockpit, the C-46 sounded very different from the DC-4. Its sixteen-foot propellers curved at the tips and, on take off, spun nearly at the speed of sound. They made the airplane roar and snarl through the air like a phalanx of enraged dragons. All C-46 pilots eventually developed some degree of deafness.

After the hefty racket of the bombers Warren had flown during the war, he didn't mind the noise much. After a while, he blocked it out or got used to it. It made conversation difficult but not impossible. What he didn't like about them was their range. Or rather, the lack thereof.

In theory, the C-46 had a flight range of over 3,000 miles. The distance between Aden and Tel Aviv is about half that, nearly 1,500 miles as the crow flies, but the flights for Operation Magic Carpet were never so direct. The actual distance could be over 1,600 miles, one-way, lasting at least nine hours or often longer. Getting from Tel Aviv back to Asmara took another five or six hours, but first came the stop at Cyprus, the only half-way reliable source of fuel. The flight from Tel Aviv to Cyprus took only about fifteen minutes. A walk in the park, provided the plane had enough fuel left.

Retaining sufficient fuel to make that last leg was something easier said than done. Given the altitude, it was impossible to take off from Asmara with full tanks, and the depot at Aden did not always have enough fuel to top the ship up, even if they were allowed to do so. In an effort to quickly move out as many refugees as possible, Wooten often ordered the passenger loads nearly doubled. The planes could be fueled to only two-thirds capacity and sometimes little more than half just to get off the ground.

Leaving Aden, the heavily-burdened C-46s might be forced to battle their way north through fierce head-winds that had the engines sucking up fuel like thirsty sponges. Encounters with ground combat were common, often requiring wide detours. Dodging the occasional anti-aircraft fire or pot-shots by angry Arabs on the ground, who wielded everything from WWII German sniper rifles to cherished heirlooms of the previous century, sometimes forced pilots to climb abruptly heavenward or to dodge and weave between hills, with a corresponding deleterious effect on the planes' fuel efficiency.

Not that the hand-held firearms presented much of a threat, and few of the pilots treated them with any real concern. "They had no sophisticated shootists, so they were shooting at exhaust or sound, because half the time they would hear us up there and just shoot through the clouds," one of the pilots later explained.[2] Planes landed with bullet holes in a wing or the fuselage now and then, but for some reason, none ever hit the fuel tanks. "I really think God was on our side," said Warren years later. "I can't think of any other reason why we didn't get hit a lot more often."

But neither he nor any of the others were willing to take the chance on a lucky shot.

Twice, after battling savage headwinds the entire length of the Red Sea, he flew into Tel Aviv without enough fuel to make it to Cyprus. He wasn't the only pilot to coast in almost dry; Clarke Cole had been screaming for a DC-4 since shortly after his arrival in October, and several other pilots issued complaints to anyone who would listen, bombarding the home offices with demands for other, longer-range aircraft. Alaska Airlines reserved the bigger ships primarily for the longer hauls out of Europe and Asia; the C-46 pilots flying out of Aden had to make do.

Spotting combat activity below during a flight and not knowing what kind of weaponry might be in play, Warren swung wide to keep out of range. The detour cost him. He didn't have enough fuel left to reach Tel Aviv.

Port Sudan had been held out as a possible option for emergency landings, though the pilots were not encouraged to use it, if any other choice existed. None of those choices were good ones. Warren made the difficult decision to try his luck at Port Sudan.[3] He called in and told the radio operator there his situation, and that he was on his way. He received an acknowledgment and changed course. The ship was practically gasping when he finally nursed it down to land.

To his alarm, armed soldiers immediately surrounded the plane. The radio operator, who had up until then seemed to understand Warren's Canadian-accented English, was suddenly unable to comprehend his identification. Or his explanation that, as far as he could tell, he'd been instructed to land by that self-same radio operator.

He finally gave up, took a chance, and opened the door to speak directly to someone on the ground below, hoping none of the soldiers, who looked anything but welcoming, would mistake him for a Jew.

The British still maintained a presence there. Perhaps their influence kept the soldiers in line, or they were uncertain of the protocol, given that it was a U.S. plane. Perhaps they simply forbore to attack an unarmed, civilian transport. In any case, Warren was able to reach an agreement with the officer in charge to refuel the plane, though they would not accept the Alaska Airlines credit card he offered. He had to pay with his personal credit card. The officer also gave him a harshly-worded warning—entirely unnecessary, under the circumstances—to keep his passengers and crew on board at all times.

The plane was re-filled by men with closed, hard faces, whose eyes when met either burned with hate or held a cold deeper than an Alaskan winter. Once he was back aboard, in spite of the smell and the heat, he kept the doors to the plane sealed and communicated with his reluctant hosts solely by radio. He didn't relax until the plane was back in the air and skimming across the border into Israeli airspace.

The situation repeated itself less than a week later, though this time a sandstorm and vicious headwinds were to blame. Again, armed soldiers waited nearby during the entire encounter, fingering their weapons and throwing speculative glances at the airplane. Only Warren was allowed to disembark to oversee the fueling. He kept his expression relaxed and fought to suppress the cold sweat breaking out along his spine. Menace hung like a stench in the air, and he prayed that whatever discipline held the men in place would continue to do so. As the airplane's wheels left the ground at last, he heaved a sigh of relief. Come hell or high water, he would never risk landing there again.

Captain By Sharp was forced to land in Port Sudan a few days later and reported to Maguire that the danger was much greater than they'd been led to believe. "The British can't guarantee our safety or that of our passengers. We need another option."[4]

Shortly afterward, Maguire himself made a similar forced landing there. Having heard from Warren and Sharp about their experiences, he was forewarned, but when he saw soldiers rushing the runway as he came in to land, he decided not to take a chance. He radioed the tower and identified himself again to the hostile radio operator. Then he added, "Please send an ambulance to meet us on the runway."

"For what do you need an ambulance?"

"We have smallpox on board. Repeat: we have smallpox aboard. Passengers require immediate medical attention. Have you got a hospital?"

The radio went silent. By the time the plane rolled to a halt, the soldiers had vacated the runway to be replaced by a fuel truck and a bevy of attendants scrambling to drag hoses to the plane. The radio operator came back on and ordered Maguire to keep his doors closed, take his fuel, and get the hell out. He was happy to oblige.[5]

Shortly afterward, official word floated down from the U.N. "They stopped us," Warren related, "because, man, when we would land, with those Lost Tribes on board, they'd be very hostile on the ground. They wouldn't permit them to get off the airplane; they'd refuel us and send us off."

Pilots and planes faced plenty of other hazards. Sharp was supposed to follow Warren from Asmara on January 12th in the second C-46 loaded with eighteen drums of oil and gasoline for the fuel depot in Aden. Given Asmara's high elevation at 8,200 feet above sea level, higher than the city itself, the planes couldn't carry much and typically took off with tanks less than half-full. Sharp was afraid the load, most of which the C-46 had already carried from Cyprus, was too much for it to lift out of Asmara, especially since one of the engines was not, to his ear, running smoothly. There wasn't much choice; the depot at Aden was all but dry, and Warren had already left with the other C-46, albeit with a slightly lighter load.

Sharp figured that the additional barrels they'd just loaded wouldn't make that much of a difference and shrugged aside his misgivings. With his co-pilot and mechanic Bob Platt on board, he taxied down the runway.

From his seat in the cockpit, Platt watched with growing alarm as Sharp prepared for takeoff. He was certain

Sharp had put the fuel mix on full rich, which on take-off would destroy the altitude control for the automatic enrichment device. "When I saw By do that, I yelled at him I wanted off that damned plane," he related years later, "but he just jammed the throttles forward and started taxiing down the runway and took off."[7]

Within moments, the plane lost an engine. Sharp managed to keep the crippled ship aloft in the thin air and nursed it around in a wide, level turn to come back to the airport. They almost made it. Would have, if Sharp had known about the irrigation ditch waiting to swallow the plane's tail wheel.

"We tore a wingtip off on a tree," said Platt, "lifted off, tore (another) wingtip off on a tree, bounced so hard that the plane broke its back, jumped over a ditch, and finally came to rest after trimming our way through a lot of trees. But we still had the engines, so By gunned them and we dragged the tail section along and went back to the field."

Miraculously, despite being shaken and slammed around in the cabin, the barrels of fuel failed to explode. The rubber-legged crew climbed out of the plane. "I got out and kissed the ground because the gas hadn't exploded and we were alive," remembered Platt. "I hailed a limo and we loaded into it, and just then Maguire came along and saw us and wondered what in the hell we were doing there when we were supposed to be flying."

Platt and the co-pilot left Sharp to explain, headed back to the hotel, and went on a bender of epic proportions.

For the rest of his life, Platt remained convinced the accident was Sharp's fault. "We weren't overloaded, but underpowered with the carburetors on that setting."

Captain John Thompson, a senior pilot who later became Chief Pilot of Alaska Airlines, disagreed. So did almost every other pilot who'd lifted out of Asmara. "I don't know anyone who could have done any more without blowing himself to Kingdom Come," insisted Thompson, pointing out that the failed engine—almost a certainty under the circumstances—on top of the load and the altitude had made a safe landing all but impossible. "There was an irrigation ditch at the north-west corner of the airport and the tail wheel hit that and broke the plane's back. He got it back to the air-port. He did a fantastic job with what he had to work with. More than I could have done."[8]

Fuel shortages were one thing, but the smell the hard-working planes soon acquired from their human cargo was sometimes worse. "The stench was ap-palling," Warren remembered, and the sentiment is echoed in the pilot memoirs time and again, often in much stronger terms.

The Yemenites were a stoic people and remained as quiet and still as possible during the flights. But many of them were still ill. Assaulted by air-sickness and fear in equal amounts, they threw up everything in their stomachs from shortly after take-off until there was nothing left. Few had ever mastered even the basics of modern plumbing during their stay at Hashed; when they could, they crept to the back of the plane to re-lieve themselves. When they couldn't, they urinated or emptied their bowels where they sat. Not understand-ing that the 15 gallon water tank in the back was meant for drinking, they sometimes urinated into that, too. The crews quickly learned not to go back into the cabin if they didn't have to.

Occasionally they had to: on more than one occasion early in the operation, the passengers, freezing in the high altitude, started fires to warm themselves. Only quick action on the part of the volunteers and crew prevented disaster.[9]

The Alaska Airlines stewardesses on the DC-4s—the unsung heroines of the air—had their work cut out for them. They did what they could, plying the passengers with water, oranges, and airsickness bags, but like the

Israeli cabin attendants who later replaced them, they could not speak the language of the Yemenites. Communicating with people who, in some cases, had lived in caves before coming to Aden, and for whom a wheel was a modern marvel, proved nearly impossible.

Spotting an elderly man about to relieve himself, one stewardess threw out the protocols and cultural taboos the Israelis had tried to instill in the Americans, took him bodily by the arm, and led him to the head. There, she lifted the lid and pointed to the waiting bowl. Utterly bewildered, the man turned away and looked for somewhere else to vent his aching bladder. She turned him back and tried again, using every trick of pantomime she could come up with.

The silent little game of charades became a contest of wills. Each time, the poor man turned away and tried to go, and each time, she seized his arm, turned him back to the waiting facility and pointed into the bowl, making every other gesture she could think of.

Finally, the old man's face lit up with comprehension. He carefully stepped into the toilet bowl, turned around, and relieved himself on the floor.[10]

The crews eventually gave up and installed sandboxes in the backs of the planes. They also chopped holes in the fuselage near the tails with fire axes so the ships could be hosed out between trips[7], and replaced the sand in the boxes each time.

The stewardesses worked almost exclusively aboard the DC-4s; there simply wasn't room in the C-46s. Israeli volunteers did their best to play hostess aboard the smaller craft and, as a result, faced some of the same hazards. In the early days of the operation, during the initial struggles to keep the fuel depots supplied, the airline made the flights do double duty. The passengers sometimes had to share space with gas drums, but the danger proved too great. During one trip, the plane hit an air pocket and dropped 2000 feet in an instant. The ropes across passengers' laps kept them more or less in the vicinity of their seats, but one volunteer slammed into the ceiling and then crashed to the floor. A flying fuel drum landed a split-second after she did, crushing her foot to pulp.[11]

After that, Maguire scheduled separate fuel runs.

Save for the roar of the engines, the flights were made in almost eerie silence. The Yemenites rarely spoke. The children did not cry. Even the babies seldom wailed.

The silence of the children bothered Warren. He'd never seen any of them laugh or play. On his occasional trips through the camps, he found them endearing. So shy, so quiet, yet so very eager for even the slightest attention.

Author Shlomo Barer wrote of his experience of the children of Hashed in words that echoed Warren's feelings exactly.

You walk through the camp and suddenly out of a tent a kid sidles up to you and smiles. If you return the smile, he pulls at your sleeve and follows, and soon there is a whole crowd of them trailing you. They smile, but they have yet to learn to laugh—it is as if these children have never laughed before; their eyes are big and sad, old before their time. Nowhere have I seen children so forlorn and wanting affection as these. They have never played, they have no toys or games, and it is pathetic the way they cuddle up to anyone who takes the slightest interest in them.[12]

Donations of food and clothing were generous, but no one seemed to have thought of toys. On his limited budget, it was impossible for Warren to supply them. He tried once, anyway; he found a store in Asmara that carried red and yellow rubber balls, and he asked the volunteers at Hashed if he could bring a few of them with him to the camp on his next trip. A nurse asked him to refrain. "There is no room for them to play," she told him, "and they would not know what to do with them anyway."

Still, it seemed like he ought to do something. The kids needed a good laugh, at least. So it was that during a stop at Tel Aviv, he wandered into a gift shop and saw a bright red fez. It gave him an idea. He purchased it and took it with him on his next flight to Aden.

Shortly after takeoff, he turned the controls over to his co-pilot and put on the fez. Twisting his face into a comically ferocious scowl, he opened the cockpit door, leaned out, and glared around menacingly, primarily at the twenty or thirty kids sitting closest to the door.

The result could have been disastrous, but Warren had judged his audience aright. The children thought it was the funniest thing they'd ever seen and burst into peels of wild laughter, their dark eyes dancing. After a startled moment or two, some of the adults even joined in. Fear and discomfort were momentarily overcome by the antics of this towering stranger. Chuckling to himself, Warren ducked back into the cockpit and closed the door.

For the rest of his life, he relished telling the story at any social gathering where Magic Carpet memories were pulled out and displayed among fellow pilots and Alaska Airline employees. And always, after the first laugh, he would wrap it up with the same line. "It oc-curred to me after the fact that if that had been a planeload of Arabs, and I'd done that wearing a yarmulke, it would have been a whole 'nother kettle of fish."[13]

1. I've been unable to discover the identity of the Commander of RAF Nicosia, but this gentleman earned the gratitude of every pilot who flew for the operation.
2. Satterfield; interview with Larry Roger, 1979.

3. In one document, he listed his destination as Khartoum, farther inland and next to an oil refinery. However, I have found no corroboration for that and have used Port Sudan instead, which was the recommended emergency landing base.
4. Satterfield notes, source unknown. I've attributed it to By Sharp, because he is the most likely candidate.
5. Maguire himself never told this story in my presence nor to Archie Satterfield, but it is repeated, in various forms, in a number of newspaper articles and in his obituary. Other pilots were also fond of telling it. It became an ongoing Alaska Airlines legend.
6. KTUU TV; interview with Warren Metzger, 2007.
7. Satterfield; interview with Bob Platt, 1979.
8. Satterfield; interview with John Thompson, 1979.
9. I heard various versions of this story from several pilots over the years, though none of Archie Satterfield's interviewees mention it. Elgen Long, navigator on Larry Currie's crew, discovered a family trying to light a gas stove aboard one of his flights. Leon Uris included such an incident in his novel, Exodus.
10. Satterfield notes, source unknown. I heard this story from Marian and several other Alaska Airlines employees over the years; it was a favorite at parties.
11. Satterfield notes, source unknown.
12. Barer, *The Magic Carpet*.
13. I heard this story frequently while growing up. While writing this book, I came across an account of it Dad had written out for some official record somewhere. To my surprise and dismay, he had written that his co-pilot was the one who had done it, thinking to have some fun giving the kids a bit of a scare. So, either my dad lied every time he told the story, or he was trying to distance himself

from the incident when recording it for posterity. Possibly he was trying to avoid giving offense, in this age of hyper-sensitivity. Perhaps it was out of a sense of embarrassment at the thought of strangers reading about his lapse in judgment. Since Dad was a stickler for honesty, and I never knew him otherwise to lie, I'm going to assume one of the latter reasons.

INTERLUDE: SHANGHAI: RESTRICTED SECTOR FOR STATELESS REFUGEES

From the early 19th Century, Shanghai had been colonized by peoples from all over the world who carved the city into districts or "concessions." France, England, the United States, Germany, Russia, India and others created areas within the sprawling metropolis that became little slices of their native lands, all overlaid and spiced by the colors and flavors of China. It was a cosmopolitan city and a major trading port known around the world for its dangers and delights.

Among the people who sought haven there were Jews escaping Germany and Russia, due in large part to its liberal immigration laws. Over the years, a small but thriving Jewish community developed in the narrow, twisting streets and colorful canal-sides. Many of the dispossessed built businesses and raised families.

They stopped thinking of themselves as refugees and more as citizens of that ancient and exotic city.[1]

During the brief period of Japanese rule, the Jews were concentrated primarily into the "Restricted Sector for Stateless Refugees," otherwise known as the Hongkou district. It was a poor area badly damaged during WWII, but this was done more to appease Japan's ally, Germany, than because of any negative sentiment on the part of the Japanese. The rulers of Japan, believing propaganda that painted Jews as part of a powerful, secret, ruling elite in the world of finance, viewed them more as distressed nobility than a victimized minority.[2] As a result, the Japanese treated the Jews with a degree of courtesy they denied the conquered Chinese.

Since re-taking control of their city, the Chinese had paid little attention to their Jewish citizens; the civil war between Chiang Kai-Shek's Nationalist forces and the Communists presented a far more urgent problem.

Chiang Kai-Shek had helped drive the Japanese from his country and believed his people saw him as a liberator and a hero. But to most of China, he was just the latest in a long line of ruling warlords. Worse, under his rule, the Chinese economy was nearing collapse. The rhetoric spouted by the Communists painted a flattering portrait of Mao Tse-Tung. The portrayal made him sound less like the murderous, power-hungry thug with a talent for terror that he was, and more like a leader for a new beginning, ushering in the dawn of a better age.[3]

Both sides were convinced that World War III was imminent, an event that would bring foreign armies and supplies flooding into China in support of Chiang Kai-Shek. The National Revolutionary or Kuomintang Army, commanded by Tang Enbo and his deputy commanders, Liu Yuzhang and Liu Changyi, had only to hold out until then. The so-called People's Liberation Army, under the command of Mao's generals

Chen Yi and Su Yu, had to take Shanghai before that happened.[4]

Though many secular Jews had been instrumental and enthusiastic proponents of Communism prior to the Russian revolution, they had learned the hard way what they could expect under the reality of a Communist dictatorship. The religious Jews, who had never supported Communism in the first place, needed no further reminder. As the People's Liberation Army closed in around Shanghai, the Jewish settlers once again packed up the detritus of their lives and sought an escape. The Holy Land beckoned, offering a promise of welcome and a home from which they would never again need flee.

1. Ron Gluckman, The Ghosts of Shanghai, http://-www.gluckman.com/ShanghaiJewsChina.html.
2. *The Jewish Refugee Community of Shanghai: 1938-1949*, Guest blog by Historicity (Was Already Taken), April 7, 2013, http://beyondvictoriana.com-/2013/04/07/the-jewish-refugee-community-of-shanghai-1938-1949/.
3. Jung Chang, Jon Halliday, *Mao: The Unknown Story*, Anchor November 14, 2006.
4. "The Shanghai Campaign," http://en.wikipedia.-org/wiki/Shanghai_Campaign.

CHAPTER TEN: MARIAN GOES TO SHANGHAI

Back in New York, Marian had hung up the phone on Mimpy's call and realized she was going to have to do some scrambling. This was going to be a long trip, and she had no clean clothes. All her clothes were at her apartment in Anchorage; somehow she'd have to squeeze in a quick trip up there before she left. She traded shifts with another stewardess, so she could take the next plane back to Seattle.

Once there, she found no way to get to Anchorage and back in time to journey to Hong Kong. The Alaska flight she'd hoped to catch a ride on had been canceled due to mechanical problems with an engine—hardly a rare occurrence. To make things worse, she was short on cash.

Girding her loins, she rushed to a small shop she knew of in Des Moines, perhaps twenty minutes south of the airport. The lady who ran the shop listened to her tale of woe and allowed her to buy a beautiful, deep blue wool suit on credit. Marian promised to pay her when she got back, adding a stack of underclothes and stockings to her bill. She rushed back to the airport and jumped on a plane to Hong Kong. "I paid her back as soon as I could," Marian later related. "It just took a lot longer than either of us expected."

After all the rush, she ended up sitting around in Hong Kong by herself, waiting for the flight she was supposed to work. The other stewardess who was to work the trip with her hadn't arrived. Another crew coming in from Amsterdam was supposed to be picking up the refugees in Shanghai and bringing them to Hong Kong. After a week of cooling her heels window shopping, since she didn't have the money to do anything else, she received a wire telling her she was going to be working both legs of the trip. Marian had to catch a ride to Shanghai, and her plane would pick her up with the refugees.[1]

Communist forces weren't yet close enough to Shanghai to be a threat, so air traffic was still flowing unimpeded to and from the city. She finagled a jump-seat on a flight hauling supplies into Shanghai and made it just as the Alaska DC-4 she was waiting for finally arrived. She was glad to find Captain John Thompson at the controls; she'd flown with him often and respected both his abilities and judgment as a pilot, as well as his genuinely kind and respectful attitude toward the stewardesses and those who flew under him.

She was surprised to find herself the only stewardess. What had happened to the two girls who should have flown the first leg of the flight down from Amsterdam? One of the crew told her only that they'd gotten off at an earlier stop. Evidently, they'd been needed elsewhere. Marian wondered if it had anything to do with her earlier assumption that this was considered a hazardous assignment. Well, those girls were just going to miss out on the excitement. She could handle it herself.

Though JDC volunteers were on hand, placing themselves in the same danger as the people they sought to help, the Chinese operators at Shanghai informed the Alaska crew that they would have to assist with getting the passengers ready to board. Marian went with the others down to the terminal and found nearly a hundred weary, frightened German Jews and a few Russians, crammed into an area that was far too small for them. Most of the people were middle-aged and had fled first Hitler and Stalin and then one conflict after another, until they had ended in a ghetto in Shanghai. They had few possessions, but what remained to them, they carried in boxes and suitcases being used as chairs and beds while they awaited rescue.[2]

While the Chinese had done their best, they were also in the middle of a war themselves; resources and personnel were equally scarce. They were relieved to turn the problem over to the JDC and the Alaska Airlines crew.

The DC-4 was one that had not been modified; it still had seating for only forty-eight passengers, though the fact that the armrests had been removed told Marian they'd be taking extra people aboard. Comfort was less important than simply getting these people out of here before enemy troops reached Shanghai. She later learned that the contract Wooten had negotiated called for sixty-six passengers, which she quite reasonably thought ludicrous.[3]

All the Alaska Airlines flights Wooten contracted were typically overloaded; he considered the planes' official capacities more guidelines than rules. But the DC-4 did have a weight limit. While they were flying with minimal fuel in order to lighten the load, extra steps needed to be taken. Marian and the others dreaded what they knew had to be done. There was no room for that much luggage, nor could the plane handle the extra weight across the distance they would have to fly.

Reluctantly, Thompson had the volunteers inform everyone in the room that they would have to leave most of their luggage behind. They were allowed one bag each, small enough to carry with them onto the plane.

The Chinese had found a scale and set it up in a side room. The refugees formed a line, and the volunteers started weighing and measuring them one-by-one, assisted by two clerks. Leaving the rest of it to the volunteers, the Alaskans headed back to the plane to prepare.

After some delay, the passengers came out of the terminal—watched by Chinese guards—and filed up the ladder and into the airplane. Marian settled them in their seats as quickly as possible, helped them get comfortable, and stored their various suitcases, though some were so heavy she had trouble handling them by herself. Her arm almost came out of the socket when she tried to take one old woman's battered, leather-strapped case; the thing had to weigh more than the woman did. "I have no idea how she carried it; she must have had the strength of an ox. This tiny little old lady who looked like she could have been my grandmother, and she carried it like it was filled with nothing but hankies. I was deeply embarrassed."

She finally asked the woman what on earth was in the case. It was filled not with clothes or dishes but with her late husband's books and papers, which she had brought from Germany; he had been a teacher and evidently a scholar of some renown before Hitler's police had taken him away.

Marian gave up and called the flight engineer back to help her with the case.

It was afternoon when the plane lifted off the runway. Marian had her hands full during the hours in the air, though her passengers were, to a man and woman, exquisitely polite and made few demands, as if afraid to ask for anything.

The Alaska crew had tried to get as many children on board as possible, but even so, most of Marian's passengers were middle-aged, anywhere from mid-thirties to mid-fifties. "Lovely people," she recalled later. Most of them spoke English reasonably well and were well-educated; it was not difficult to strike up conversations with them. "I knew they'd been through hell, but they didn't want to talk about their experiences. They were just grateful to get out with their skins after fleeing the Germans and then the Communists."

They were very willing to talk to her about Israel. To a man, woman, and child, they were anxious to get to the land they had never seen but thought of as their homeland.

Several she spoke to planned to remain only long enough to obtain Israeli passports, which would enable them to travel on to the United States or other places where they had relatives waiting. They, too, spoke of the future, not the past. "They looked forward with great hope to starting new lives, good lives, for themselves and their children," Marian related.

Her natural friendliness and honest concern coaxed some of them into opening up just a little; the stories she heard nearly broke her heart. "They didn't say a great deal about what they'd seen or lived through, but just the few words one or the other would let fall would just wring your heart. I had to go forward several times so I wouldn't cry."

More than one had spent time in concentration camps, and over and over she heard hints of lost wives, husbands, children, parents in those terrible places. Not one, it seemed, had escaped the loss and misery of the Holocaust. Most had lost nearly everything, every material possession they had ever cherished, save what they carried in those bags.

And yet, they remained hopeful, even optimistic. It was as if, when the war took everything else from them, it had also removed the capacity for fear. "One man had saved a fur coat," she remembered. "That was going to be his grubstake. There were others carrying jewelry or mementos that they were going to sell and live on. It seemed a small thing to hang your whole future on, but no one seemed worried at all. They knew God would look out for them."

The scheduled route was from Shanghai to Hong Kong, from there to Calcutta, on to Bombay, then to Aden to offload their passengers and refuel, and then to Asmara; another plane and crew would take the passengers on to Tel Aviv. The DC-4 could fly greater distances, but with such heavy passenger loads, it was wiser to keep the tanks only partially filled and fly only as far as each half-tank would take them. Fuel was readily available at every stop along the way; why risk fighting the weight?

They landed in Hong Kong to find the second stewardess had finally arrived. Marian was secretly relieved not to have to handle the rest of the flight alone. But to her surprise, Captain Thompson announced they'd be staying the night.

The British Overseas Airways Company (BOAC), which ran virtually all the airfields in that part of the world, closed all their radio stations at sundown and, sensibly, went home for the night. Flying at night meant a pilot was utterly on his own and often flying over hostile territory; the war had left most nations—large and small—nervous of large planes flying through their airspace. Many of them still had anti-aircraft guns aimed heavenward. Night flying, in that era, was not something done without good reason.

Alaska Airlines had a very good reason. Planeloads of them, winging through the dark to reach the safety of a land they'd never seen. Of all the airlines in that entire region during the whole operation, only Alaska Airlines flew at night, hiding their mission under the cloak of darkness.[3]

Like the other Alaska pilots, Thompson had maps with areas to avoid carefully marked. But he was tired. He'd been at the controls since Amsterdam, and he and the rest of the flight crew very much needed a rest. He intended to take off as early in the morning as possible to take advantage of the cooler temperatures.

The refugees were supposed to be housed in the airport, under guard. Instead, a kindly local businessman offered lodgings for the entire planeload—crew and refugees alike—in his hotel, though there were insufficient rooms. Some slept on sofas or the floor in the lobby. Marian and the rest of the crew left it to the Hong Kong authorities to worry about and gratefully accepted the offer.[4]

The mighty DC-4 was still being refueled in the pre-dawn darkness when Marian and the others returned to prepare for the next leg of the journey. They cleaned up the plane, re-stocked the galley, got everything ready, and settled in to wait for their passengers. And wait. After a while, Thompson made a call to find out what the hold-up was. He was told that because the refugees had been housed elsewhere overnight, they needed to go through security checks again. There was nothing the Alaska crew could do; they settled in and continued to wait.

It was still early, but the sunlight was already swimming through the hot, muggy air before the passengers arrived, much refreshed. The crew got them loaded as quickly as possible, and the DC-4 trundled down the runway.

It seemed to Marian that the big bird had to put some extra "oomph" into the take off, but that wasn't all that odd, given the size of the load and the heat. It was over a 1600 mile flight to their next stop in Calcutta; at least eight or nine hours later, they landed, re-fueled, and took off again as the day cooled toward approaching evening.

It was little more than an additional thousand miles to Bombay, but by the time they landed, the day's hard labor had taken its toll. One of the engines had developed an oil leak, and they would have to spend the night.

The passengers were allowed to go into the waiting room at the airport—a real terminal as a change from many of their stops. However, the Indian airport authorities passed on a warning not to step off the sidewalks because of a local pest called krait snakes that lived in the gutters; small but deadly.

It was getting late, and the snake warning discouraged Marian from going out to explore. The other stewardess chose to grab the opportunity to stretch her legs in the terminal. Marian decided to stay on the plane and take a quick nap while she could.

She had barely closed her eyes when she was awakened by one of the mechanics, a young Indian man, who came into the cabin not realizing she was there. He introduced himself as R.L. Raja, and was, she decided, very good-looking. Surprised and delighted to have a chance to talk to the lovely young American woman, he lingered until, in the interest of helping speed repairs, she agreed to accompany him to the cockpit while he worked. She remained nearby, chatting with him long into the evening about nothing in particular.

When his work required him to leave the plane, she bade him farewell, waved him off in search of the troublesome leak, and laid back down. She did not wake again until Captain Thompson and the rest of the flight crew returned to prepare the ship for take-off the next day.

Months later, she would receive a passionate and beautifully written love letter from Raja, in which he spoke of his fervent hope that she returned his love, and that they would be together someday. He seemed to have enshrined every word, every moment of their brief meeting in his heart; certainly, he remembered it much better than she did. Torn between bemusement at the thought that she had unintentionally inspired such devotion and chagrin at the thought of hurting his feelings, she added the letter to the shoebox full of similar trophies, which she could never quite bring herself to throw out. Warren would later read it and ask, "My God, what did you do to him?"

. . .

John Thompson had found a message from Jim Wooten waiting for him on arrival in Bombay, warning him to buy enough fuel to be able to fly non-stop to Asmara. A fresh eruption of violence in the area meant there was a danger of Arabs seizing the plane and passengers if they landed to re-fuel at Aden.[5] They would have to tank up to the DC-4's maximum capacity in order to make the distance.

Captain Thompson knew the ship couldn't do it. They would have to shed weight in some other way.

He asked Marian to break the news to their passengers. Her heart sank, but she knew there was no choice. She squared her shoulders and went into the airport's waiting area to inform their passengers that they would have to leave their luggage behind. She tried not to think of how much these people had already lost. She met each pair of eyes with a smile, unable to forget their stories, knowing how much the little that remained meant to them. There was no choice.

They were supposed to have taken off in the pre-dawn darkness, not only to make it easier on the plane to get off the ground but also to ensure they could still make a daylight landing in Asmara. They could not remain overnight at Tel Aviv, and Asmara, like Aden, had no runway lights. But the Bombay ground crew would not pump fuel during the worst heat of the day for fear of fire. It was late afternoon when they finally brought out the hoses and fed the hungry DC-4.

Thompson and the Alaska crew waited still longer for evening, hoping things would cool off. It was still sweltering when the DC-4 finally lumbered down the runway, using every inch of it to finally attain lift-off.

Marian, strapped in her seat, heard the roar of the engines deepen, felt the plane's leaden response and knew instantly that something was very wrong. "The plane staggered into the air," she recalled. "The other girl and I just sat there, gripping our seats until our knuckles were white, and smiling so the passengers wouldn't know anything was wrong."[6]

The plane continued to groan and lurch skyward, as if fighting for every inch. Marian, still smiling, un-buckled her safety belt and headed for the cockpit.

Thompson, wrestling with the controls, was unac-customedly terse. "We're still overloaded," he said over his shoulder. "Go back there and see if you can spot anything that doesn't belong."

Marian returned to the main cabin, still smiling and poised, trying to imagine how anything she found could make a difference. It would take several thou-sand pounds of extra weight to make the powerful DC-4, the workhorse of the air, labor like this. Surely the additional fuel alone was responsible.

Despite violent tremors shaking the cabin and its entire contents, she strolled down the aisle, seeing to her passengers' needs, her hazel eyes scanning every face. Every one of these people had already flown with her from Shanghai; she knew their faces, their names. No new ones surprised her. No bags or pack-ages had mysteriously appeared anywhere, either.

She noticed one man sweating profusely, despite the cooling temperature within the unheated aircraft, and stopped to see if he was all right. The man rose and began removing his pants. Flustered, she tried to stop him, only to realize he wore a second pair under the first. And another under that. He removed three pairs of pants and wore still another.

The other stewardess waved to catch Marian's at-tention and gestured to an older woman she was helping out of a heavy coat. The woman was wearing at least four layers of clothing under her coat and had a pair of shoes in each pocket.

The two girls made a thorough investigation and found that, after being told they could not bring their luggage, every passenger on board had donned all garments, jewelry, and sundries they possibly could and stuffed their other belongings into pockets, sleeves, socks, and hats. Books and papers filled every available gap in every conceivable article of clothing. None of them had any idea that the restriction was not an issue of room but of weight.

Marian trotted back to the cockpit to inform Captain Thompson of her findings. The pilot was known for his sometimes colorful turns of phrase, but this time he just shook his head and sighed. "Good thing we didn't try to leave any earlier, or we'd have never gotten off the ground. Well, we'll be all right once some of the fuel burns off. Provided we can stay aloft until then."

The mighty DC-4 labored upward to 5,000 feet and hung there, unable to rise further. Buffeted by turbulence, it fought to stay in the sky for two and a half hours, until enough fuel burned off to enable it to climb above the worst of the roughness. It was longer still before the engines' pitch settled at a more comfortable level and the crew stopped sweating.

Marian and the other stewardess scrambled back and forth with air sickness bags and towels, all the while assuring their passengers that everything was fine, fine, this was normal...

"Thank God (and I do mean Thank God)," she said later, "we had no more engine trouble. All four purred the entire time." The passengers finally dropped off to sleep, one by one, and Marian finally let her breath out and relaxed. They were on the last leg of the trip; the rest, she hoped, would be smooth sailing.

The big plane flew alone through the night above a darkened landscape, skirting the borders of hostile countries and aiming for a land out of legend, a long-cherished hope that filled the dreams of the sleeping passengers.

They landed at Asmara, Eretria, in the early afternoon and rolled to a final halt. Marian was first at the door and opened it with practiced ease, gratefully breathing in the warm, fresh air.

"Hey, Marian!"

She didn't recognize the voice and looked down. The familiar face of a ground crewman she'd last seen in Alaska greeted her. He grinned up at her and waved. "Hey, Metzger's in Tel Aviv, but he'll be down tomorrow." In a company as clannish and close-knit as Alaska Airlines, it hadn't taken long for people to make assumptions about her relationship with Warren.

She'd known, of course, that he was working one of the legs of this airlift, but given the chaotic nature of her airline, that could have meant anything. Until that moment, she had no idea where in all the world he might be. Her heart gave a happy leap. She hadn't seen him in weeks. Imagine finding one another again on the other side of the world!

The ladder rolled up to the plane, and she went back to help her passengers prepare to depart for their flight to Tel Aviv. After so long in their company, many felt more like dear friends than strangers she would likely never see again. She wished each of them a joyous "homecoming," hoping that they would find the good lives they had awaited for so long.

One elderly gentleman paused beside her and actually picked up her hand, patting it gently. She did not realize at the time how unusual a gesture that was; Jewish men did not touch strange women, especially not gentiles. He told her, in excellent English, how deeply he and his fellow passengers appreciated all she and the crew had done. And added, "You are the kind of young lady that a man would marry even without a dowry."

She thanked him sincerely; he surrendered her hand and made his careful way down the ladder. For the rest of her life, she cherished the odd compliment, always relating it with her ready laugh. "Evidently, I'd done a pretty good job on that trip."

When the passengers were all gone, she and the rest of the crew descended and headed for the hotel for a well-deserved rest. But she lay awake on her bed for a long time, listening for the distinctive roar of a C-46 in the sky.

1. It is unclear whether Marian flew both legs of this trip, starting in Shanghai, or only one, starting in Hong Kong. Since ASA crew schedules were often changed at the drop of a hat, I'm guessing a similar situation must have happened to Marian.
2. The Jewish refugees awaiting transport often had little notice and bundled what they could into whatever luggage was available. They were forced to wait around in the airport for their rides out, sometimes for days.
3. Satterfield; interview with John Thompson, 1979.
4. 60 years after the fact, Marian could not remember the gentleman's name or the name of the hotel, but it was almost certainly Sir Horace Kadoorie, a wealthy Capitalist and philanthropist, who helped the refugees and airline crews on several flights with unstinting generosity. In relating this incident, Marian was also uncertain if it had happened on that particular trip or another. For the sake of simplicity, I've inserted it on this trip. I have heard similar stories from Elgen Long and other sources, who remember the gentleman with great respect for his kindness and generosity.
5. Back in Asmara, Clarke Cole received what was probably the same warning at around this time. Neither pilot knew the specific details of the

problem in Aden. This may have been when a series of riots broke out in the streets of the city, and several people—Arab and Jew—were killed.

6. Marian remembered this happening on take-off from Hong Kong; Thompson remembered it happening on take-off from Bombay. Since Thompson's version was recorded 30 years before Marian's, I've opted to use his.

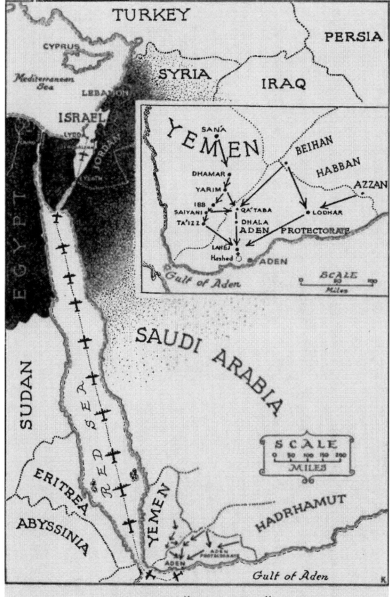

MAP SHOWING THE "MAGIC CARPET" ROUTE

The black and shaded parts show the inner ring of the Arab League countries at war with Israel at the time of the flights.

1. Map of the air route for the Operation Magic Carpet flights 1948–1950 (Barer, Shlomo, *The Magic Carpet*, Harper & Brothers, New York, 1952).

2. James Wooten, CEO and President of Alaska Airlines from 1947 to 1949 (courtesy Alaska Airlines).

3. One of the two C-46 airplanes used in Operation Magic Carpet (courtesy Alaska Airlines).

4. From L to R: LeRoy Johnson, Hal (?) Stewart,
Harold McCoy, in Asmara with a C-46
(courtesy Alaska Airlines).

5. The nose of a C-46 on the ground at Lydda
(courtesy Alaska Airlines).

6. Alaska Airlines DC-4 (courtesy Alaska Airlines).

7. Yemenite refugees waiting to board in Aden
(courtesy Alaska Airlines).

8. Alaska Airlines C-46 over the Red Sea
(courtesy Alaska Airlines).

9. Yemenite family in Hashed (courtesy Alaska Airlines).

10. C-46 tire, victim of Egyptian bombs
(courtesy Alaska Airlines).

11. A camel parked in the streets of Asmara
near the market, always a source of fascination
(Metzger collection and Alaska Airlines).

12. Travel sticker from the Albergo Ciaao Hotel in Asmara, home base for many of the pilots and crew throughout Operation Magic Carpet (Metzger collection).

13. Refugees disembarking at Lydda from one of the planes sent by Alaska Airlines, logo and lettering removed (courtesy Alaska Airlines).

14. The tail of this DC-6 is broken in the same way as By Sharp's C-46 after his unfortunate landing (Metzger collection).

15. Yemenite refugees awaiting transport at Hashed (courtesy Alaska Airlines).

16. A Jewish refugee ship, possibly the Athalanthe.
Many refugee ships reached Israel only to be
prevented from offloading by the British, who feared
both dire diplomatic consequences from other
countries and repercussions from the Arab League
(courtesy Alaska Airlines).

CHAPTER ELEVEN: FLIGHT

Throughout the month of January, the refugees kept coming, appearing out of the desert like tattered ghosts, "looking like prophets out of the Bible," as Hank Mulleneaux described them.[1] Starving and often ill with dysentery, malaria, and a host of other diseases, they followed their dreams and a murmur of destiny no louder than a whisper on the wind. Truckloads of them, scooped up from whatever part of the city of Aden they had reached, arrived daily at the gates of the camp. The trucks dumped them there before driving back to the city proper for the next load.

At Hashed's gate, they stood or squatted in almost universal silence. They were unfamiliar with chairs and tended to topple over if they tried to sit in one. Their huge, night-dark eyes were wide with wonder. They watched, wary or trustful by turns, while a bevy of doctors, nurses, and well-intended but awkward volunteers from many countries assessed their physical condition. Separating the worst injured or most ill for immediate treatment, they tried to make all feel welcome.

The culture shock was mutual. Only a tiny handful of the volunteers spoke the Yemenites' language—mostly, those who were themselves of Yemenite origin or whose families had immigrated to Palestine a few years before. None of the Yemenites spoke Hebrew or English. Centuries surrounded by Arab customs had altered some Yemenite customs in turn. Multiple wives were not uncommon, and the volunteers were shocked by mothers as young as twelve years old and brides of eight or nine.[2] The Yemenites married orphans in order to keep them from being taken and converted to Islam, as required by the laws of Yemen, and to ensure they did not starve. Nevertheless, it appalled the Israelites, Americans, and British who worked with them.

For their part, the Yemenites were taken aback not only by the bewildering array of technological advances to which they were so abruptly introduced, but by the almost immediate changes the constant exposure to new customs, new sights, new experiences began making in their own culture. Even at the dawn of its existence as a modern nation, Israel prized education above any other commodity and held men and women to an equally high standard. Almost as soon as they reached camp, Yemenite girl children were shuttled into makeshift schoolrooms and, for the first time in history, had books put into their hands.

The adult Yemenite women learned, too. Their dark eyes saw things unimagined in their old lives, such as women working side-by-side and on an equal footing with the men. And this led to a quiet revolution. "The example of the women working in the camps has led to some of them (Yemenite women) suggesting to their menfolk that the old order should be changed—to the distress of their husbands," reported one newspaper with forgivable smugness.[2]

Meanwhile, Israel's economy was tottering under the burden of the influx of immigrants. Rough calculations showed that the state needed some $3,000 for the absorption of each immigrant, which meant that the state required about $700,000 for the whole campaign. The entire state budget was considerably less than that.[3]

Generous donations collected by the JDC as well as other charity organizations, primarily from the United States and South Africa, helped considerably, but it was still a crippling load. Israel offered what help it could to Alaska Airlines and the crewmen and women struggling to fulfill the contract and bring the wandering tribes home, but there was nothing to spare. The British, too, helped in whatever way they could, though they were forced to do so covertly.

Though Israel and England had frequently been on opposite sides of the struggle for Israel's independence, the two nations tried to find ways to work together in overcoming the various problems the refugees presented. "The political situation made for strange bedfellows. That's kind of a cliché but it's a good way to put it," said Larry Roger, one of the Alaska Airlines pilots who flew into the area for supporting missions during Operation Magic Carpet and became well acquainted with its troubles. "The Israeli government contacted the British in Aden for a little hard cooperation in getting these people from Yemen into Aden and into that area where they were inoculated and cared for, and on their way."[4]

With characteristic *noblesse oblige*, England stepped up and shouldered the burden. "In fact they were so helpful," remembered Roger, "they were more helpful than the Jewish cadre there in Aden were at times, at least when I was over there."[4]

The High Commissioner of Police, one A. E. Sigrist,[5] was neither the governor of Aden nor the governor of the trust territory in Asmara, which the British had confiscated from the Italians. But the Alaska crew soon learned that he was the *de facto* head of government there. "What he said was what happened," remembered Roger, "and he was very helpful."[4]

In the end, it was up to Alaska Airlines and the men and women working under its auspices to get the planes into the air, find the fuel, fix the problems. A plane's crew was "on" for twenty-four hours—the length of a complete run including refueling—then "off" for the next twenty-four, time spent resting and preparing themselves for the next trip.

As badly as he wanted to be rated as a Captain in the DC-4, Warren didn't envy Flahart, Patton, or the others the hours they were racking up. The lone DC-4 that Alaska Airlines had dedicated to the Aden to Tel Aviv runs almost never touched the ground. Every time it limped into Lydda, the mechanics scrambled to make it airworthy again. "All the maintenance you could get on it was about four to five hours a day at Lydda," remembered one mechanic, "so you couldn't do anything except pre-flight it."[6]

The remaining C-46's tag-team schedule allowed the plane 24 hours of downtime for maintenance, and it needed every minute. The all-pervasive sand ground its way into every gear, joint, and crevice; rare indeed was the trip when all instruments kept working the whole way. Engines gave out on a regular basis.

By mid-January, "the smell" had become so much a part of all the planes that Warren hardly noticed it anymore. After each trip, the crews hosed out the interior, changed the sand in the box at the back, and threw disinfectant around like perfume. It made little difference. Urine leaking through the floorboards corroded wiring and control cables, and the mechanics tore their hair out trying to find ways to patch it up.

Wooten raged about the damage whenever he was in town; the mechanics learned to shrug and shut him out. They were doing the best they could with what they had to work with. The planes stayed in the air; what more could anyone ask?

Wooten hired a few free-lance pilots who had their own planes, but few made more than one or two runs.

Most lost engines to the devouring sand, and though Wooten had contracted with KLM to perform maintenance, it meant getting the planes to KLM hangers, where KLM mechanics could work on them, which was more than most self-employed pilots could readily do.

While Wooten scrounged around for more planes, Maguire put the word out along every channel he knew that they needed pilots who could fly commercial aircraft. A few answered the call and joined up, still officially as Alaska Airlines sub-contractors. For some, it started out as just another paid flying gig. Others approached it as a divine opportunity to do God's work. Almost all, eventually, became obsessed with the mission itself and the need to "get these people home, and do it fast." Like Maguire, they came to sense the clock ticking.

Maguire, determined to keep the mission on track, learned early on that the flying schedules simply could not be cast in stone. Even when planes and crews were ready to go, some unforeseen circumstance might ground them for an extra day or more. Enemy action halted a number of flights, but by far the most common hold-up was the refugees' refusal to fly on the Sabbath or on any holy days. Between the various tribes, there were a lot of holy days. "We have holidays," remembered one crewman, "but the Jewish people have holidays and holidays and holidays. It was always a problem."[7] Even Rabbis couldn't always convince the Yemenites of the necessity of boarding the planes, and not all Rabbis were willing to try.[5]

Finally, there were times when the operation had to halt until someone, somewhere, scrounged up fuel. Generous though they were, the RAF base at Cyprus couldn't produce enough to fill their own needs as well as those of the airlift's at the drop of a hat.

Stanley "Buddy" Epstein, an American-born Israeli pilot and maintenance specialist, heard about the

Operation while airlifting supplies from Czechoslovakia to Israel.[9] When he delivered the last load, he ran Maguire to earth and got himself hired on just before Christmas, 1948. He wasn't a religious man, but he firmly believed in the necessity and the rightness of the Operation.

It didn't take him long to decide the mission had to have been blessed by God. The way he saw it, the possibility of any of the airplanes being successful was pretty remote.

"There was rioting in Yemen over the concentration of Jews. The British—who controlled Aden as a colony—were putting pressure on us to get the airplanes turned around and get the refugees out of there," he related in an interview.[9]

Epstein was up to the challenge, but it came as a surprise—one he soon deeply appreciated—to realize that his new fellow pilots felt the same way. The danger, the ongoing hurdles that had to be overcome, seemed endless and at times insurmountable, but no one faltered. "The plight of the Jews is what drove everyone to keep going forward," he later said.[9]

"For the English-speaking volunteers in Israel, the story of the Jews from Yemen was just another amazing story of the gathering of the Jewish people in their homeland. If there was a single reason felt by all of the English-speaking flight crews and other volunteers, it was a feeling of 'never again' after the press and other news media dramatically revealed the stories of the Holocaust."[9]

All the pilots seem to have shared the sense that what they were doing was bigger than they were. They took pride in being rewarded with something more than their paychecks. Maguire never forgot the Yemenites' singing and crying out blessings as they flew into Israel nor the grateful expressions on their faces. "It was so touching you almost don't want to remember," he recalled. "When you've been privileged to see something that people don't see very often...I was lucky, I was blessed that God had given me the opportunity to be there."[10]

All the pilots were piling up ridiculous numbers of hours, far more than would have been allowed had they been flying in the U.S. or in other than emergency conditions. Warren put in over 150 hours in January alone. Maguire himself was flying between 270 and 300 hours a month while trying to run the operation and start up a new airline at the same time, all without adequate fuel, planes, or parts.

Alaska Airlines had every plane it owned in the air somewhere in the world, but the post World War II world was full of pilots and airplanes looking for work. Trying to stay one step ahead of Wooten, Maguire set himself to hunt up more airplanes. At one point, he tried to procure surplus military aircraft, and only later found out he'd been bidding against Wooten for the same planes. It was impossible to keep the business threads from tangling and still make the number of flights he needed to.

He knew Wooten was in an awkward situation: effectively running his own company in order to lease planes and personnel from another company of which he was still president. Usually, Wooten couldn't pass up a chance to turn the slings and arrows of outrageous fortune into hilarious anecdotes with himself as the ultimately triumphant hero. This time, he was being less than transparent about where he was in the process of getting Near East Air Transport ready to take over from Alaska Airlines.

And he was almost impossible to get in touch with, zipping between continents like a hyperactive mongoose. He would sometimes descend upon Tel Aviv or Asmara for no more than a few hours before zooming off to some other destination, temporarily absconding with a plane and crew in the bargain. He no sooner returned to Asmara in December with re-fitted planes when he headed back to the states because of some legal trouble that was brewing, about which he apparently told Maguire little, downplaying or dismissing entirely the gravity of his situation.

In the middle of January, payday came—and went. Warren wondered how he'd been overlooked and asked around. He wasn't alone. Clarke Cole hadn't been paid, either, and neither had anyone else Warren asked. He made up his mind to track down Maguire as soon as the Chief Pilot returned, but Maguire remained characteristically tight-lipped. "Just charge what you need to Alaska Airlines," he told Warren and Cole. "It'll get straightened out." Exactly what that meant, Warren had no idea.

He knew nothing of the existence of NEAT or of Wooten's plan to run the airlift under the new business. He and the other pilots had little leisure to worry about it, but the uncertainly left them uneasy.

Not as uneasy as getting shot at by furious Arabs, suspicious and trigger-happy Israelis, or even the RAF made them, though. Warren and all the Alaskans were constantly and often rudely reminded that there was a war going on all around them, disrupting communications at the most inopportune moments, causing emergency blackouts, forcing planes to change course to avoid areas of combat, and generally sowing confusion that impinged on every aspect of the crews' efforts, in and out of the planes.

Bob Platt was flying with Maguire for the first time since his arrival, when the plane took a hit. "We had to take off just before sunset—some Arabian rule or law—and we came in to land at Tel Aviv before dawn." He settled in to nap for the duration of the flight, but was rudely jarred awake. "(I) felt the plane bouncing around needlessly and grumbled to Maguire to straighten it up and fly right, then figured out what it was." The cause turned out to be that they'd been shot. "We had to patch some holes from shrapnel."[6]

That was the second time the hyper-vigilant Israelis had given Maguire a close call; the third time, it was the Egyptians, or so he surmised. He dodged the bullets—literally—by dropping down behind a higher range of hills and weaving his way through the passes until he was out of firing range.

Not long after his initial close call coming into IAF ace Slick Goodlin's sights, Clarke Cole watched apprehensively as two twin-engine British fighters came at him head-on. He dropped down, hoping to hide in the thick cloak of sand filling the air, but they flashed past without slowing. He realized belatedly that the sun at his tail had saved him; flying straight into its burning light, the pilots hadn't seen him.[11]

An Egyptian bombing raid surprised a young co-pilot, who was up on the wing of his C-46 refueling in the black of night when the first bombs fell. Shrapnel struck one of the airplane's tires; the explosion shook the plane so badly that the young man thought it had been hit. He leaped to the ground, dashed to his rental car and drove like a madman into Tel Aviv.

Screeching to a halt at the hotel, he ran inside and headed straight for the room in which he knew Jimmy Wooten was staying. He pounded on the door until Wooten opened it. "I'm through," he shouted. "Give me a ticket back to New York. I quit." Ironically, he was killed a year later on Long Island while demonstrating light aircraft at an air show.[12]

John Thompson watched tracers go by the windshield on his way into Aden. He called the British radio operator at Khormaksar. "Are you people having any combat exercises going on right now?"

The operator replied that, no, none were scheduled.

"How about target practice. Any of that?"

Again, the operator replied with a negative.

"Well I didn't have anything to report; I just wanted to know who the hell's side you're on," snapped Thompson.

Later, he recalled, "I told Wooten I wanted combat pay."[13]

Larry Roger had a few tough moments when his radio operator repeatedly failed to contact Israeli flight control as the plane they were flying crossed the border. "It really gets your attention, you know," Roger said later, "to have those tracers go by the cockpit when you're on approach." He dealt with the problem with his usual cool-headedness until the third time it happened. Then he opened up a channel to the tower and politely but firmly berated his own hapless radio operator, by name, to the Israeli controller, who relayed the message to the ground troops. "It went out to all the ground forces to lay off the airplane."[14]

The crew flying in the first phases of the operation, in October of 1948 and again from December 1948 to March of 1949, took the worst of it, facing fire from Arabs and Israelis, sometimes on the same flight. Wooten loved to tell the story of when he himself was on a flight that was hit by anti-aircraft fire. The ensuing attempts to cope turned what could have been a fatal tragedy into a keystone cops-style farce.

A direct hit caught the #1 engine on fire. The pilot ordered the co-pilot to hit the extinguisher, but the flustered co-pilot hit the wrong one and extinguished the #4 engine, leaving the airplane flying with only two engines, one of which had also taken a hit and was faltering. Fortunately, Lydda was close at hand, but as they turned on the final approach, the injured engine caught fire. Again, the co-pilot reached to extinguish the blaze, but the pilot stopped him, preferring to risk the flames rather than have the co-pilot kill the wrong engine again. The pilot eventually got them safely on the ground, and Wooten lived to tell the tale.[15]

Warren never faced any significant fire; he didn't consider angry tribesmen with rifles on the ground as much of a threat, and he was careful to stay out of range of the known anti-aircraft emplacements. But he dreaded nights when active combat along the route caused Lydda to shut down the airport and damp the runway lights.

He could cope with landing in the pitch black at Asmara or Aden, when he had to. But seeing nothing but dark, apparently empty landscape where one was used to seeing welcoming lights and civilization made him uneasy. For one thing, it meant something, somewhere, was wrong, and that could mean anything from a bombing raid to armed troops actually exchanging fire in the vicinity. Not a happy thing for an unarmed commercial aircraft with a load of defenseless and highly vulnerable passengers. For another, it made the Israeli military even more jumpy than usual, and more than one flight was greeted by Israeli soldiers armed to the teeth. "You never knew what kind of welcome you were going to get," Warren later admitted.

Bob Platt remembered one such instance, coming in from Aden in the much-abused and badly overloaded Skymaster, only to be greeted by a total blackout where their destination was supposed to be. "Still don't know how Maguire managed to land that thing without runway lights, but he found some hills on the maps we had and lined it up, then the tall blond co-pilot[16] said, 'Well, here we go,' and landed," Platt recalled in amazement. "We had 76 women and kids on that flight. When Bob got her down where he thought land must be, he turned on the landing lights and there it was. We were met by some military trucks and they made us haul out our ID and passports; they thought we were Egyptian bombers."[6]

Many of the pilots who survived World War II and continued to fly were hardened adrenaline junkies, addicted not only to flying but to the thrill of danger. Alaska Airlines seems to have had more than its fair share of that type in its roster. It was almost a requirement, considering the conditions under which they flew, in and outside of Alaska. "The bravest pilots in the world fly for Alaska Airlines," one young co-pilot told his Captain upon tendering his resignation from the company. "How you have any nerves left is beyond me."[17]

Perhaps that is why so few of them gave up and went home. Whatever else it was, Operation Magic Carpet was never boring.

Cole and Warren were both in Asmara in January when a wire came in addressed to Clarke. The younger man held it out so Warren could read it over his shoulder: "ADVISE COLE WAR HALTS OPERATION WAITING WORD WOOTEN WILL ADVISE."[18]

Warren knew that his friend had assisted Maguire during a lot of the operation's set up, but given the growing bad blood between Wooten and Cole, he'd assumed Cole was as out of the loop as he was. "Again?" he asked aloud. "What the hell does that mean?"

Cole wadded the note up and stuffed it into a pocket. "I don't have a goddamned idea," he growled. Then he shrugged and looked up at Warren. "Got any money?"

"Not really."

"Me neither. Let's go back to the hotel and get drunk on Bob's credit."[19]

1. Barer, *The Magic Carpet*, p15.
2. "Entire Yemen Jewish Community Being Transferred to Israel", *The Palestine Post*, November 8, 1949.
3. "Operation Magic Carpet," Allan Keller, staff writer, *New York World Telegram* and *The Sun*, May 27, 1950.
4. Satterfield; interview with Larry Roger, 1979.
5. Parfitt, *The Road to Redemption*, p165-167.
6. Satterfield; interview with Bob Platt, 1979.
7. Satterfield; interview with Hank Bierds, 1979.
8. Barer, *The Magic Carpet* and multiple other sources.

9. Magic Carpet Pilots, Alaska Airlines: https://www.-alaskaair.com/content/about-us/history/carpet-pilots.aspx.

10. "Jews Discover an Unsung Hero," Christiana Sciaudone, *Los Angeles Times*, June 19, 2004.

11. Satterfield; interview with Clarke Cole, 1970.

12. Satterfield, multiple interviews, 1979. The young man may have been Dick Whiting.

13. Satterfield; interview with John Thompson, 1979.

14. Satterfield; interview with Larry Roger, 1979. I also heard Larry tell this story in person on several occasions.

15. Satterfield; interview with James Wooten, 1979.

16. Almost certainly Hank Mulleneaux. He was a DC-4 captain in his own right, but also Maguire's frequent co-pilot as well as a good friend. Later, Maguire asked him to act as his Chief Pilot when he became President of Near East Air Transport. They ran the business together for several years.

17. Satterfield, as related by Capt. Forrest Wood, 1979.

18. This is apparently the same warning received by Capt. Thompson when he landed in Bombay at the same time. Wooten was reacting to reports of rioting in Aden.

19. Author; interview with Warren Metzger, 2008.

CHAPTER TWELVE: TOGETHER AGAIN

Warren landed in Asmara late in the evening. Whatever difficulty in Aden had inspired the wire to Cole had apparently caused no more than another temporary hiccup. He saw the silhouette of a DC-4 against the darkening sky. As their lights brushed over the fuselage, he realized he was not looking at good old 915 but at 667, the plane he'd heard was coming in from Calcutta. That was a bit of good news, as they could sure use the help. Hopefully this one would stick around.

As he neared the bottom of the ladder, Dick Carlson, one of the mechanics, reached up and clapped him on the back. "Hey, Metzger, Marian's here. She came in on 667 yesterday. She and the others are at the hotel."[1]

Warren's tiredness vanished in a warm glow. His half-joking wish, scrawled out at the end of a letter he'd mailed almost two weeks before, had been granted.

The desk clerk at the Albergo Ciaao Hotel was happy to tell Warren what room Marian was in. She was sharing a room with Jean and Shaina; the other two girls were almost never in town at the same time, so adding a third wasn't an issue. The desk clerk warned Warren politely but sternly not to disturb the young lady, as she was resting. Then he gave Warren a meaningful head-to-toe look-over. "Perhaps the young sir would like to freshen up before the young lady rises?"[1]

Ouch. Warren accepted the reminder gratefully and bounded up the stairs to his own room, which he shared with a revolving cast of other pilots or crew, usually Gene Wheeler or Noel Grout, though both were out at the moment.

Unbeknownst to him, while he was "freshening up," the desk clerk, whom Marian had asked to wake her when Warren arrived, made a hasty trip upstairs, tapped on her door, and gave her the good news.[2] When Warren came down again, having showered, shaved, and changed to fresh clothing, it was to find Marian waiting for him, newly washed, curled, scented, and made up, her eyes dancing above her high-wattage smile.

They ate dinner and spent the evening regaling one another with their adventures, laughing uproariously over what had been hair-raising escapades. Marian learned about the letter he'd written that was out somewhere in the Alaska Airlines pipeline, making its circuitous way to her, and she filled him in on her adventures and all the news from "back home," or as much of it as she knew; she had been away from Anchorage and Seattle almost as long as he had.

They went out walking, despite the lateness of the hour. Asmara boasted modern streets and buildings lit up like holiday decorations. There were gardens everywhere, scenting the balmy air with night-blooming flowers. In places, the buildings gave way to trees, flowering shrubs, and tall, tough grass. One could look up and see the night sky in all its glory almost as if one were out in the country. The moon silvered the heavens, where stars in unfamiliar arrays glittered like diamonds. Neither was terribly worried about being mistaken for Italians; by now, most of the locals could identify many of the American flight crewmen-and-women on sight.

They ran out of words and wandered aimlessly, holding hands, both secretly wishing the night would go on forever.

Warren realized he'd been thinking of this moment for a long time. Knowing what he wanted to say from the moment he met her, but denied to himself out of fear that she didn't feel the same way. Somewhere during the last few hours, the fear left him, and he realized it wouldn't have mattered if it hadn't.

There they were, and the time was right.

What the hell.

He broke the prolonged silence by clearing his throat. "Say, if we can do it, do you want to get married tomorrow, or the next day?"[1,2]

Marian looked at him with her head tilted playfully to one side; she smiled as a bubble of warmth swelled inside her. Silly to think they could pull it off on such notice, of course, and given their schedules, the next few days probably wouldn't work out much better. That didn't matter; a little to her own surprise, she had no doubts this time. "Sure. Why not?"[1,2]

She stopped and pulled his head down for a kiss.

The hotel lights had dimmed, but the desk clerk was still on duty when they returned. When they stopped and asked him how they might go about getting married, his white smile broadened in his dark face. "In the morning, you must go to City Hall," he told them. "Ask the people there, and they will help you."[2]

Knowing they would need witnesses, they headed for the hotel bar to see who was still up.

Captain Massey[3] and co-pilot Hershal Patton[4] were there, and they invited the couple to join them in finishing off the bottle they were sharing. Warren and Marian had flown with both men and liked them tremendously; both had a reputation as pranksters, even among the wild Alaska crew. The two men quickly agreed to accompany Warren and Marian to City Hall in the morning, on the condition that Massey be allowed to be Marian's Maid of Honor and Patton the Flower Girl. Since all the other stews were out on flights, Marian agreed with a laugh.[2]

Warren was left needing a Best Man; Clarke Cole, riding as co-pilot to John Thompson in the DC-4, had already taken off for Rome with Wooten riding shotgun, which was probably just as well. When he voiced a protest at Massey and Patton's defection, Massey waved him off. "Hell, Warren, *anyone* can do that. You can take your pick in the morning. Good Maids of Honor don't grow on trees."[2]

Accompanied by Massey, Patton, and Dick Carlson, whom they'd picked up on the way out the door, Warren and Marian made the trek bright and early the next morning to City Hall, and there a very large, very polite Italian man who spoke English told them the mayor could marry them, and that he would arrange it. The appointed hour was set for just after noon. That left time for a few arrangements.

They all returned to the hotel, where Massey, Patton, and Carlson, taking their tasks seriously, left Marian and Warren to eat lunch. The trio raced off to pound on doors and hunt down the rest of the Alaska crew.

Everyone turned out their pockets and pooled their resources. Pickings were pretty slim; a nickel here and a buck or two there, as no one had gotten a paycheck in a while. When they figured they had enough, Massey and Carlson ran to the only jewelry store in town[5], where they paid $9.00 for a twenty-four carat gold ring. Patton and several others hunted all over town for flowers. The only fresh flowers available in any quantity were pink carnations, so they scooped up as many as they could and headed back to the hotel.

The hotel manager, his wife, and the hotel staff threw themselves into the project. They went wild with candles, ribbons, and flowers in the dining room, turning the rather utilitarian space into a spring garden. The sweet scent of the carnations filled the air.

Warren hadn't brought a dress uniform or much of anything else appropriate. With the help of the hotel manager and by borrowing bits and pieces from other pilots, he descended to the lobby in a sharp-looking suit and a silk tie, his shoes freshly polished, and sporting a pink carnation boutonnière.

Marian's beautiful new wool suit was much, much too hot, and it was all she had aside from her uniform. Fortunately, Jean Cusy[6] had returned that morning and produced a lovely, flower-print, off-the-shoulder sundress with flowing skirts that fit Marian almost perfectly. Also fortunately, she wasn't a bit put out by being usurped by Massey and Patton. She thought having them fill the roles of Maid of Honor and Flower Girl was hilarious, and she yielded with grace and a ready laugh. She spent the morning helping the bride fix her hair and pinned a spray of carnations at her temple.

The manager's wife came to the room to see if Marian had all she needed and shook her head. With a flurry of rapid-fire Italian and effusive hand gestures, she managed to make Marian and Jean understand the enormity of their oversight: it was not possible for a lady to be married without a headdress of some sort. She dashed off and returned moments later with a beautiful, black lace mantilla and arranged it on Marian's thick, auburn hair.[2]

It was totally wrong with the sundress but stunning. Marian thanked her profusely and headed down the stairs.

The big clock over the door was just hitting noon when Warren and Marian—followed by nearly every Alaska Airlines employee in Asmara—trekked down to the Mayor's office.

The mayor, Signore Eduardo Dionesio, was a charming little man with two goatees and enormous, curling mustaches, which amazed her and elicited Massey's open admiration. Marian privately thought he looked like one of the Munchkins from the film, "The Wizard of Oz." He spoke no English, but offered them effusive assurances of his joy and delight in florid Italian, his dark eyes sparkling as he ushered the couple and their attendants into his office.

Marian knew just enough Italian to understand that their wedding was, apparently, the talk of the town and *the* social event of the colony's season. Evidently the Alaskans had done a thorough job of spreading the word as they dashed through town on their mad shopping spree.

With Fred Perino providing music on his harmonica and Patton strewing the floor with carnation petals, Warren and Marian walked arm-in-arm to the Mayor's desk, signed the certificates, and said their vows on January 24th, 1949.[7]

.   .   .

The party put the Albergo Ciaao Hotel on the map for months to come. The crew was long overdue to blow off some steam, and Warren and Marian had just given them the best excuse possible.

Bob Maguire started off the festivities by tapping his glass for a toast, somewhat to everyone's surprise, since he wasn't part of the wedding party. Without fanfare and in his dry, spare style, he announced that the whole shindig was on Alaska Airlines' dime. He paused, obviously trying to think of something to add. "Have fun," he finally said and sat down.

His words brought a roof-shaking cheer and a round of popping champagne corks; to a man and woman they were—especially after scraping up funds for the ring and flowers—all but penniless.

At least twenty guests sat down to the feast around a giant banquet table the hotel covered with a gorgeous Irish linen tablecloth that, the manager assured

Warren and Marian, was reserved only for "special occasions." He also leaned in between them as he refilled their glasses and assured them that the hotel had arranged for them to have their own room—something the bride and groom both knew had taken a lot of shuffling by the crew.

After a lavish dinner of spaghetti—the chef's specialty—the guests polished off in short order the champagne and the Chianti that had been served with the meal and started in on stronger spirits. The hotel provided a cake, the frosting decorated with—surprise!—more carnations.

The manager had closed off the dining room, reserving it solely for the wedding party, but somehow more and more people kept finding their way in. The other tables quickly filled up as total strangers presented the newlyweds with congratulations, blessings, and gifts. The latter ranged from bouquets of flowers or baskets of fruit to a caged songbird and a live kitten, which Marian accepted with delight and only very reluctantly gave to the hotel manager's wife at the end of the night.

The mayor and his wife, who actually *had* been invited, arrived early on; Marian found him "very charming and a marvelous dancer," even if the conversation was somewhat limited. Hank McCoy brought the young Israeli lady who had been hired to drive the crews in the company jeep back and forth from the airport. They held hands and looked suspiciously starry-eyed for the rest of the evening.[8] Several local couples dropped in just to congratulate the bride and groom and share in the fun. One lady, Doris Sivek, who came with her husband and later became quite a good friend, invited Marian out to her uncle's ranch. Her uncle bred Arabian horses, and Doris insisted Marian come riding with her in the near future.

The hotel manager beamed through it all, though probably with some difficulty, as the glasses started being flung into corners with cheerful abandon, shattering to the accompaniment of increasingly robust and intoxicated cheers. Maguire made no attempt to stop the destruction, but he made the manager's night a bit better by signing for glasses in batches of a dozen before slipping quietly away.

Marian, for one of the few times in her life, let the alcohol get the better of her, but she was more drunk on the moment than on the champagne. She danced with her new husband and what seemed like every man in the room, until her feet wouldn't hold her up anymore. She sat next to Warren, holding his hand and laughing for no reason at all. He beamed at everyone in warm good-fellowship, happy just to be there with all of these people—and especially with this woman, his wife.

He leaned over her, savoring the scent of her hair. "Hey, Mrs. Metzger. Want another glass of champagne?"

Her eyes looked as blue as the Mediterranean and sparkled like sunlight on water. "I've had enough, thanks. What say we blow this joint, Mr. Metzger?"

1. Author; interview with Warren Metzger, 2008.
2. Author; interview with Marian Liscomb Metzger, 2008. Who served as Best Man is uncertain, but probably Dick Carlson.
3. Captain Massey left a deep and very fond impression on many of the Alaska crew; several have related anecdotes featuring him. No one, however, seems able to remember his first name.
4. Pilots who were full-fledged captains often flew as co-pilots for others, though usually only on planes on which they'd not yet been certified as "Captain" themselves. Patton seems to have been a DC-4 captain at this point, but several remember him flying as a co-pilot with them.
5. Or, at least, the only one that had a plain gold wedding band, which was all they could afford.

6. By this time, Marian and Jean may have been the only two stewardesses left. Shaina may have left at some point prior to this; lacking evidence, I've chosen to leave the matter in doubt. Marian mentioned on several occasions that Jean was out on a trip, which was why Marian had no female attendants. But Jean played witness in the Mayor's office and attended the wedding dinner, and Marian wore a dress borrowed from her, so I'm assuming Jean returned post-planning but pre-wedding.

7. They married again after returning to the states, on March 31, 1949, and had a plethora of reasons as to why. Their favorite was that the first wedding wasn't legal in the United States, and they didn't want their children to be bastards. Their second favorite was so that they could celebrate two wedding anniversaries per year.

8. Harold McCoy ended up marrying the young lady —whose name is not recorded in any of the pilots' interviews—and staying in Israel. He later went to work for Near East Air Transport, and afterward for El Al, Israel's first airline.

1. The wedding party: best man (probably Dick
Carlson), groom, bride, maid of honor Capt. Massey.
The flower girl, Hershal Patton, took the photo
(Metzger collection).

2. The wedding party in the Mayor's office L to
R: Dick Carlson (?), Warren, Marian, Jean Cusy,
Capt. Massey (Metzger collection).

3. Signore Eduardo Dionesio, Mayor of Asmara, signs papers before the ceremony (Metzger collection).

4. Fred Perino plays the wedding march on his harmonica (Metzger collection).

5. The Wedding dinner, L to R: Mrs. Stoppe, Perry Karafel, Red Elliot, Hank McCoy, Ray Stroup, LeRoy Johnson, John McKenzie, Jean Cusy, Bud Gessner, Warren, Marian, Bob Platt, Fred Perino, Bob Newman, Paul Arnold, Jack Morris, Dora Sivek, (unknown), Tony Gjessing, Joe McKloskey (Metzger collection).

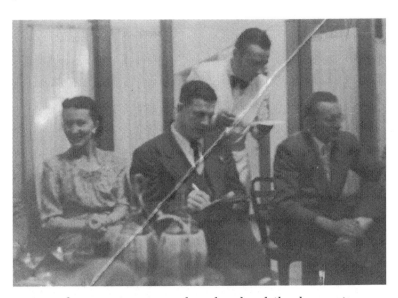

6. Bob Maguire signs the check while the maître d'hôtel watches anxiously. Also pictured: Mrs. Stoppe and Hank McCoy (Metzger collection).

N. 556 *Reg. Certificati*

Amministrazione Municipale di Asmara

CERTIFICATO DI MATRIMONIO

L'ufficiale di Stato Civile sottoscritto

CERTIFICA

che nel giorno **ventiquattro** -- del mese di **gennaio** -----

dell'anno mille**novecentoquarantanove** ----1949 - - - - -

in **A S M A R A** ----------------- - - - - - - - - - -

sono stati uniti in matrimonio

WARREN Carl Metzger di George Lewis e di ELSIE May,

di anni trenta, pilota - - - - - - - - - - - - -

nato a **Lethosige Alberta(Canada)** residente a **Asmara** - - - - -

e

LISCOMB Marian Frances di Paul E. e di MARY H. LISCOMB,

di anni ventisei, impiegata,, -- - - - - - - - - - -

nata a **New Brighton** residente a **Asmara** - - - - -

come risulta dall'atto inscritto nel registro degli atti di matrimonio di **questo**

Municipio - - - - - per l'anno 1 **949** -- al N. **2** -----

Parte **I** ----- Serie - - - -

Si rilascia il presente **per ogni legale effetto.-**

Asmara, li **25 gennaio** 194 **9**

ESATTE L

L'Ufficiale dello Stato Civile
-Dr.E.Dionisio-

WP 357 - 1000 - II - Tip Zuco gest. Iacovacci

7. Certificato di Matrimonio. Note the incorrect date, entered by the clerk, which caused a few problems later (Metzger collection).

8. The new Mr. and Mrs. Warren C. Metzger
(Metzger collection).

9. The honeymooners in the courtyard of the
Albergo Ciaao hotel (Metzger collection).

10. Together in Asmara (Metzger collection).

11. Back to work; one of a series of publicity photos taken during Operation Magic Carpet, directly after the wedding. (Metzger collection and Alaska Airlines).

12. Another of the unreleased publicity photos
(courtesy Alaska Airlines).

13. Unreleased publicity photo (Metzger collection
and Alaska Airlines).

14. Marian and Doris Sivek in Asmara; Doris showed
Marian around Asmara while Warren was flying
(Metzger collection).

15. Marian and Doris Sivek's uncle, with one of his
Arabian horses (Metzger collection).

CHAPTER THIRTEEN: BLUE SKIES, DARK CLOUDS

The honeymoon was brief, however idyllic. Warren and Marian were still in the middle of a war zone and on a mission. Both were scheduled to fly out the next day: he to Aden, and she on another run to Shanghai. They made the most of what time they had.

Warren enjoyed showing his new wife around Asmara; Marian had a layman's interest in architecture and anything new and different. They sipped coffee and tea in a little café with a shaded, outdoor garden, making sure to say, "Hi," to all the native staff. They ran into Doris Sivek again, who insisted on having her picture taken with Marian and renewed her invitation to come out and ride her uncle's horses. And they talked about their future, made plans, and named the children they would have.

Neither wanted to leave Alaska Airlines, but the company faced an uncertain future, and the mystery of the missing paychecks was hardly reassuring.

For once, Marian wasn't looking forward to the adventure of her flight to Shanghai the next morning. It was one thing for Warren to be taking off for a full day and a night; at least he'd be coming back to Asmara. When she left, she'd be gone for at least three days, maybe more. And after that, who knew where she might end up?

Jim Wooten's lovely and long-suffering wife, Phyllis, widely regarded as "one of the nicest people you'll ever meet,"[1] met them at the door of the hotel upon their return. "Marian, would you mind very much if I took your place on the flight to Shanghai? I so want to do some shopping in Hong Kong, and this might be my only chance. I'm sure Bob will approve it."

She could have gone to Hong Kong virtually any time she liked, and was unlikely to have time to shop if she worked the flight. Marian recognized the offer for what it was. In any case, she was not about to look a gift horse in the mouth. "Would you? That would be wonderful!" The sudden freedom emboldened her. "Do you think he'd okay it if I rode along with Warren on his flight tomorrow?"

Phyllis looked taken aback. "Well, I can't see why not. Why don't you ask?"[2]

Permission was readily granted on the condition that Marian remain in the cockpit unless absolutely necessary. She did not speak the language, would only get in the way of the Israeli volunteers or, worse, intimidate the passengers. Somewhat miffed, Marian nevertheless agreed. Warren patted her hand. "You'll be glad for it," he assured her. "Trust me."

It wasn't that she didn't believe him; by now, she'd heard numerous stories from the other stews who'd flown the Aden to Tel Aviv trips. But for all the hardship, it sounded like a real adventure, and she longed to experience it for herself.

Her first glimpse of the Yemenites fascinated her. Though most of them were even smaller than she was, and usually dressed in a bizarre mish-mash of cast-off clothing supplied by the JDC, they seemed exotic and fascinating, like something out of an ancient tale. They were a stoic people, Warren assured her, inured to hardship. They would have to be, she thought. Every face among them told a story of courage and endurance she could hardly imagine.

Some of the children nearly made her weep. Their bones pushed up against their skin from prolonged starvation, as if about to burst free. And yet, their shy smiles enchanted her. She now understood why Warren spoke so often of them.

She briefly held an orphaned little girl who had been close to death when she'd arrived at the camp but was now officially pronounced out of danger. The girl's huge eyes, dark as midnight, stared up at her with wonder, and a tiny hand, as small as an American infant's, shyly touched Marian's cheek. "I melted," she later remembered. She handed the girl back to the nurse with great reluctance. "If I could have, I'd have been tempted to take her with me."[2]

Her enthusiasm suffered a bit of a setback as she climbed aboard the plane. Even forewarned, the smell the C-46 had acquired and now wore like an extra coat of paint rocked her back on her heels. "The stench was absolutely foul," she said later. "And it got worse as the flight went on."[2]

Despite her orders to remain in the cockpit, she did have to go back to the passenger head at one point. She used the opportunity to do what she could en route. After all, she wasn't exactly disobeying orders by smiling, handing cups of water to people who looked like they needed it most, or helping the volunteers pass out oranges along the way. And holding air sickness bags while hoping her uniform would somehow remain unscathed. She'd had a lot of practice, but this was a real challenge. She avoided the sand box at the back of the plane, and somehow managed to not step in any of the accidents elsewhere.

She longed to really help, but she had to admit, there was little she could do. After one or two forays, she confined herself to the cockpit for the majority of the trip, as ordered.

As they swept down for a landing at Lydda and the wheels hummed against the tarmac, she heard voices raised in song. She did not recognize it, but the emotion came through loud and clear; joyful and celebratory.[3] She leaned forward to touch Warren's shoulder. "Listen! They're singing!"

He smiled over his shoulder. "They do that almost every time. The volunteers tell them when we're about to land in Israel. It's a homecoming song."

Marian's eyes stung, and she sat back, intensely grateful to have had the opportunity to witness this moment and play a part in it, however minor.

As they taxied slowly toward the terminal, Warren threw another smile over his shoulder. "Hey, honey, if you really want to help out, go back and open the door once we stop. The volunteers always have a bit of trouble with it."

Happy for something to do at last, she waited until the plane came to a halt before heading back into the cabin. The change in the Yemenites delighted her. "All the passengers were so happy," she remembered, "it seemed a miracle to them." Their dark faces glowed, and their eyes shone with an inner light caused by more than tears of joy.

As Marian made her way back to the cockpit, one little old lady reached out to her with a thin, wrinkled hand. Marian paused, and the woman caught the hem of her jacket, raised it to her shaking head, and kissed it. "She was bestowing a blessing, thanking me, as if I'd personally made this all possible," Marian remembered later. "It made me feel half-an-inch high on the one hand, because I had done nothing. And at that same time, I felt ten feet tall, as if God had, for just a little while, made me one of His angels." She knew the gesture, however heartfelt, was not for her alone. "We were the wings of eagles. We'd brought them home. And she was thanking me for it."[2]

·   ·   ·

Even in the midst of a war for its existence, Tel Aviv was a beautiful city. Established as a suburb of the ancient port city of Jaffa in 1909, it engulfed the older, Arabic town during the war for Israeli independence and emerged as a modern hybrid, hiding its older origins behind brick and barbed-wire walls. The Tel Aviv of 1949 still wore a sheen of newness: white-washed walls nearly pristine of smoke or dirt, streets lined with trees and flowering shrubs, buildings designed by modern architects beginning to rise into the air with every evidence of pride and confidence.

The waves of immigrants engulfing the city since the end of World War II had set off another building frenzy. Housing was desperately short, and new construction was hopelessly unable to keep up with the ever-growing demand.

As a result, the Alaska crew usually ended up encamped on the roof of the Yarden hotel. Warren and Marian nevertheless tried to talk the manager into finding a room for them, just this once. The manager was terribly sympathetic to the newlyweds, but he had displaced families and high-ranking bureaucrats filling every nook and cranny. There was simply no room to be had at any price. They would be sharing the roof with eight or ten other pilots.

Resigned, the two lovebirds headed out to find something to eat. Even then, Tel Aviv's night-life was famous and infamous in equal measure. One of the crew, Red Elliott, had almost gotten himself killed in a brawl in one of the dives his date, a rather daring Israeli beauty, dragged him to.[4] But Warren and Marian found a slightly more upscale place where they ate dinner and even danced. It was a favorite hang-out for pilots, and they ran into several whom Warren knew. Among them was a fighter pilot named Blackstone who was known to all and sundry as "Blackie."

Blackie greeted Warren with a grin, eying Marian with a look of none-too-subtle interest. "Back already? You just left this place."

"Blackie, I'd like to introduce you to my wife, Marian," Warren said proudly. "We just got married."

Blackie made polite noises and shook Marian's hand. "But I could tell he didn't believe him (Warren)," Marian later laughed. "I don't think he ever did."[2]

When they got back to the hotel, they discovered that the staff had walled off part of the roof with blankets and set up a beautiful bower within. The lovers would be able to watch the stars, if they wished, and still have some privacy from the other pilots sharing the roof with them.

The next day, they returned to Asmara, and life assumed what was to become their normal routine. Every two or three days, Warren left to fly to Aden and would be gone for two more days.

Marian asked Maguire to assign her flights on the DC-4 or one of the other planes making the Yemenite run, but he told her the other stewardesses were being sent home; the Israeli nurses and other volunteers could do what was needed for the refugees during the flights. She shrugged and decided to make the most of it. She said goodbye to Jean and Shaina and had the room to herself, except for the crew women sometimes sweeping in from Shanghai. She visited her new friend, Doris, rode horses, saw the sights, wrote cheery letters to her family, and "loafed around and ate spaghetti."[2] And waited for Warren.[5]

·   ·   ·

In order to prevent Clarke Cole from being sent back to the U.S. or, more likely, fired outright by a fed-up Wooten, John Thompson used the trip to Rome at the time of Warren and Marian's wedding to give Cole a check flight that, by the end of it, made the young pilot the newest DC-4 captain.[1]

Never one to hold a grudge, Cole accepted Warren's victory with good grace, and decided to view his "promotion" as a just and well-deserved compensation. And, yes, he rubbed Warren's nose in it a bit.

On his first trip as a DC-4 captain, the camp assistant who had once asked Cole to double his load in the C-46 now asked him how many he could get into the modified DC-4.

"Up to 110, now," Cole replied.

"See if you can get 150 in, why don't you?" the man urged. "Then take her up and see if it will work."

Cole wondered if he'd heard right. "110 is all she'll take. That's more than twice what she was originally rated for. If I take her out to try it, we'll never make it back. A lot of people get killed that way."[6]

The man looked disappointed. "Well, it might be worth a try. We're simply not moving them out fast enough."

Riding along on another flight during a brief visit, Wooten, receiving the same challenge, tried to meet it. He overrode his pilot's protests and squeezed 148 Yemenites—adults and children—onto the plywood benches of a DC-4.[7] The plane wallowed and groaned its way successfully to Tel Aviv, whereupon the pilot told Wooten, "Never again."

Unbeknownst to Warren, Marian, and the Alaska Airlines crew busting their humps and dodging bullets in the sand-laden skies between Asmara, Aden, Tel Aviv, and Nicosia, more trouble was brewing, this time back in the States.

The number of pending lawsuits piling up against Alaska Airlines—and Wooten personally—finally started rolling down in an unstoppable avalanche, with a roar even he was unable to ignore any longer.

More than one of his opponents had taken his counter-suit, now entering its second year, as a declaration of war. Juan Trippe of Pan American Airlines made a point to seek out Wooten while they were both at the Wings Club, an exclusive aviators' gathering place in Washington D.C. Trippe and Wooten were usually on fairly friendly terms, but this time Trippe was boiling over.

According to Wooten, Trippe cornered him after a few bourbons. "Jim, I'm gonna put your ass into jail, and don't take this lightly; I'm tired of you being the flea in the elephant's ear. You've cost me millions of dollars, and I'm gonna put your ass in jail."[7]

Wooten couldn't really argue; he certainly had cost Trippe a fortune in attorneys' fees, if nothing else.

Back in 1948, while he and the CAB were first flinging suits and counter-suits at one another, Pacific Northern (another small Alaskan Airline run by former bush pilot Art Woodley) had filed its own suit, asserting that Alaska Airlines was running scheduled flights between Seattle and Anchorage as well as other destinations up the Alaska coast. In fact, they were. Wooten, confident of immunity from censure, had even begun advertising a flight schedule in local newspapers: four flights per day. The charge was entirely true, and they were hardly the only flights to and from the Lower 48 openly advertised by Alaska Airlines in local papers.

Wooten had lumped the case with all the others, thumbed his nose at the lot, and left them entirely in the hands of his law team. He was certain his agreement with Jim Landis and Oswald Ryan of the CAB would protect him, and that the CAB would grant him an exemption to run flights as needed.

The CAB didn't see it that way. In the fall of 1948,[8] just as Wooten and Maguire were gearing up to get Operation Magic Carpet into full swing, the court supported its earlier decision and threw out the agreement as "not legal or binding." The ruling signaled the first defeat for Alaska Airlines, but it was quickly followed by others.

Another less significant but painful blow landed in November, 1948, while Wooten and the leased Alaska Airlines planes were in Anchorage being refitted for the second phase of Operation Magic Carpet. A Los Angeles company, Pacific Airmotive Corporation, sued and won—probably justifiably—for lack of payment of a bill for $63,528.19; a staggering amount of money for the financially strapped airline, and one even Marshall couldn't ignore. Though he could have paid it himself, he tried to pass the buck, literally and figuratively. He demanded that Wooten return to New York at once and pay the fine, threatening to fire him if he didn't.

Wooten, trusting his luck and the protection of his political allies, ignored the summons and continued his work on Operation Magic Carpet and the other charters. But with the survival instinct he had honed over years of skating on thin ice, he started hedging his bets by hunting down airplanes he could buy on his own and put in the name of NEAT when the time came.

The Flying Tigers were having financial difficulties, and for a time, it looked like the hard-working freight airline was about to go under. Wooten contacted the president, Bob Prescott, and ended up bidding on five planes they were about to put on the market. As a bonus, he talked Prescott into coming to work for NEAT once things were up and running, and promised him a place in his planned offices in Rome.

Alaska Airlines legal battles were mentioned now and again in the financial sections of newspapers back in the U.S., but none of those newspapers made it into the hands of the employees overseas. Not a whisper reached the ears of the pilots and crew wondering where their paychecks were. Larry Roger and John Thompson, who touched down at home base now and again, knew the airline was in bad odor with the U.S.

State Department, but had no specific information. "They thought we were a bunch of renegades," was Roger's assessment.[9]

No one in Asmara knew it, but time was running out for Alaska Airlines.

Warren's next inkling that something beyond the normal politics was seriously amiss was when the long-awaited new DC-4 finally landed in Tel Aviv at the end of January 1949, not long after the mysteriously worded cable to Clarke Cole. It carried a fresh Alaska Airlines crew, but the familiar logo and lettering on the sides had been painted out. The ship was a sleek, silver blank.

The crew on the plane could provide no explanation; they'd simply been told to fly it over. The interior was already equipped with the by-now-expected plywood benches. Was it a lease from another air service, perhaps, or a new purchase? How, when everyone knew the airline was broke?

Shortly afterward, Warren learned from the mechanics that they'd been told to paint out the Alaska Airlines logos and lettering on all the planes. The proud eagles over the doors were long gone, but the removal of the company's logos felt almost like an attack, as if someone sought to erase the record of their struggles and accomplishments. He tried not to take it personally or let it spoil precious hours he spent with Marian in Asmara, their strange and wondrous paradise.

In the evenings, pilots and ground personnel gathered in the bar of the Albergo Ciaao to trade rumors and ideas. They knew that they were flying way over the number of hours they'd have been allowed in the U.S.—with loads far above the legal limit for their planes.

Was the State Department trying to shut them down? Had the airline been sold? Was Alaska Airlines still in business? Would they have jobs when they got home? Everyone had heard some rumor about legal troubles and most were convinced that Bob Maguire knew the whole story. They waited for an explanation, but true to form, he maintained silence on the subject. Without money or sufficient fuel, hoping their faith in their airline would be justified, the Alaska crews buckled down and kept flying.

Almost certainly, Maguire was under orders from Wooten to say nothing about reasons for the missed paychecks, re-painted planes, and so forth; probably, he did not have all the facts. Near East Air Transport wasn't ready to make its debut, and removing Alaska Airline's logos from the planes would hardly hurry its launch along.[10] Perhaps the U.S. State department didn't want the publicity of an American airline working on the side of Israel during a war. The ever-lengthening list of lawsuits piling up against Alaska Airlines was almost certainly a factor, as was the veil of secrecy surrounding the entire operation. The airline's owner, Raymond Marshall—now gearing up for open war against Wooten over the operation—added to the complications, though that was not public knowledge, either.

For whatever reason, the name of Alaska Airlines was being forcibly disassociated from Operation Magic Carpet.

1. Satterfield; interview with John Thompson, 1979.
2. Author; interview with Marian Liscomb Metzger, 2008.
3. The song was most likely "HaTikvah" ("The Hope"), the Israeli National Anthem; Israeli volunteers often taught it to the new immigrants while still in camp.
4. Satterfield; interview with Bob Platt, 1979.
5. Marian made a second flight to Shanghai, but the timing is unclear; it may have been the last flight out of Shanghai, after she and Warren had returned to the U.S. She did not believe the flight to be part of Operation Magic Carpet. Technically, she was correct; the Chinese rescue flights were part of another contract but were evidently later

lumped together with the Yemen flights as part of Operation Magic Carpet.

6. Satterfield; interview with Clarke Cole, 1970.
7. Satterfield; interview with Jim Wooten, 1979.
8. The dates on this are unclear; I have found several references to this decision but not a specific date or paper trail to support it.
9. Satterfield; interview with Larry Roger, Sam Silver, and John Thompson, 1979.
10. Marshall called a special Alaska Airlines Executive Committee meeting on March 25, 1949, which Wooten attended. Asked for an account of what was happening with the airlift, Wooten reassured the Committee that everything was fine. There is no mention of ending Alaska Airlines' role in the airlift at that time, nor of the fact that by that time the original Hashed had been virtually emptied and was set to be demolished. In fact, Alaska Airlines signed a second contract with the JDC to continue the airlift a few weeks later, before the new camp had even been built. *Minutes of Meeting of Executive Committee of Alaska Airlines, Inc.,* March 25, 1949.

CHAPTER FOURTEEN: OUT OF THE FRYING PAN

Early in February 1949, Wooten made another of his flying visits through the area; Warren and several of the other pilots tried to pin him down, but he avoided them when he could and brushed them off when he couldn't. Something was up, but no one among the crew was much the wiser.

The free-wheeling business wizard was still a force to be reckoned with, and still a miracle worker when it came to opening doors and untangling knots. But in some ways, having him on site was more of a hindrance than a help. Whatever was going on behind the scenes, the stress was clearly wearing on him, and he took it out on Bob Maguire as well as anyone else unfortunate enough to be in his vicinity.

A rumor went around the airline—accompanied with many a sideways glance—that Wooten had more than a business interest in Maguire. If so, his feelings weren't reciprocated, and they didn't stop him from making life as tough for Maguire as he did for everyone else.

Even in the face of disaster, Jimmy Wooten couldn't help being Jimmy Wooten. For all his brilliance and bursts of generosity, some of his worst traits began to appear on a regular basis. He infuriated the taxi drivers in Tel Aviv and Asmara by paying them only half their fares. He overrode the pilots' safety concerns and ignored the mechanics' requests for assistance. Worse, he alienated suppliers with his financial sleight-of-hand.

Warren was right beside Wooten when, having loaded $4,000 worth of aviation fuel onto the C-46, Wooten pulled out a wad of cash and waved it at the seller. "Look, I can give you $3,000 here and now, if you'll call it square; it's all I've got on me." Rather than risk not getting paid at all, the seller reluctantly accepted. Even before he and Warren got back to Aden, Wooten had filled out a reimbursement slip billing Alaska Airlines for the entire $4,000.[1]

Warren heard similar stories repeated by other pilots who ferried Wooten to and from various fuel sources. More than one seller refused to do business with him twice, eliminating desperately needed sources. Maguire was furious and frustrated, but evidently unable to rein in his errant partner. More than one seller refused Alaska Airline's credit, forcing pilots to use their own; they did so, determined to keep the mission flying, but Wooten's name became almost a curse word among many of them.

It was second nature for Wooten to play his cards close to his chest. The pilots and crews, most of whom had served in WWII, were still accustomed to simply accepting orders without much question. For the most part, they shrugged off the various difficulties and uncertainties as just part of the job. The Alaska Airlines employees in Asmara were unaware of what was happening with their company in the rest of the world, and it seems to have been mutual.

Irritated by constant nagging from the JDC that the airlift wasn't moving refugees out fast enough, Wooten freed up more DC-4s by early February 1949 and brought them into the operation. Not that he ever told their crews exactly what they were doing. Captain Larry Currie and his crew, which included Elgen Long,[2] a young navigator fresh from the Flying Tigers and still working on getting his commercial pilot's license, were in Tokyo with a DC-4 when they received a crew schedule change to go to Hong Kong instead of flying back to the U.S. Accustomed to their airline's oddball orders, they headed for Hong Kong and cooled their heels for two weeks before getting further orders. From out of the blue, Currie received a cable telling him to fly to Shanghai to pick up a load of Jewish refugees and take them to Tel Aviv.

When they landed at Lunghwa airport in Shanghai, Currie and his crew were informed that their passengers were stateless individuals, without any national documentation, identity papers, or passports. They were also warned against landing anywhere except at ports of call known to be friendly to the U.S. or an active British RAF station. Landing in any Muslim country was to be avoided at all costs, and "Under no circumstances were we to land, or even fly over, any Muslim country that was at war with Israel," Long remembers.[3] Considering how much of the long journey to Tel Aviv was over Muslim countries at war with Israel, Long had his work cut out for him charting a course that would keep their plane relatively safe.

They took on 52 passengers, which with a full crew that included 2 stewardesses, totaled 60 souls, well over what the unmodified DC-4 was set up to carry. They took off for Bangkok in the late afternoon.

After zig-zagging across Southeast Asia and India, they landed at RAF Khormaksar at mid-day. Since the whole crew had been sleeping in 3-hour shifts since leaving Shanghai, Currie decided to wait until the following morning to make the final flight of the trip, so everyone could get a full night of real sleep in an actual bed. They dashed to the Crescent Hotel, got up again at 3:00am, and headed back to the plane for the last leg of the journey.

Homer's Rosy-fingered Dawn had yet to put in an appearance as they approached the airfield the next morning. The sky was just light enough that Long, looking out the car window, saw to his astonishment people crawling out of the caves peppering the cliffs along the roadside to make preparations to begin their day. "They obviously lived there," he later recalled. The juxtaposition of a stone-age culture living a few miles from a modern RAF base amazed him. It was only later that he learned that many of those people were Yemenite Jews who had fled from villages all over Yemen to seek a way into Aden and the hope of escape to Israel.

Before Currie and his crew took off for Lydda, the base operations officer at Khormaksar passed on a polite but firm warning about the dangers of landing anywhere between Aden and Lydda Airport. No peace agreement had been officially signed between Israel and the countries of the Arab League. Shots were still fired at unexpected intervals and, oh yes, five British airplanes had been shot down by Israelis in late January. Feelings were a bit touchy all around.

Ralph Cheatham, the mechanic aboard the flight, found a couple of oil leaks. By the time repairs were made, passengers re-loaded, and the plane again ready for take off, it was nearly noon, and the temperature was in the 80s. The DC-4 rolled up her sleeves and heaved herself into the air. Long sweated over his outdated charts, trying to keep them on the safest course.

Halfway up the Gulf of Aqaba, the Radio Operator, Elliot Judd, tried to raise the radio station at Lydda and was met with silence. Currie tried using the VHF radio when they reached Beersheba after the sun had vanished over the horizon. Now somewhat nervous, they awaited a response but again received only silence. The night was moonless and pitch-black, and they were still more than half an hour out from Lydda. Hoping that someone was at least listening and could identify them, they kept on course.

When they saw the lights of Tel Aviv, they knew they were no more than 10 minutes away from the airport, but no airport lights were visible. The land below was like a featureless black ocean. Currie and Judd both tried to raise the tower at Lydda on both radios, asking them to please turn on the lights. No response. Knowing the airfield was down there somewhere, Currie unknowingly followed in the footsteps of Warren Metzger and Bob Maguire, turned on his landing lights and circled the area looking for a landmark. He spotted a runway, headed for it and eased the plane down. The whole crew gave an inward sigh of relief when they touched ground.

They were taxiing up the dark runway when they spotted the lights of a ground vehicle coming toward them. It pulled in front of them and signaled the plane to follow, so they fell in behind what they thought was a follow-me vehicle to a ramp at the terminal, where they parked. They finally got a good look at what they'd been following, which turned out to be an armored car with its mounted gun pointed ominously at the cockpit.

Once the initial awkward "who-the-hell-are-you" business was cleared up, the Israeli Army personnel were prompt, courteous and friendly, and quickly brought up equipment for off-loading passengers and luggage. They provided electrical power to the plane, so the crew could see what the hell they were doing. The Americans learned that thousands of Jews were pouring into Israel from all corners of the globe. The officer in charge apologized for the necessary precautions taken by Israel, which had so stretched the crews' nerves, and thanked them for making the arduous flight. "It is a good thing you have done!" he told them.[3]

An Israeli radioman came to the plane and told them that they'd received all the DC-4's calls, but ground forces were on high alert due to the danger of imminent attack and so could not risk a response. Should the Alaska crew return to Lydda in the future, Israeli radio operators would respond with a single letter of the alphabet in Morse Code. If the letter were anything but "X," all was well and they were safe to land. If the letter was an "X," the airfield was under attack, and the plane would need to land somewhere else.[3]

The DC-4 was low on fuel, but there was none to be had, so Currie decided to take off immediately and head for Nicosia. That flight went without a hitch, and from there, they hop-scotched their way north to Amsterdam.

Ten days later to their surprise, they were back in Shanghai to pick up another load of Jewish refugees. Even more to their surprise, this time another Alaska Airlines crew under Captain John Thompson was there waiting for them.

Thompson warned Currie about the hazards awaiting him from the heavy load in Shanghai and got right to the point. "When you're in trouble with this load, do what I do; dump all your flotation gear off the aircraft. But not the life raft for the flight crew."[4]

"I can't do that," Currie protested. "That wouldn't look very good."

"Well, make your choice. If you don't, I don't think you're going to fly far."

Currie did as Thompson advised and was later intensely grateful, as the overloaded plane wallowed over the Mediterranean. As soon as they were unloaded at Lydda, Currie and his crew were ordered to fly to Asmara. They had no idea why, but they found out as they came in for a landing.

Long stared in astonishment as he saw an Alaska Airlines C-46 with a broken back beside the runway. "We never saw, or knew, there was another Alaska Airlines plane within 5,000 miles of us," he said later.[3] "On our first arrival in Asmara, when our landing lights illuminated a bent and broken Alaska Airlines airplane parked on the ramp in Asmara, we were completely dumbfounded. Until then we had believed we were the only Alaska Airlines plane in the Middle East."

The first question they asked the fuel truck crew who came to meet them was what the hell an Alaska Airlines C-46 was doing in Asmara, and they learned of the wreck a few weeks previous. The ground crew knew nothing about other Alaska Airlines personnel, and as soon as they were refueled, Currie and his crew left none the wiser.[4]

Meanwhile, John Thompson contacted Wooten and told him what he'd done; Wooten was less than pleased. Thompson let Wooten bellow but stuck to his guns.

"We've got to have lighter loads," he insisted when Wooten paused for breath.[4]

"Well the contract says we can't do that."

"Well, the only alternative is to get more fuel stops."

Wooten bristled. "Well, maybe you don't want to fly it like that."

"Not particularly, Jim."

"Maybe I'll have Maguire take this next trip."

Thompson refused to be buffaloed. "Jim, I wish you would. But when he goes down, I'll be on your front doorstep."[4]

Wooten backed down and found more fuel stops, so the DC-4s could keep their tanks half-full or less.

Three DC-4s were now making runs between Aden and Tel Aviv, as well as Shanghai and Tel Aviv, along with the old C-54 plus several other aircraft on lease. The lone C-46 was clearly becoming more trouble than it was worth. In mid-February, Maguire finally relegated the tired old ship to fuel runs and assigned Warren to fly as co-pilot in the DC-4s. Warren hoped to get checked out as Captain but knew his chances were small under the circumstances. Going back to co-pilot status meant a reduction in pay, but it wasn't like he was getting paid anyway, so he wasn't going to complain. At least he was still getting to fly.

Even with multiple flights a day, Hashed's population wasn't dropping fast enough to suit the Aden authorities, the British, the Israelis, or the JDC.[5] Harry Vitales complained to Maguire and Wooten, insisting they find a better solution.

Wooten pointed out that discrepancies in payments the airline received from the JDC were one of the biggest problems, since he could hardly hire more pilots or planes if he couldn't pay them.[6] He didn't mention that the U.S. State Department had been adding its voice to his list of detractors with rumbled warnings of his stepping outside the bounds of what was permissible in an American airline. Wooten cited back to them the international codes for "emergency exceptions," but he did order Maguire to schedule more flights.

Maguire held his ground; planes and pilots alike needed the down time, and they were already well past the legal limits for pilot flight hours and airplane maintenance time tables. But like Wooten, he was determined to make the airlift a success. He called a small British air service which had made occasional flights for them; it had an Avro Tudor and a refitted Halifax bomber. The company needed the money and accepted, despite earlier problems with their craft.

The Tudor was a beautiful four-engine plane capable of carrying more passengers than the DC-4, but it had a fatal weakness: the Rolls Royce engines. Fine-tuned and flawless, they were such high-precision machines that the sand in the air over the desert burnt at least one out on nearly every flight. Which meant that after every flight, the company had to send for another engine from England.

On one flight to Tel Aviv with a full load of refugees, three of the four engines on the Tudor coughed to a halt over the Red Sea. The pilot, knowing the plane would float about like a brick, made for the closest land—the Egyptian coast. Thinking quickly, he radioed Maguire for help.[7]

Maguire called the Naval Attaché in Cairo, identifying the downed plane only as a British cargo plane sub-contracted to Alaska Airlines. The Naval Attaché warned him that the Arabs would, of course, claim the plane once they found it. "You will lose your cargo and it would take me at least 30 days to get your crew released," he added.

Knowing what "losing the cargo" would really mean in this case, Maguire scrambled a crew and absconded with a DC-4. Before appropriate orders even filtered their way through the ranks of the Egyptian military, the Alaska crew had rescued crew and "cargo" and left Egypt behind.[7]

The British company knew they were unlikely to ever recover their plane; they took another hit shortly afterward when the Halifax bomber choked and died coming in for an emergency landing at Port Sudan and landed on its belly. They couldn't afford those kinds of losses and withdrew from the airlift.

Hearing of the rescue incident, Vitalis called Maguire in a rage. "Why didn't you call me?"

The crews had learned the hard way that the JDC representative never responded unless some publicity was involved that reflected well on him. "Vitalis had a rule," said one Alaska employee years later with a snort of derision. "Nobody called him."[7]

Maguire answered with characteristic bluntness that there was nothing Vitalis could have done, since there'd been no reporters around.[8]

Wooten was still insisting on more and more flights, and he was the boss. Maguire grudgingly scheduled half the additional flights Wooten wanted. The two men quarreled openly now; the tension filtered through the ranks, keeping the Alaskans ducking and looking over their shoulders.

With housing disappearing on a daily basis, many of the crews frequently lived, ate, and slept in the cockpits of their planes. Unshaven and red-eyed, sometimes unable to bathe for days at a time, they made a less-than heroic appearance. It didn't matter. The planes needed to fly, the people needed to get home, and the clock was still ticking.

Warren lived for the days he got to spend in Asmara with Marian. He knew she was growing restless, eager to fly again, eager to help out. She was also eager to work off the spaghetti; she'd put on weight and her uniform was in danger of no longer fitting. She volunteered for flights to Shanghai and was promised work. But nothing else seemed to matter on his days off, when they could wander the streets of Asmara and dream of a life together.

They both wanted to make their home in Anchorage rather than Everett, and Marian wanted to keep flying as long as possible; she hadn't finished seeing the world yet. They both also both wanted children and knew that would mean the end of her flying career.

It all made the world of Hashed, of Tel Aviv, of the long hours over the Red Sea or fighting the sand-saturated air somehow distant, almost unreal, and certainly more bearable.

At the beginning of March, Maguire met Warren as he climbed down from the DC-4 after another exhausting run and told him he was sending both Metzgers home. Maguire had more than enough pilots for the one remaining C-46, and the incoming DC-4s were fully crewed. There was a flight leaving for Rome the next day. Warren was to take the co-pilot's seat; Marian would take over for one of the stewardesses. Checks would be waiting for them in Anchorage.

"Your part's finished. You've done a great job," he told Warren. "Now go home."

Warren knew questions would be futile. He nodded, shook Maguire's hand, and headed for the hotel.

The next day, he and Marian climbed aboard a spotless DC-4 along with what seemed like most of the rest of the Alaska Airlines crew and a few passengers. Marian, smartly turned out in her overly-snug stewardess uniform, got everyone seated and locked down the galley. She threw a smile at Warren on her way to shut the door as he moved forward into the cockpit, and she promised to bring him coffee after takeoff. She paused, one hand on the door's handle, and took a long, last look at Asmara.

For all the headaches, she'd been happy here, but she was quite ready to leave and begin the next adventure. She pulled the door shut, latched it, and went to check that all was in readiness with her passengers before belting herself in for take-off.[10]

Settling into the co-pilot's seat, Warren was busy checking instruments until take-off. As the plane lifted off the runway, he took a glance out the windows at Asmara spread out like a colorful carpet below him. He hoped whoever was left would be able to get the job done, however long it would continue, and wondered what would become of the remaining Yemenites back in Aden, who had been forbidden to leave.[8,9] He turned his thoughts toward the skies ahead.

Neither he nor Marian heard anything more about Operation Magic Carpet. It remained an adventure interwoven with mysteries over which they would occasionally wonder for the rest of their lives.

.   .   .

Flying blank, silver-sided DC-4s, John Thompson, Larry Currie, and a few others continued to bring refugees in from Shanghai and Aden to Tel Aviv through March and April.

In mid-March, Captain Currie and his intrepid crew landed at RAF Khormaksar and found an officer, Group Captain Keens, waiting for them at the ramp.[2] Keens all but begged Currie to take up a series of emergency flights. Refugees who had flooded into the area, even as Hashed was demolished, were refused entry into Aden and had nowhere to go. The crew had only a vague idea that an ongoing rescue operation existed, had never heard of Hashed, and knew nothing about the politics involved. All Currie knew was that his faithful, overworked DC-4 could carry up to 60 of the stranded, sick, emaciated refugees away from near-certain death awaiting them if they remained exposed and helpless in the desert around Aden. He had to get them to Israel.

He and the other men aboard had already been everywhere in the world over the previous two months and had been hoping for a wire from Alaska that would tell them they could finally come home. But turning away from so many in need was not an option. The crew resigned themselves to living in the DC-4 for a while longer. They did not know it, but they would one day be honored at the airline with the moniker "The Ironmen Crew" for the sheer number of virtually non-stop emergency rescue missions they flew from Aden to Tel Aviv during the rest of March and early April.[2]

Maguire and Mulleneaux quietly resigned from Alaska Airlines, but few of the Alaska pilots who flew with them were aware of it, since they still worked with them and saw them on a regular basis.

The crowd of refugees in Shanghai dwindled as the planes bore them load by load to Tel Aviv. There were only fifty or so left when, on the morning of May 18th, 1949, John Thompson came in for a landing at Hungchow (Hangzhou) field, west and south of town.[4,11]

He saw flashes on the ground at the same time a chaotic racket blasted from his radio; he made out explosions and shouting. He heard a frantic Chinese voice and grabbed the mike again, identifying himself and his plane. "What the hell is going on down there?"

Finally, an English voice came through. "Alaska Airlines DC-4, do not land at Hungchow, repeat, DO NOT LAND. The Communists have it now."

Thompson pulled back and aimed the plane for the clouds above, hopefully out of range of any missiles. He wasn't surprised; he knew the war had been going badly for the Nationalist Chinese. Nevertheless, he felt a chill. "Where are my passengers?"

After a moment, the voice returned. "There's another airfield in the center of Shanghai—Lunghwa. It is still open. Your passengers will be waiting there."

Thompson acknowledged and circled back toward the center of Shanghai, landing safely a short while later. To his deep annoyance, his passengers did not appear. He was informed that they were not ready to board. His requests for an explanation went unanswered; the Chinese authorities had other matters demanding their attention.

Marian Metzger, one of the two stews on the flight,[10] came forward to find out why they'd suddenly been re-routed and what was going on. She lingered in the cockpit, waiting with the crew. Like them, she listened to the sound of small arms fire, no longer coming in over the radio; she could hear it outside the plane. She wasn't especially nervous, but she found the pop and chatter of gunfire so close at hand disturbing. Just how close was it? A stray bullet could strand the big plane here. What would happen to them then?

Her cherished secret fantasy of dashing up to the cockpit to take over as pilot or co-pilot and fly them all to safety withered in the face of reality. The idea of Captain Thompson or any of the crew being injured or killed was unthinkable. Besides, the truth was, she had too few hours in the air; there was no way she could fly this bird, even if she had to.

She aimed a silent prayer skyward, hoping that her increasingly tardy passengers would come out of the terminal soon.

She drifted back into the cabin, but she and her fellow stew had already done everything needed until their passengers arrived. The other girl was even less sanguine about the situation; her nervous twitches every time the sound of an explosion reached them began to wear on Marian's calm. Lacking anything else to keep her mind occupied, she headed back up to the cockpit, though she knew Thompson would inform them if the situation changed.

She got there just as Thompson picked up the radio. "Is everyone aware this field is going to be coming under attack shortly?" he asked the Chinese operators.

Someone finally responded with less-than-reassuring information that the Communists would not claim the field until after dark. Thompson gritted his teeth and sat back.

"Guess we can all relax," he drawled. "They think we're fine for a while yet."

Whether he believed it or not, Marian didn't know, but he didn't seem as nervous as she thought he surely would be if danger were imminent. On the other hand, she knew from long experience that pilots were a pretty steely-nerved bunch.

Since Thompson didn't order her to return to the cabin, she stayed at the back of the cockpit, listening in growing uneasiness and irritation to gunfire all around the airfield. Where the hell were their passengers? Were they hiding in the terminal or something? What on God's Green Earth were they doing in there?

Morning passed, afternoon waned, and still no passengers appeared. Finally, an especially loud report echoed through the cockpit. "That sonofabitch is close," the co-pilot muttered.

"That does it." Thompson grabbed the radio. "Alaska Airlines DC-4 to operator. We're leaving in fifteen minutes whether we're loaded or not. Pass it on."

Moments later, the last Jewish refugees in Shanghai scurried out of the airport and across the tarmac to the waiting plane, dragging their bags behind them. Marian and her cohort got everyone seated as quickly as possible and then dashed forward again. As soon as she informed Thompson that everyone was aboard and accounted for, and the door closed, Thompson taxied the mighty DC-4 down the runway and took off.

Marian wedged herself next to a window and watched as the plane lifted from the ground. The engines' roar drowned the rattle of gunfire but didn't disguise smoke rolling over the end of the runway, or the deadly firefly flashes in the gathering dusk beneath her as the DC-4 soared overhead.

After the Communists took over, they permitted one, final plane to leave: a Pan American Constellation loaded with airline personnel, American citizens, and a few Chinese officials. They filled every seat; those who couldn't get seats sat in the aisles. The overloaded Connie took off, wallowing over the ocean on full power and headed south to Hong Kong and safety.[11]

1. Satterfield; interview with Warren Metzger, 1979.
2. Elgen Long, author of *Amelia Earhart: The Mystery Solved (1999)*, is a world-famous aviator with a legendary career. His memoir, *On Eagles' Wings*, contains his own account of his adventures during Operation Magic Carpet.
3. Author; Interview with Elgen Long, 2013.
4. Satterfield; interview with John Thompson, 1979.
5. Parfitt, *The Road to Redemption*, p186. Parfitt claims only 1,000 Yemenites had been flown out by the beginning of January. But by mid-March, the camp's population had dropped by nearly half. However, authorities feared that a fresh wave was imminent, so were desperate to get the camp emptied and closed before they arrived. Plans for a new, better camp were underway. In the meantime, many new arrivals were barred from entry and left with

nowhere to go; most camped wherever they could in the open desert around Aden.

6. Parfitt, *The Road to Redemption*, p186, and Wooten's own recollections.

7. Satterfield; interview with Bob Platt and Van Ostrander, 1979. Harry Vitalis was undeniably a great man whose passionate dedication to his personal mission of getting Jewish refugees from all over the world safely to Israel is evident. He made herculean efforts, moved mountains, and pulled rabbits out of hats to get it done. However, any request made of him by Alaska Airlines crew tended to be completely ignored. Most felt that he let them down every time they dealt with him. Their overall impression of him was that, unless there were reporters and cameras present, he was "useless as tits on a boar," to use Warren Metzger's colorful analogy.

8. Author; interview with Warren Metzger, 2008. Warren returned in late March or early April to fly a few additional fuel runs.

9. On March 2, 1949, the Imam granted permission for the 860 men of military age and the 120 so-called "ineligibles" to leave. Parfitt, *The Road to Redemption*, p186.

10. Author; interview with Marian Liscomb Metzger, 2008. Marian Metzger made at least one other flight to Shanghai after returning to Alaska, but the dates are uncertain. If she was indeed aboard this last flight, as she believed, she was substituting for another stewardess. Nor did she believe this flight was part of the same series of rescue operations that included Operation Magic Carpet. In this, she was correct. Only flights that carried the Yemenites from Aden to Tel Aviv were part of Operation Magic Carpet. The flights from Shanghai and other places were carried out under separate contracts and were only later grouped under that heading.

11. Satterfield, *The Alaska Airlines Story*.

INTERLUDE: CLIPPED WINGS

Operation Magic Carpet came to a standstill in the spring of 1949. Governor Champion ordered the demolishment of Hashed, saying that leaving it open would only attract more refugees, which he was 'determined to keep out of Aden at all costs'.1

Rumor at the time and assumptions made after the fact have tainted Champion with the label of "anti-Semite." This is inaccurate and grossly unfair. He dreaded another typhus outbreak or some equally lethal disease caused by an influx of hundreds and thousands of people from the farthest reaches of the Yemen, not to mention the crippling burden a mass of starving people would place on the Protectorate.

He also had good reason to fear riots; the murder of two Arab girls[2] had led to mass arrests and beatings of Jews, raids on several towns by various Arab tribes seeking booty from the undefended Jewish settlements, increasing unrest among the Yemeni Arabs, and had inspired a full-fledged pogrom.[3]

Champion was a learned man with a great deal of experience in dealing with both the governments of

Yemen and of Palestine.[4] While he was far too intelli-
gent to believe that peace and order in Aden could be
achieved and maintained if the Yemenite Jews stayed
put, he was well aware that the problem would become a disaster for all concerned if the floodgates
were opened and unrestricted emigration was granted
to the Yemenite Jews all at once.

There is little doubt that the Imam Ahmad was aware
of the same difficulties and complications. He had,
sometime earlier, made token efforts to halt the exodus
of the Jews from their towns and villages to Aden. While
this created a host of other difficulties, it gave the airlift
a chance to catch up; by the end of January, only a little
over 5,000 refugees remained in Hashed.

The Imam Ahmad had a number of reasons for his
sudden interest in arresting the flow of immigrants;
part of it was due to a reason neither the JDC nor the
British had anticipated. The Jews in Yemen had been
used to clean the streets and collect refuse for years,
but that was a small matter. Most of the coffee and tobacco farms were owned and operated by Jews, but
that, too, could be overcome. A far greater loss was
that of their roles as builders, craftsmen, and artisans.
Many of the Yemenite tribes were incomparable silver
and metal smiths with skills dating back centuries;
Jewish and Arab homes alike were liberally furnished
and decorated with the fruits of their labors, and men
and women of wealth draped themselves in the artwork coming from Jewish smiths. The Arabs had become abruptly and painfully aware that they were
losing the world's greatest artists and craftsmen. The
Imam issued the provisional ban partly in order to
force the Yemenite Jews to teach their skills to Yemeni
Arabs before they could be allowed to leave.[5,6]

None of these reasons stopped the Yemenites from
trying to escape. Hundreds, having already made the
exhausting and terrible trek across Yemen, were arriving destitute, worn, starving, and ill at the borders of

the Protectorate, trying to reach Aden and what they imagined was safety.

In February of 1949, the Jewish Agency in Israel, which was in charge of immigration quotas, established that 1949's quota would be 250,000; all Israel could absorb without completely destroying its economy. This was probably already far too many, but memories of the Holocaust were still fresh and bloody. Many in the Israeli government believed the only way to halt another was to bring every single Jew from everywhere in the world into Israel. The head of the immigration department, Y. Raphael Werfel, in his single-minded dedication to the cause, ignored the quotas and did everything in his power to bring the scattered children of the Diaspora home at last.[7]

The JDC, fully aware that Israel was in no condition to absorb thousands more refugees but desperate to save the now-homeless wanderers from being abandoned, had been tirelessly working with the Jewish Agency in Israel to raise both funds and awareness around the world. Harry Vitalis relentlessly petitioned the British to keep Hashed open. Failing that, he begged them to allow construction of another, better appointed camp for the same purpose.

Despite a reputation for ruthlessness and cruelty earned during his father's reign and his own struggles to claim his rightful place after the assassination, the Imam Ahmad was, in his own way, a fair-minded man. He frequently accepted and even heeded petitions from Jewish community leaders to help counter persecution and injustices, and intervened directly to halt the worst of the evils. His good intentions and good works were sometimes derailed by his younger brother, Prince Sayf al-Islam al-Hassan, a religious zealot and notorious xenophobe. Prince Hassan made no pretense of remaining neutral in what he saw as a great religious war taking place a short distance from his home. He not only wielded power in his own right, he held a great deal of influence over his brother, and threw repeated complications in the path of a smooth and well-orchestrated exodus.

Eventually, the Imam reached the only decision he could and bowed to the inevitable. In April of 1949,[8] he lifted his ban and proclaimed that any Jew who wished to emigrate would be allowed to do so. He even ordered his Arab subjects to purchase Jewish homes and holdings at a fair price. The news, spread through hand-delivered letters to individual communities throughout the Yemen, didn't reach British, Israeli, or the JDC authorities until weeks later.

By that time, the mass of refugees on the move had become a juggernaut.

The British, bowing to necessity and moved by genuine humanitarian concerns, began construction of a new camp, also called Hashed but which came to be known as *Geulah Beth:* Redemption.

1. Quoted by Harry Vitalis in Parfitt, *The Road to Redemption*, p187.
2. The murder was never solved, but an Arab woman supposedly later confessed to the crime. It was never clear if she had done so of her own volition. The Jewish community was initially blamed for the murders, because propaganda brought into Yemen from other Arab lands revived the old tales of Jewish blood rituals and human sacrifice.
3. The Yemeni Arabs had co-existed more-or-less peacefully with their Jewish neighbors prior to the war in Palestine, later Israel. They were, for the most part, benevolent masters. They even took a perverse pride in "their" Jews, boasting of their artistry and piety. All of this changed with the outside influence of Palestinians and other Arabs seeking refuge in Yemen, spreading their own less tolerant views and a hatred freshened by recent

bloodshed. The availability of affordable radios, new to the Yemen, also spread inflammatory news broadcasts coming out of Palestine.

4. Parfitt, *The Road to Redemption*, p178.
5. Parfitt, *The Road to Redemption*, p205.
6. Barer, *The Magic Carpet*, 179.
7. Parfitt, *The Road to Redemption*, p179.
8. Imam Ahmad gave his verbal consent to lifting the ban somewhere near the end of April, 1949. The news was communicated directly to Jewish community leaders and passed on from there, which is why no one knew about it at first. Confirmation didn't reach Vitalis until May 25th.

CHAPTER FIFTEEN: NEAR EAST AIR TRANSPORT

In the spring of 1949, while Hashed was being de-molished, Jim Wooten was back in the states fight-ing legal battles he was finally starting to take seri-ously. He still believed in an eleventh hour reprieve, but even his self-confidence was being shaken.

The CAB, forced by circumstances they could no longer overlook and the relentless pressure from Pan Am and other airlines, ordered Alaska Airlines to im-mediately cease all overseas flights. They followed up by threatening to shut the airline down due to an over-whelming number of safety infractions.[1]

Mechanical wizardry could do only so much; CAB inspectors had discovered engines on at least three planes being used far in excess of the established overhaul time limits. They cited the airline for failing to provide an adequate number of check pilots, for al-lowing pilots to fly wildly over their legally allotted hours, for not allowing pilots adequate rest periods, and for using crew who were technically not qualified for the airplanes they flew. The CAB also restricted the airline to scheduled flights during daylight hours, claiming the pilots were unqualified for instrument flying at night.

Some of the charges were true.

Certainly between Marshall's parsimony and Wooten's ambition, the planes' engines were never overhauled as legally required. But the mechanics had, in fact, been keeping the planes air-worthy, doing whatever it took, up to and including dumpster-diving for discarded parts through other airlines' trash and machining their own parts when Marshall wouldn't give the airline money to obtain them any other way. They steadfastly refused to send planes out they considered unsafe.

Furthermore, nearly every pilot could and had flown every plane in the airline's diverse fleet under some of the most challenging flying conditions in the world. The shortage of check pilots or legal certifications was due solely to Marshall's refusal to pay for anything he didn't consider necessary, and he saw no need to allow his pilots to qualify for pay increases due to the number and types of aircraft on which they were legally certified.

As for the charge of the pilots being unqualified for instrument flying at night, it took only one night flight from Anchorage to Fairbanks with John Thompson at the controls to get that charge dropped. Thompson casually wound the plane through canyons and mountain passes so tight the wings nearly brushed the sides, all while keeping fastidiously within established flight procedures, while a CAB inspector in the cockpit gibbered and desperately tried not to dampen his dainty drawers with terror. After landing, the rubber-legged inspector agreed to order the restriction rescinded. Then he found himself another way back to Anchorage.[2]

The airline's protestations over some of the other charges didn't cut ice with the CAB, however. On paper, Alaska Airlines was guilty as hell. The CAB leveled a $34,000 fine against the airline and an additional

$1,000 against Wooten himself. Wooten filed more counter-suits but, while the issue was still being contested, dared not openly defy the Cease and Desist order.

This didn't stop him from signing—on behalf of Alaska Airlines—another contract with the JDC[3] to pick up the airlift as soon as the Imam's ban was lifted. The British balked at restoring Alaska's landing rights in Aden due to a conflict of interest with BOAC[4], who wanted the contract for themselves. In late June, Alaska preempted the entire issue by sending in a DC-4 to Aden and scooping up 108 Yemenites, and 98 more on a return flight. Hashed was officially empty.

Within days, hundreds more had arrived, and the new camp was barely started; Ramadan had slowed the pace of work by the Arab contractor.[5] Nevertheless, it was declared open on July 4, 1949, when it was little more than a bare patch of open ground, and the first inhabitants were installed, once again, in tents. New Hashed/Geulah Beth had, as its core facilities, another WWII British army camp which was mere yards from the old Hashed camp.

The Jewish Agency in Israel never envisioned a mass migration; they foresaw instead a gradual influx over a period of several years and made exacting plans to support just that. A report filed in June of 1949 and circulated among the offices of the JDC and Israeli government, using information based on the best estimates of British intelligence as well as Jewish authorities, stated that the JDC would be handling the entire operation of the exodus from Yemen. It was expected that the entire Jewish population would wish to emigrate. Estimates of numbers were given as somewhere between 25,000 and 50,000. The authors assumed that not more than 700 Jews per month would be coming into the new camp, with a maximum of 10,000 in the year. The new camp was designed for a maximum capacity of 1,000 inhabitants, with a single resident nurse and a visiting doctor on hand to minister to those requiring medical care.[5]

Yosef Zadok, a Yemenite Jew from Israel, was assigned as the new director and immediately started issuing complaints about the inadequacies of the unfinished camp.[5] Though he was aware of the structure and plans the Jewish Agency had laid out, Zadok was dedicated to the idea of an immediate mass migration, and did everything he could to bring one about. He wrote letters and sent messages and messengers to the farthest reaches of Yemen, exhorting the Yemenites to leave everything and go—go now.

Throughout May and June, word of the Imam's lifted ban spread. Zadok's letters, fluttering across the Yemen throughout July, were opened, read, and passed from hand to hand. The floodgates opened.

By the end of July, hundreds of refugees were once again arriving daily at the gates of the new camp.

The poor old C-54 Skymaster had at last given up the ghost and been sent limping home, and the unmarked DC-4 waited in Rome for a new engine. With the CAB breathing down their necks, Alaska Airlines wasn't about to send more DC-4s. The airline and its affiliates held their breath, waiting to see how the chips would fall. Caught between a rock and a hard place, Alaska Airlines was, for the time being, unable to fulfill its contract, which left Maguire in a kind of limbo.

True to form, Wooten apparently kept Maguire out of the loop on a lot of the legal shenanigans; all Maguire knew for certain was that Wooten was in trouble and had neither the energy nor the attention to give to Operation Magic Carpet and Near East Air Transport.

Maguire spent his days trying to line up more planes and put a team back together. Not all the Alaska Airlines employees had returned to the States. Mechanic Hank McCoy stayed and married his Israeli sweetheart; he had a job waiting for him at El Al, Israel's first airline, which had started up in September of 1948, but he wanted to stay with Alaska Airlines—or, rather, NEAT, as a sub-contractor—until the operation was finished.

Ralph Cheatham, Alaska's VP of Maintenance who had come over in March as part of Larry Currie's crew, and remained to try and straighten out the various maintenance problems, agreed to stay and help NEAT get off the ground, literally and figuratively. He hired additional mechanics and even subcontracted another group from a British outfit, but they arrived empty-handed, having left their tools behind in England.[6] Cheatham's time wasn't entirely wasted though; he met, fell in love with and married a dark and dashing Italian countess.[7]

Captain Massey, the devil-may-care C-46 pilot, was still around—somewhere—and Stanley Epstein and several others hired specifically for the airlift remained at hand, poised to fly and waiting for orders.

Maguire decided to take the leap and re-start the airlift as Near East Air Transport, but he needed help on the business end. Within Alaska Airlines, only he and Wooten knew of the existence of NEAT and wanted to keep it that way as long as possible. Technically, the airlift still belonged to Alaska Airlines. NEAT was just another sub-contractor until the roles could be officially reversed. But Maguire needed someone to help with the financial management end, someone who could actually keep his eye on the books and not on the thousand other details Maguire had to juggle. Someone who could also keep a secret.

Maguire knew just the man for the job: Alaska Airlines' Purchasing Director, Van Ostrander. Wooten agreed, approached Ostrander, explained the situation, and asked him to go help out.

Ostrander wore a lot of hats at Alaska. Something of a Jack-of-all-trades, he'd been a ceramics engineer and had worked with Wooten frequently when Wooten had owned a trucking company. When Wooten switched gears to start up the cargo division at American Airlines, he talked Ostrander into coming to work for him. When Wooten left, Ostrander followed him to Alaska Airlines. He soon found his job title meant little; his role in reality encompassed almost every aspect of airline and financial management at one time or another, juggling half-a-dozen crises of differing natures at any given time.

Like many scrupulously honest men, Ostrander was fascinated by rogues and scallywags, and found it impossible to say "no" to Wooten, who made life such an endless adventure. Years later, he admitted, "For years, I lived in fear he'd show up one day and say, 'Come with me, I've got this great idea,' and I would go." [8]

Wooten offered Ostrander the temporary position of treasurer for Near East Air Transport, which meant making sure both airlines got their proper cut for as long as Alaska still officially held the contract. And that Marshall didn't hear any of it; the crafty Chairman was already prowling around looking for evidence to bring a lawsuit against Wooten and trying to find a way to re-direct all the operation's profits to his own pockets.

Wooten told Ostrander that the job would be of fairly short duration, and offered him ten percent of the gross profits on top of his regular salary to do it; the same deal he'd offered Maguire. "There's only maybe 1,000 refugees left; it won't take more than a few weeks," Wooten said. "It'll be like a vacation. Bring your bathing suit."

As an added bonus, he agreed to also hire Ostrander's wife, Thea. Van and Thea often worked as a team, but Wooten was a little wary of her; she had a head for numbers that equaled—or perhaps exceeded—her husband's, but she brooked no funny business. She also knew her husband's weakness for Wooten's proposed schemes and adventures, and she didn't trust Wooten as far as she could throw him. She signed on, probably in order to watch her husband's back. Ostrander was also supposed to get $500 a month per diem; her first act as a subcontractor was to buffalo

Wooten into tacking on an additional $400 for her own share.[8]

As a final benefit, Wooten promised them a weekend layover in New York en route, so they could visit Ostrander's parents.

Unbeknownst to the Ostranders, Wooten was finally ready to make the change. He quietly informed Maguire that NEAT was a go. On August 7, 1949, Maguire informed Harry Vitalis that Alaska Airlines had transferred the airlift contract to Near East Air Transport. Alaska Airlines was officially out of the overseas charter business.[9,10]

The Ostranders scrambled to get their house rented and the details of their lives arranged. Wooten, wanting to leave as little "paper trail" as possible, planned to rely on cash transactions and made Ostrander responsible for this. And so it was that, in late August of 1949, Van and Thea Ostrander set out for Israel with Wooten and a handful of others in a DC-4, carrying a suitcase full of greenbacks and a bathing suit.[8,11]

The DC-4, recently purchased by the JDC, had been newly repainted with "NEAR EAST AIR TRANSPORT" stretching down its sleek, silver sides. But at the helm was a pilot who had missed out on the earlier part of the mission and was looking forward to satisfying his curiosity.

In December of 1948, Captain Sam Silver had been asked to go over to fly C-46s. But he knew he'd make a lot more money if he stayed behind and flew DC-4s on the routes up and down the Alaska panhandle and into the interior.[7]

Still, he heard fascinating rumors from time to time of his fellow employees flying for the Jewish airlift—at that point, he was unaware of the official title—and paid especial interest in what was going on "over there." A Jew himself, though hardly devout, he had a personal interest in Israel's struggles and his airline's part in them. Finally, his curiosity got the better of him.

With Alaska Airlines now restricted to flights within the Alaska Territory, the airline had little use for most of its DC-4s. The two re-fitted DC-4s formerly used in the operation were still over there on lease, and Sam expected NEAT or somebody to buy them sooner or later. He wasn't entirely surprised when he learned that the JDC had purchased another DC-4 that had been side-lined in Everett. He asked Wooten if he could ferry the ship to its new owners; it would give him a chance to see for himself what was going on over there.

He was supposed to fly Van and Thea Ostrander, along with several others, over to work with the new air service after a weekend in New York. At the last minute, he received new orders and another, less pleasant task. He was to stop at St. Louis, Missouri, to drop off the body of an Alaska Airlines mechanic who had been killed in a flying accident while hunting in the Alaska Range.

That duty cast a bit of a pall on the journey and ate up a full day. Finally, he and his passengers took off, heading for Teterboro. As if depressed by its task, the plane lost an engine en route, and Sam had to feather it all the way to Teterboro. A one-man repair service, Willis Fixed Base Operator, used up the rest of the weekend changing the engine.[12]

Disgruntled, the Ostranders settled for a phone call to Van's disappointed parents, while Silver filed for Tel Aviv and immediately ran into trouble with customs. "Customs would not let us leave for Tel Aviv; they said we were flying into a war zone," Sam recalled. "We tried to convince them that this was a commercial airplane and nothing to do with the war, but they refused to believe it. So there were some telephone calls between Teterboro and New York and Washington."[7]

The customs official kept shaking his head. "Do you have any idea what you're getting into?" he asked Sam.

It seemed a stupid question at the time. "Yes," he replied. "I'm taking this airplane to Tel Aviv."

The customs inspector fixed him with a steely glare. "If it's used in a war zone, you are going to be responsible."

At the time, Silver was glad for the chance to finally settle his passengers and lift off. Later and to his chagrin, he admitted that the man was right.

As usual, once in the air, he enjoyed the flight, especially the company. One of his passengers, a newly-hired pilot and mechanic named Larry Raab,[13] had flown in Israel before and during the war. During the long hours of the night, as the Atlantic Ocean passed below them, Raab regaled Sam with some of his experiences. One tale left a deep impression.

On his last flight, Raab had been flying from Czechoslovakia to Israel in a DC-4. Having gotten a late start, he arrived over Israel after dark. Two of his engines were losing oil, and the control tower at the Tel Aviv airport, expecting Egyptian bombers at any moment, refused to turn on the landing lights. He circled until he finally had to land, and put the plane down in the surf off the beach of Tel Aviv. Silver, who had heard tales from some of the Alaska pilots about the perils of flying into Tel Aviv after dark, privately thought Raab had gotten off lightly.

The next morning, Silver brought the DC-4 safely down at Lydda. Maguire was waiting for them and made a surprising offer. "Want to stay and fly this ship between Tel Aviv and Aden? We need another DC-4 pilot."

Silver hadn't planned on doing anything other than heading straight back to Alaska to resume his career. The thought of being involved in the whole endeavor seemed like a welcome opportunity, almost a gift. Why not? "Well, if Seattle agrees, and you pay my expenses, sure I'll stay. I'd be glad to."[7]

Maguire nodded. "Is it okay if you use some of the American fighter pilots from the Israeli Air Force as co-pilots? Maybe check some of them out, if you think they can do it."[7]

It didn't sound like a terribly onerous task, so he agreed. He, Maguire, and Ostrander worked out a deal: Sam would get $100 a trip on top of his regular salary, provided Wooten approved the deal.

Permission was, of course, granted. "Ostrander wired New York," Sam recalled. "They didn't care, said, 'just do as you want over there.' So they sent the rest of my crew back to the states, and I started flying from Aden to Tel Aviv and back."[7]

First, the plane had to be refitted. It took two days to pull out all the seats and replace them with plywood benches and rope safety belts. Silver watched the process in bewilderment. The benches filled the interior like a deck of cards on its side. How on earth could people fit in them? The installation of a sandbox at the back of the plane reminded him of stories he'd heard from other pilots. They'd been funny at the time. Now he hoped the situation had improved since the earlier part of the airlift.

The situation had not only not improved, in some ways it had deteriorated. "We were promised four planes and 1,000 refugees," Van Ostrander later related. "Things progressed very well, except when we got there and it was two planes and 10,000 refugees."[8] In the weeks the operation had been at a standstill, the influx of refugees staggering out of the desert had not stopped. The status at New Hashed was worse than it had been at Old Hashed back in October of the previous year.

Van and Thea never did get to use their bathing suits. The job was demanding, with every day bringing new challenges that had to be somehow overcome. Over the course of the next several months, Thea lost 30 lbs, and Van lost 15.

One thing had changed. For the first time, Ostrander actually had money to throw at situations. "It was a totally new experience for me, having the money to spend when I needed to," he recalled. Although having to keep it in a large but still very portable suitcase proved nerve-wracking for both of them. "We didn't dare leave it anywhere. We took it with us every time we went out the door. The whole time we were there, Thea was asking, 'Where's the suitcase? Where's the suitcase?'"[8]

But handy cash did make some things easier. Ostrander finalized the purchase of the five planes Wooten had claimed from the Flying Tigers, got them refitted, tracked down one or two replacements, and ended up able to present NEAT with a ready fleet of eight aircraft, including the Alaska Airlines C-46. He secured more fuel sources, paid off old bills, and soothed ruffled feathers. He also found more sub-contractors. One small air service, Flying Caribbean, was hard-working, but Ostrander didn't think much of their maintenance. The Flying Tigers, still in business, he rated as "Top notch."

"Flying Tigers, of course, they were a good bunch, they brought their mechanics down with them and dug in," he recalled.[8]

Jim Wooten flitted in and out, always on his way to somewhere else and always running on what seemed to be raw nerves. While his negotiating skills remained unparalleled, and he was still NEAT's main point of contact with the JDC, he moved into more of a background role, mostly to keep the U.S. State Department off the new enterprise's back. In October, he told the NEAT team that he had resigned as President of Alaska Airlines; from now on, NEAT was on its own.[14]

To Maguire, he remained distant, at least in front of others. Maguire never spoke of the collapse of his long-standing friendship, and if it pained him, he never showed it.

Marshall was officially out of the picture, Wooten tied up stateside. With adequate funding at last, the obstacles and problems that had beset Alaska Airlines melted away under the capable hands of the team Maguire had put together for NEAT.

Vitalis, who had been instrumental in getting the JDC to purchase the DC-4, had at last likewise formed a capable team of assistants, who did their best to produce whatever NEAT needed at any given time.

As in the old camp, New Hashed was still short of food, clothing, medicine, and funds, but not anywhere near previous degrees. The new co-Director, Max Lapides, who had replaced Dr. Feinberg in January 1949, proved himself a master of logistics and organization. In addition, he had been given a broader range of authority and was at last able to institute many long-overdue changes and improvements.

By the autumn of 1949, New Hashed boasted actual buildings with shower facilities, kitchens, and bunkers for housing. Conditions in the camp continued to improve dramatically. The mortality rate for infants—appallingly high up to now—finally subsided, to the relief of the volunteers. In the new camp, the refugees even began to put on weight, and incidences of disease declined.

But the Ostranders, Silver, Cheatham, and the others began to wonder if it would ever be over. The two months stretched to four, and then five. Van and Thea had expected to be home by Thanksgiving, but November came and went with no end in sight. The first phase of the airlift had moved over 5,000 refugees.[15] The second phase reached that number in the first three months, and still more kept coming.

It wasn't over by a long shot.

1. Satterfield, *The Alaska Airlines Story*, p113.
2. Satterfield; interview with Larry Roger, Sam Silver, and John Thompson, 1979.
3. Parfitt, The Road to Redemption, p210.
4. BOAC: British Overseas Airways Corporation; now British Airways.
5. Parfitt, *The Road to Redemption*, p208-209.

6. Satterfield, *The Alaska Airlines Story*, p106-107
7. Author; interviews with Sam Silver, 2008—2015.
8. Satterfield; interview with Van Ostrander, 1979.
9. Barer, *The Magic Carpet*, p191.
10. Parfitt, *The Road to Redemption*, p214.
11. In *The Alaska Airlines Story*, Archie Satterfield claims the Ostranders and Capt. Silver went over in January 1949, which Van Ostrander also said at one point during his interview. However, Sam Silver insisted that it was late July or August 1949, the middle of summer. Other evidence supports his claim, including other things Ostrander said in his interview. I'm guessing Ostrander made a slip of the tongue that Satterfield took at face value.
12. Willis Fixed Base Operator was actually a man named Charlie "Whiskey" Willis. In one of those weird coincidences that litter the history of Alaska Airlines, Willis was the President and CEO of Alaska Airlines from 1957 until 1972 and proved even more controversial and colorful than Wooten.
13. Larry Raab also found the love of his life in Israel, married her, and became a citizen of Israel.
14. Wooten resigned his position with Alaska Airlines on October 14, 1949, his overwhelming legal difficulties having made it impossible for him to continue in that role. He also wanted to keep NEAT from being tarred with Alaska Airline's brush.
15. Parfitt, *The Road to Redemption*, p186-187 gives the number at around 7,000 by early May.

CHAPTER SIXTEEN: SAM SILVER

On the day of his maiden flight for Operation Magic Carpet, Sam Silver met the first of his new co-pilots, Slick Goodlin, who had months ago asked Clarke Cole and Warren Metzger about the possibility of flying for the airlift. The war was officially over and the IAF was mostly idle. Slick wanted to help his adopted country, and he wanted to keep flying. The airlift gave him the chance to do both.

Another man might have been intimidated; Slick was already an aviation legend. Perhaps Silver thought it more peculiar than ironic, but finding the famous aviation soldier-of-fortune in the seat next to him ready to take instruction did tickle his funnybone. "I'd tell him, 'Keep your hands in your lap,' and away we'd go," he said later.[1]

This became his teaching style with all the IAF pilots, which included Lou Lenart as well as Goodlin. "I gave them a 10-minute cockpit check out. 'Here's the brake. Here's the rudder. Here's the throttle. Keep your hands in your lap and don't touch anything until I tell you to.' It worked out pretty well." It seems to have, as some of the men later became sufficiently competent to become certified DC-4 captains.

They flew to Aden and, early the next morning, went to the airport for the first trip. Sam was astounded by what awaited them there. "I saw the Near East DC-4 parked in front of the small Aden terminal," he recalled. "And under the wings, I saw what looked like 500 people squatting on their heels. I asked the ground people who were running things, I said, 'How many are you planning on putting in there?' They said, 'Oh, about 140, plus or minus a few'. I said, 'that's not possible', but when I saw the size of the Yemenites—none were over 5 ft tall or weighed more than 100 lbs, and there were children and babies involved—I thought, well, if they can find room on the benches, we can go safely within limits. So they loaded the 140, plus a couple, more or less, and closed the doors and Near East flew the first load from Aden to Tel Aviv."[1]

Apparently, Maguire hadn't learned a lesson from the prior flights; he'd ordered stewardesses aboard for that first trip, borrowed from another airline. "We carried some stewardesses the first trip," Sam recalled, "and then we never did carry any more. I opened the door and walked back and I just had to turn around and come back up and stay up there."

According to other pilots, it took at least six months to get the last of the odor out of the planes used on the Aden to Tel Aviv portion of the airlift; this plane, the very one Marian and Captain Thompson had flown out of Shanghai, now received its first baptism from the Yemenites. "Oh, God, it was terrible," Sam groaned. "They wouldn't use the back biffy there, they went on the floor, didn't know how." After a moment, he added, "We had a sandbox by the back door, and they would use that part of the time."

But no one lit any fires, no other unpleasant surprises awaited him in the air, and he touched down nine hours later at Lydda without incident. Sam offloaded his passengers and set out for Asmara.

At the front door of the hotel downtown, a tall, lanky fellow dressed in desert khakis and a desert hat stood waiting. He introduced himself as Captain Massey; Silver didn't know it, but this was the same man who had acted as Marian's Maid of Honor back in January. Massey had been so impressed with Mayor Dionesio's handlebar mustache that he'd grown one of his own; it was the first thing Sam noticed about him. Massey lit up at the sight of the Alaska Airlines uniform.

"Do you have any paychecks for me?" he asked.

Taken aback, Silver answered, "No."

"Any mail or instructions?"

"No."

Massey sighed in frustration and vented; he'd heard nothing from Tel Aviv for weeks. Where the hell was everyone, and what was going on?

Though he didn't mention it to Sam until a bit later, and not in so many words, Massey's time off hadn't been entirely unproductive. Left on his own, Massey, for lack of other orders, had alleviated his boredom by taking out the left-behind Alaska Airlines C-46 and booking his own charter flights with it.[2]

Along with two other crewmen who had evidently been either forgotten, disowned, or abandoned by Alaska Airlines, and whose names are now lost to history, he flew into towns up and down the Malaysian peninsula, the African coast, and into Australia, as well as Italy and Greece. In each town, he advertised in the local papers that he was taking passengers to Tel Aviv. When he got a planeload, he'd take their cash and fly them in. By all accounts, he did it almost solely for love of the mission; he made just enough money to pay his bills, using an Alaska Airlines credit card to buy fuel.[2]

But the airline finally stopped him by cutting off the credit card. Once again, he was frustrated, alone, and bored. Having Sam turn up at least promised some kind of change. And Sam ended up liking the maverick pilot as much as everyone else who'd worked with him. "He turned out to be quite a droll fellow, quite a likeable guy," Sam recalled.[1]

He reassured Massey that he was about to be needed again. Sure enough, Massey was soon called back into active duty, flying the C-46 in service to Near East Air Transport. Sam lent him a few fighter pilots. "It's on me," he told Massey.

Every other day, Sam arrived at the airport and saw much the same sight: a horde of small, dark-eyed people watching him from the shade of the DC-4's outstretched wings. Even in the early mornings, the September sun was punishing, and the refugees had long since lost their fear of the giant birds. He learned to greet them with a smile and a wave, always returned, before hurrying up the shallow, wooden gangplank to the waiting cockpit of the DC-4. "They were so patient, didn't seem to mind the heat much," he said. "I guess that's what comes from living in the desert." Thinking it over, he amended the thought. "Or maybe they did mind, but they were so eager to finally get home, it didn't matter."[1]

Alternating with another crew, Sam's schedule quickly fell into a pleasant routine. He enjoyed the landscape, so very different from Alaska's, as it rolled away beneath him. "We would take off in the evening about 8 o'clock from Tel Aviv, climb up to 10,000 feet, and fly across the Sinai Desert with Jordan on the left and the Bay of Aqaba to our right. We'd fly over Eilat, the small fishing village, at the entrance to the Eilat canal," he remembered. Eilat would later become a very famous resort, renowned for snorkeling and skin diving. At the time, however, it remained an undiscovered treasure, just another pretty sight from overhead.

"It was mostly dead reckoning flying, and all visual flying. We could see the Red Sea below us. We'd land at Aden in the morning and fly back the next day.

Sometimes, on the northbound flight in the afternoon, we'd see a sunshine haze ahead of us."[1]

Some things had changed since the earlier part of the airlift; Tel Aviv had become safe to use as a base again. Sam and Massey were told to move into town.

Once again, the Yarden had no vacancies, but many individual homeowners had rooms to let, and the hotel manager located two of them. The one Sam took turned out to be only a few blocks from downtown and even had a private entrance.

Sam liked his hosts well enough and quickly got used to stepping over the sandbags around the entrance. But it did bring home the fact that these people were still at war. "One evening, I was talking to the man of the house, a fellow in his early 40s, and I asked him if he was in the Israeli army," Sam recalled, "and he said 'no, but I'm in the reserve. I have a gun and ammunition and if we are invaded, my post is the corner ditch outside the house, and my orders are to stay there until killed or relieved.' The war was a matter of survival for the Israel people at that time."

Every day brought more reminders of the violence with which the people of Israel still lived. So did the nights; the infamous Tel Aviv nightlife could be hazardous for more than one reason. Sam's chivalrous instincts almost landed him in hot water. "Blackie" Blackstone, the American fighter pilot Warren had also known, had a fight with his girlfriend and walked out, leaving her alone in the hotel lounge. She lived several blocks from the center of town, a daunting distance in the blackout. Sam offered to walk her home. "I left her at her doorstep and started for my place," he later related. "As I was crossing one of the streets, a jeep came flying around the right corner and before I could say, 'boo', I was spread-eagle over the hood by two MPs and I was patted down."[1] Fortunately, he was able to convince them that he was an American pilot working the airlift and not a terrorist. The MPs drove him home, but he was careful never to go out alone after dark again.

He loved the serenity of the sky; the only flies in the ointment were his restless, fidgety co-pilots. Fighter pilots are an energetic breed by nature, and neither silence nor stillness come easily to them. Sam, blunt-spoken and somewhat acerbic by inclination, quickly taught them to enjoy long periods of meditative silence.

Over time, he developed friendships with several of them, especially Slick Goodlin, with whom he flew more than probably any other. Slick had the ability to re-tune himself to the task at hand, and Sam thought he had the makings of a pretty good airline pilot. He eventually grew comfortable enough to ask the ace about an incident he'd read of in the paper back in the states.

During the early part of the Arab/Israel war, the British had sent up a flight of RAF Spitfires to patrol the Sinai border. At some point, they'd strayed over the Israeli border and were promptly jumped by a flight of Israeli Messerschmitts,[3] which shot down two of the British fliers. "There was no stink in regards to that," Sam recalled, "but there was no information in the papers whether the Israeli pilots were Israeli or perhaps the American volunteers who were serving in the air force."

As they were flying north up the Red Sea in the late afternoon one day, he decided to push the limits of the new friendship. He turned to Goodlin, napping in the co-pilot's seat. "Slick, was that you that shot down those two Brits?" he asked.

Goodlin's eyes opened. "No, I didn't shoot anybody down." He paused. "But I was in the air that day."[14]

Sam often spent the evenings at the hotel lounge, a favorite gathering place for pilots, and enjoyed swapping stories. One of his co-pilots, a fighter pilot named Tom, told him of how he loaded a bomb aboard a Norseman, a single-engine aircraft of a type frequently used by Alaska Airlines and others as a bush plane.

Tom took off at night and flew over the Sinai Desert until he found an Egyptian army camp. There, he opened the door and managed to push the bomb out. Sam loved passing the story on with the tag line, "How's that for strategic bombing?"

He also spent time with the young woman he'd walked home from the bar, who had been sufficiently impressed by Sam's good manners that she'd dumped Blackstone for him. Young and adventurous, she and a girlfriend once coaxed him into spending a morning exploring the suburb of Jaffa. A Palestinian suburb of Tel Aviv with a population of over 50,000 people at the start of the war, it had been evacuated by the Israeli army. Deserted, it had the haunted air of a place where tragedy had left its invisible but indelible mark.

"As we walked the narrow, cobble-stoned streets, winding here and there, it was like being transported back to Biblical times 2,000 years ago," Sam recalled. "We wandered through the streets and there wasn't a sound. On the left and right were the two-story sand-stone walls and an occasional door or a second-story, Muslim-type window, barred, with a dried flower-box.

"The girls led me through a corridor into an open square surrounded by four walls; it was a small half-a-block, quarter-block, open area enclosure with palm trees and dried shrubbery and a dried fountain. It must have been a very attractive place at one time."

Sam found the experience fascinating and saddening at the same time. He could not help but feel for the plight of those who had been driven from their homes and put in refugee camps with other Palestinians. "They're still there, even after some 60 years," he said, still regretting the injustice. "They're still in the refugee camps and the problem has not been solved. The Palestinians have still not formed a state and there has been no legal, no peace treaty between the Arabs and Israel that ends the war. As of now, the Palestinians are fighting amongst themselves, the Jaffes in the Gaza strip and the Palestinians in the West Bank, those that are left, are killing each other and the Jaffes in the Gaza strip are still firing rockets into Israel and Israel is retaliating with bombs and cannon fire."

He pondered it while flying his missions; the people he bore aloft to a new life had also been persecuted, driven from their homes and imprisoned. Yet now, at last, they had a chance to redress old wrongs and start anew with a fresh life. The world had changed, and he was helping to change it. Perhaps in a way, restoring the Yemenite Jews to the land of their forefathers balanced the scales.

The flood of refugees coming in from the desert slowed to a trickle. The numbers waiting in Hashed gradually dwindled. Many of the refugees who had been in Aden for some time now had finally returned to health and began to gain weight. It meant cutting down the numbers that could be squeezed onto the DC-4s, but still, the flights were making headway.

In late December, Maguire told Sam his next trip would be his last; after that, he was free to go home. Sam had accumulated so many hours that he would have to take the next six months off, with pay, in order to be legal to fly again, but that certainly was nothing to complain about.

Massey was there with the last C-46, and Maguire gave him his orders in front of Sam. "Go back to Asmara and pick up everything you can from that '46 Sharp crashed. Alaska wants as much of it back as you can scrounge. When you're loaded, come back here and pick up Sam. You and he can fly back to the states together. You'll have a couple of passengers, but that's it."

By 7:30 that evening, Massey was taxiing down the runway and heading for Asmara. Sam lifted off on his last flight for the airlift about 20 minutes later and had one final wartime scare. "We leveled off in the darkness at 10,000 feet, and a few minutes later, I saw ahead of us and to the right the flashing lights of an airplane. Had we caught up with Massey, or was it an Egyptian night fighter?" After a few tense moments, Sam decided to err on the side of caution. "I veered to the left and turned off our navigation lights, left the plane to the right and behind us."

He suffered no further moments of uncertainty and completed his mission with an impeccable record. It was time to go. Van and Thea Ostrander and Ralph Cheatham had left a week or two prior; there was no one at NEAT aside from Maguire and Mulleneaux he needed to say goodbye to. That night, he had the chance to raise a farewell glass with many of the former fighter jocks who'd flown as his co-pilots.

Two days later, Massey returned in the C-46, its cabin packed with all the salvageable spare parts of the dead C-46 that had lain all those months by the runway in Asmara. Side-by-side in the cockpit, he and Sam took off for home.

Naturally, there was a problem. They were no longer working for NEAT. That meant they had no money, not even an Alaska Airlines credit card. Fortunately, one of their passengers, a young lawyer from Miami named Rex, had been given a large amount of cash in order to buy automobiles. He agreed to buy the fuel instead and pay some expenses for the trip; Alaska Airlines would reimburse him once they got home. *Or so we hope*, Sam privately thought.

Shortly before take-off, Massey told Sam he'd had to replace the right engine on the C-46. Fortunately, the helpful Israelis had found a Pratt and Whitney R-2800 engine that had formerly powered a Republic Thunderbolt, a WWII fighter, stocked in a cave. Sam was a bit hesitant about flying the North Atlantic in a two-engine airplane with a so-called fighter engine on the right side, but Massey had assured him that the engine had been performing very well all during the summer. With a shrug, he took the other pilot's word for it, and they took off.

They flew to Rome, where the next morning they were approached by two young Americans, a pilot and a mechanic who had been working for a carrier called Trans-Caribbean[5], which had been flying charter work in Europe. "Trans-Caribbean had gone out of business and the two chaps were stranded in Rome," said Sam. "We didn't need a pilot, but I thought a mechanic might come in handy, so we put them aboard."

The merry band, now enlarged by two, took off again, this time for Lisbon as their next port of call. Somewhere en route, Sam looked over and saw the radio operator, Frank, slumped over in his seat. Roused, the young man muttered the happy news that he thought he had malaria. There was nothing to do but continue to Lisbon. Once there, local agents whisked them all away to Estoril; a far from dire fate, as it happened. Estoril was a seaside resort about 30 miles west of Lisbon and the home of many displaced royalty of the Balkans who, during World Wars I and II, had been taken and locked up in Portugal, there to languish in the wonderful climate and sunlit beaches.

The crew were housed at a casino hotel where Sam called a doctor. The doctor was able to relieve their minds somewhat; Frank didn't have malaria but dysentery. He gave the sufferer a couple of pills that seemed to help and told him to rest for a few days. Sam reassured the doctor and sent him off secure in the belief that the patient was in good hands.

The next day, the crew packed poor Frank back into the plane and flew from Lisbon to Santa Maria (Gaua) via the Azores, where they fueled, checked the weather, and filed for Gander, the base in Newfoundland and Labrador, Canada. Naturally, their escape wasn't permitted to go as planned.

As they were getting ready to start the engines, the weatherman came running out with a sheaf of papers in his hand. A new weather report just in predicted 40 knot headwinds over the Atlantic. There was no point in even trying, so Sam and Massey shut down and the whole crew stayed overnight in Santa Maria. Divine Providence was evidently on the lookout for Frank.

By the next morning, the winds had abated. Sam and Massey filed for Lagens (Lajes), a small island about 200 miles west of Santa Maria. They topped off their tanks there, checked the weather and the emergency frequencies, then flew to Gander. At Gander, they filed for LaGuardia in New York.

"We sent the necessary dispatch, which was required in those days, to LaGuardia, telling them of our anticipated arrival at 3:00 in the morning. We landed at LaGuardia at 3:00 a.m., parked the airplane, and were led to the immigration and customs offices. Lo and behold, there was nobody there; the place was empty. We went in and waited."

The wait stretched on, during which the two vagabonds they'd picked up in Rome scrounged through some desks, looking for documents they thought they might need, then disappeared without a goodbye.

It was another twenty minutes before a very irate, very Irish immigration officer showed up. Mallory Remeal immediately laid into the two pilots. "What are you guys doing landing here at 3 o'clock in the morning? Don't you know this airport closes at 11 o'clock?"

Sam apologized. "Well, we thought that this was New York and the airport would be open 24 hours a day." He backed up the apology with a bottle of Italian cordial he'd stashed, and the offering seemed to mollify the immigration officer a bit.

Finally, he growled, "Okay fellas, you're back in the United States. Disappear."

Sam Silver and Massey were home.

The next afternoon, their load bolstered by office furniture that Marshall wanted them to take to the west coast, they took off again, heading for Chicago. "As we were flying west over Pennsylvania on a clear, sunny afternoon at about 8,000 feet, we received a call from United 4. They said 'Alaska C-46, we're 6,000 below you and behind you and have you in sight. We saw a piece fall off your airplane. Are you okay?'"

This is never something a pilot wants to hear. Massey and Sam looked at each other. Sam picked up the radio and thanked United 4 very politely, assured them that all seemed to be well at the moment, and promising to check it out at their next stop.

Nothing seemed amiss when they looked the plane over after landing in Chicago, so they shrugged it off. The next day, they flew on to Great Falls, Montana. After refueling, they filed for Everett, Washington; almost home. Only a few more hours...

Sam wasn't big on prayer, but he crossed his fingers and hoped nothing more would go wrong.

"That evening, as we took off in the dark, the right engine, the Thunderbolt engine, started burp-burp-burping," Sam said. Massey, who was flying that length, turned around and landed back at Great Falls, and they shut down for the night. Even the most foolhardy Alaskan pilots wouldn't have risked trying to fly over the Rockies and the Cascades in the middle of the night with an engine that was huffing and puffing like an asthmatic rhinoceros.

The next morning, Alaska Airlines sent a mechanic from Everett to Great Falls. He tinkered with the carburetor, ran up the engine, and made dozens of tests, trying to find the problem. The engine purred like a large, happy cat the entire time, giving no indication of anything amiss. The mechanic finally shrugged. "Well, it looks like it's okay," he told the pilots. "It's running all right."

With that assurance, Sam and Massey took off for Everett.

All was well until they had crossed the Cascades and came out atop some clouds at around 9,000 feet, over the Everett beacon with the airport practically below them. "Massey throttled back the engines to land at Ev-

erett, and what do you think happened? The Thunderbolt engine started huffing and puffing and burping, as if
to say, 'Fellows, I've flown you from the near east across
Europe, across the Atlantic, across the United States. I'm
not an airline engine, I'm a fighter engine. I think I need
a rest,'" Sam remembered. He could hardly begrudge the
engine its complaints; he felt exactly the same way.

They managed to bring the tired old bird safely in to
land.

Much to Sam's relief, Alaska Airlines promptly reimbursed Rex in full and paid Massey before officially re-
lieving him of duty; his free-lance escapades with the
C-46 had not been overlooked after all. Massey
shrugged, tipped his hat, and headed back to New York
to look for another job. No one at Alaska Airlines heard
from him again.

Sam felt as if the adventure were officially behind
him. He checked in with the airline and took his well-
earned, six-month vacation.

Flying his scheduled runs between Anchorage, Fairbanks, and Seattle was like coming home all over again,
but he had no regrets for the time he'd spent on the
airlift.

"Thinking back, it wasn't my intention or rather I
didn't expect to be involved in the Flying Carpet incident. My job, and I did it, was to fly the Near East DC-4
from Everett to Tel Aviv and then return to the states
and continue my normal career. But oddly, once I was
there and they needed my help, I was glad to oblige,"
Sam said. Much later, he learned that the idea of what
might happen if an Alaska Airlines Jewish Captain and
a load of Jewish immigrants were forced down in Islamic territory had caused no small concern among
some of the company officials. Fortunately, the question had never been answered.

Sam could look back on those days in the sandy,
bronze skies over the Red Sea as a great adventure.
"When they asked me to fly the trips, I was glad to do

so, and I'm happy to say that I flew about 1,000 Yemenite Jews back to their home in Israel. When I made my first flight for Alaska Airlines with Captain Flahart on a cold, clear December day in 1943, little did I dream as we flew by Mt. McKinley that someday I would be flying the Magic Carpet."

.   .   .

Less than two weeks before Sam made his last flight, Van Ostrander, pausing in Amsterdam on the way back to the states, got a call from Jim Wooten. "Hey, I'm back in Paris. Phyllis and I are here with the kids. Why don't you and Cheatham stop by on the way home? We need to settle up, and I've got an idea I want to run past you. Put Thea on the plane home and come on down."

Ostrander almost laughed. "Have you got rocks in your head? She isn't about to leave and go home without me; I wouldn't put her on that airplane."[6]

Wooten yielded with suspicious ease. "Okay, bring her with. I've got an idea I want to talk to you guys about."

Ostrander knew what that meant: another adventure lay in store. He took Thea and went with Ralph Cheatham—who was traveling without his countess— back to Paris to meet with Wooten.

Wooten did indeed have a wonderful new scheme lined up involving flying hordes of Catholic pilgrims from South America to Rome in 1950. Ostrander would be stationed in Bermuda, a mid-point refueling stop.

This time Thea put her foot down. No more running after Wooten. It was time to go home and take up new lives. And this time, Van agreed. "No, Jim," he told Wooten. "I'm going home and going back into ceramics."

Wooten surrendered, knowing he couldn't win against Thea. It was time to settle accounts and part ways. "What do I owe you?" he asked.

Van smiled. He and Thea had kept very careful track of his promised 10% over and above his salary. "$40,000."

Wooten threw his hands in the air. "What do you want, my right arm?"

"Sure, I'll take your arm. But I'll still take my $40,000."

Thea was ready to burst; she had never been so proud of her husband. Van had finally stood up to his charismatic boss. For the first time in years, she and Van were going to have a life without riding the Wooten roller-coaster.

Secretly, though, Van was already missing Alaska Airlines. Forever afterward, he would look back on his job as the most exciting time of his life. "I almost lost jobs over it," he laughed. "People got so sick of hearing Alaska Airlines stories, they'd tell me to shut up or get another job."[6]

1. This and all other facts relating to Sam Silver's adventures are taken from Satterfield's interview with Captain Silver in 1979 and the author's interviews with him between 2008 and 2015.
2. According to former Alaska Airlines Purchasing Officer Henry "Hank" Bierds in a 1979 interview with Archie Satterfield: "They were getting bills for years from East Borneo trading company for gas for that guy who was on his way down to Australia to pick up some refugees."
3. Avia S-99; the Czech version of the well-known German fighter, the Messerschmitt.
4. Slick Goodlin is still officially credited with shooting down two British planes and an Egyptian Spitfire on January 7, 1949.
5. This may be the same airline Ostrander remembered as Flying Caribbean.
6. Satterfield; interview with Van Ostrander, 1979.

CHAPTER SEVENTEEN: THE RECKONING

While Sam Silver, Massey and the others were still ferrying refugees from Hashed in the fall of 1949, Wooten was back in Washington D.C. for the Federal Court's final ruling. He listened with disbelief to the decision he'd fought for a year and a half. "The Ober Dictum of his (Tony Dimond's) decision is one of the greatest eulogies of me I've ever read," he said later, "but the decision was that 'the Civil Aeronautics Act of 1938 said an applicant had to have a Certificate of Necessity and Convenience before commencement of operation and the defendant here did not. So I have no alternative but to find him guilty.'"[1]

The CAB, tired of Alaska Airlines kicking sand in its face and eager to follow up the courtroom victory, slammed the airline with a massive fine of $500,000 and ordered the airline to shut down. They levied an additional fine on Wooten himself for $200,000, and added insult to injury by throwing in a sentence of ninety days in jail. Wooten's contempt for authority and his grifter tricks with the system had finally caught up with him.

He hastily filed an appeal then headed for the comfort of the Stattler men's bar to drown his sorrows. According to him, he ran into an old friend, Matthew J. Connelly, Appointment Secretary and Aide to President Harry Truman. Matt listened to his tale of woe and promptly took him to the White House.

Jimmy Wooten was known to be a great raconteur, a spinner of yarns so splendid that listeners rarely cared about their veracity. As a former Alaska Airlines executive once put it, "Don't believe half of what Wooten tells you. And double check the other half."[2]

But Wooten maintained to the end of his days that his old pal Harry Truman saved the day over cards and whiskey.

"Took about an hour before we got in to see the old man," he later said. "Harry asked if they wanted to go upstairs for a round of poker and bourbon. Then he says to me, 'I understand you got a problem,' and I said, 'I sure do,' and he said, 'that's what I'm here for.'"

Wooten's narrative, related during a colorful (and probably slanderous) interview made three decades later, can only be told in his own words.

"By this time it was about 9:30," he related. "We played a few hands of poker, chewing the fat. Nick Bez[3] was saying, 'He's a crook, Mr. President. He's a sorry, no-good bastard" Nick was a Yugoslav, spoke with a pretty heavy accent. 'Don't pay any attention to him; he ought to do a little time.'

"Finally the Pres said, 'Nick, I'm the President of the United States, I think I can handle my job without the assistance and the negative annoyance of my so-called friend, Nick. Now you go over in the corner and shut up.'"

According to Wooten, Truman had him call in Welch Pogue, a highly respected and capable attorney in Washington D.C., who had also at one time been chairman of the CAB. Welch was already in bed when he received Wooten's call and at first refused to believe him. Finally, an impatient Truman snatched the phone from Wooten's hand.

"So he says, 'Welch, what's your problem?' Harry says, 'Okay, 45 minutes will be fine. I'll get ahold of Howard McGrath in the meantime; you come on to the White House and come in to the east entrance. A pass will be waiting for you.'"

The drama unfolding in Wooten's colorful narrative grew in scope. "So, he called Howard McGrath. Now, J. Howard McGrath was the US Attorney General, and had been a Senator from Rhode Island, and had been Chairman of the Democratic Party that had tried to sell Harry Truman down the river to salvage the Democratic Senate, and Truman knew all this. So he got McGrath on the phone and told him he was going to have Welch Pogue write out this order and that Welch would have it in his office at 8:00 in the morning and he wanted Howard there at 8:00 to sign it. And Howard says, 'I won't do it.' And Truman says, 'You're fired.' And he was absolutely livid.

"Well, Vaughn and Matt Connelly and Nick and another guy had come in, another one of his secretaries, and they were all trying to tell him, 'We're not in any shape to have an inter-party fight here, because you just got through blasting reporters for saying Margaret had a voice like a sour owl. Mr. President, please, we can't afford this.' Meantime, while they're working on him, Howard calls back and talks to Matt and says, 'I'm sorry, tell the President I'm sorry, that I apologize. I don't want to do it, but he's the President and I'll do what he says.'

"Matt told him to stand by and he'd see if he could get the president to talk to him; call back in another 15 minutes and we'll see what happens.'

"Well, finally Harry cooled down; he'd had another bourbon and he was getting sleepy. He said, 'All right, the sorry sonofabitch; get him on the phone and tell him that apology of his had better be a deep one and a

very sincere one, or I've sure had a bellyful of that con-
niving snake.' So, believe me, Howard made him a pro-
fuse and a deep apology, and he (the president) says,
'You had better be here at 8'clock and I don't mean 8-
oh-one. And you sign this, and don't you make one
change in whatever Welch has written.'"

Apparently Welch Pogue, Matt Connelly, and one of
the President's lawyers worked with Wooten until
3:00am on the Consent order, had it typed up and, at
8:00 in the morning, J. Howard McGrath came in and
signed it. James Wooten and Alaska Airlines were off
the hook for the fines and the jail time.

Wasting no time, he took his hard-won prize directly
to R.W. Marshall's office and slapped what amounted
to a Presidential Pardon on the desk. "Here's the Consent order,' I said to him, 'I saved Alaska Airlines
$500,000.'"

For the first and only time, Marshall thanked Wooten
for all he'd done.

The overturn of the fines and jail time did not negate
the CAB Cease and Desist order. Marshall, faced with
losing an enormous amount of business, was ready to
make deals, and Wooten, desperate to keep his charters in the air, was ready to take them.

It was clear to both men that Wooten could not remain as President of Alaska Airlines. They were probably equally relieved when he formally tendered his
resignation on October 14, 1949.

Wooten offered to buy the two converted DC-4s
he'd been using, plus others that had been used strictly
for cargo, leaving Marshall with two remaining DC-4s
that had been used only for passengers. Alaska Airlines
would soon have its certificate of operation for within
the Territory of Alaska restored, but the time to flaunt
CAB rules was gone forever.

Wooten claims he warned Marshall to put the planes
in for their long overdue overhauls and rehabilitation
as soon as possible—something he himself had never

gotten around to pushing for during his entire tenure. "If you're not going to be cooperative with me I'm going to tell the President don't give you the certificate," he remembered saying. "Let's just lay it right smack out on the table. I don't want anything from Alaska Airlines that they can keep. Near East Air Transport is mine; it was mine to begin with, I paid for it, and I'm going to keep it."

Marshall accepted the deal, certain Wooten would fail without the additional support of Alaska Airlines' planes and personnel, and unaware of the work Maguire had already done and the deals Wooten had made with the Flying Tigers and Bob Prescott. Near East Air Transport was still in business and would remain so for a while longer.

·   ·   ·

In late September of 1950, the official last flight of the airlift included 26 Jews from Sana'a. The last of the community was flown to Aden in one of the Iman's two private planes as a goodwill gesture. Operation Magic Carpet was finally over.[4]

There were still Jews in foreign lands begging for rescue, and Maguire was still determined to get them to Israel. With the able assistance of Hank Mulleneaux, he committed NEAT to other airlifts, hauling Jewish refugees from Iran, South America, and other parts of the world well into the 1950s.

He didn't realize how much his efforts had cost him until his health began to fail, and a doctor's examination gave him the chilling news. At some point while swimming in Aden, he had acquired a parasite that left him with a damaged heart. He could no longer be licensed to fly. His career was over.[5,6]

Maguire could no longer run NEAT, and without him, NEAT couldn't operate; the assets were sold to the JDC, and he returned to the states. He rolled up his sleeves and went to New York to settle accounts with Wooten, from whom he'd now been estranged for some time.

Neither he nor any of the others who signed on with NEAT had written contracts, but Maguire had accepted the position and title of President of Near East Air Transport on the same 10% over-and-above arrangement Wooten later made with Ostrander.[7] Maguire was unaware that Wooten had already snookered him out of any profits he would have made from NEAT beyond his paycheck as president. When he tried to collect, he learned the bitter truth.

Wooten owned a number of paper corporations, of which NEAT was only one. He had legally arranged it so that all profits for services rendered by NEAT went to one of the other dummy corporations. NEAT had essentially worked for nothing. At some point, when Maguire was in a frenzy of paperwork, Wooten had simply shoved the agreement under his nose; trusting Wooten, Maguire signed his rights away without reading what he had signed.

Hearing about it later, Ostrander was convinced the paper had been meant for him. "I think this paper that Maguire signed was one Jim meant for me to sign. If he'd said, 'sign this,' I would have signed it without thinking anything about it. And Jim knew that. So he thought, 'Well, it's better to have the president (of NEAT) sign it.'"[7]

Maguire took Wooten to court over this, but the damning paper with his signature at the bottom was undeniable. Whatever grievance Wooten had against his former friend, he had certainly extracted a thorough and intensely satisfying revenge.

To the end of their lives, both men continued to take pride in what they had done. An entire people had been moved by the men and women of Alaska Airlines and Near East Air Transport between October 1, 1948 and September 30, 1950. More than 40,000 of them were carried between June 1949 and September 1950.[8] It remains a feat unparalleled in aviation history.

1. Satterfield; interview with James Wooten, 1979.
2. Satterfield; interview with Hank Bierds, 1979.
3. Nikola Bezmalinovich, millionaire supporter, fishing buddy, and friend of Truman.
4. Parfitt, *The Road to Redemption*, p285.
5. "Robert Maguire Jr., 94, Pilot Who Airlifted Yemenite Jews, Dies", Margalit Fix, *Los Angeles Times*, June 18, 2005.
6. *Magic Carpet Pilots*, Alaskaair.com.
7. Satterfield; interview with Van Ostrander, 1979.
8. Parfitt, *The Road to Redemption*, p283.

EPILOGUE

A few Jewish stragglers—perhaps as many as 2,000 —continued to live in the Yemen, some by choice, more because they could not afford the cost of the journey to Aden. The directors of New Hashed—Yosef Zadok and Max Lapides—continued to campaign tirelessly for their succor; the camp remained partially open, waiting to welcome home the last children of Israel.

For those who completed the exodus, after a slightly rocky start, the Lost Tribes found their place in Israel. Successful in a variety of enterprises unimaginable to their immediate forefathers, they and their descendants have flourished not only in Israel but around the world.

Bob Maguire settled with his family in California and became wildly successful, first in pension-fund banking and then in real estate.[1,2] His children went on to forge their own paths to success, in which he took enormous pride; his son eventually took over the business. He retained close ties throughout the aviation industry; he and the Metzgers traded Christmas cards every year, and spoke over the phone at least once a month.

In 2004, Maguire was awarded a medal of valor from the Simon Wiesenthal Center.[1] One of the attendees, Ely Dromy, a successful businessman in California, was only 6 months old when he was flown with his mother and two sisters from Aden to Tel Aviv. He came to the ceremony for the chance to express his deepest gratitude to the old pilot, then 93. He'd grown up with stories of the airlift.

"My family had never seen an airplane," Dromy said. "They called it 'the eagle.'"[1] In his view, his entire family owed everything they had, including their lives, to Maguire.

Maguire's entire family, including eight grandchildren and eight more great-grandchildren, were at the ceremony at the Simon Wiesenthal Center to watch their patriarch being honored with justifiable pride.

Robert Maguire died in 2005, at the age of 94.[2]

Warren and Marian moved to Alaska, had three children and six grandchildren, and stayed married for 60 years through all life's ups and downs. Warren died on Mother's Day of 2009; Marian, determined not to be left out, followed him on the last great adventure four months later. All three of their children learned to fly at an early age, and their eldest son, Warren Jr., became a pilot for an Alaskan emergency medical airline.

After three children, Jim Wooten's marriage collapsed; Phyllis had had enough. He married again, but failing health forced him to retire from his position as president of U.S. Airlines, a cargo and air freight service. Praised by David Ben-Gurion for his instrumental part in directing the airlift, he died at age 71 in 1985.[4]

In 2012, Sam Silver, then well into his 90s, was in Hawaii with his daughter and granddaughter, who were on vacation. Sitting in his wheelchair at an outdoor market, he saw a beautiful new hotel in the distance and asked a nearby young lady what it was. She replied that she didn't know; she was not from Hawaii. She looked Hawaiian to Sam, so he asked her where she was from. "Israel," she replied. Within moments, he learned that her mother and grandmother had been carried from Aden to Tel Aviv on the Magic Carpet, and she discovered that he was one of the pilots who had taken them there. She threw her arms around him and insisted on having her picture taken with him. "Thank you for saving them," she said.[5]

It is almost the only acknowledgment Sam ever received for his part in the airlift, but he cherished the memory of that encounter more than any award he could have been given. In 2013, he was an honored guest and speaker at the opening of the Operation Magic Carpet exhibit at the Alaska Jewish Cultural Heritage Museum in Anchorage, Alaska, along with Elgen Long and the author of this book. He died in July of 2015 at the age of 99.

At the Operation Magic Carpet exhibit opening where Sam had been a speaker, this author and my two brothers were approached by a young man from Chicago. He eagerly introduced his own children to them and wanted the families to be photographed together. "Your father flew my mother into Israel. He saved her life," the young man said, his eyes shining. "None of us would be here today without your father."

At the same gathering, another older gentleman whose family had been transported on the airlift sought out the younger Metzgers to introduce himself. He gestured to the gathering of hundreds, many of whom were descendants of refugees airlifted out of Aden and Shanghai. "All these people here, all of this, is because of your parents. They made this possible."

Pan American Airlines, Northwest, TWA, and the other giants who once dominated the skies are all gone. Alaska Airlines is still here, now one of the largest, best-respected, and most successful airlines in the world. It's no longer the small, clannish company it once was. But the spirit of those earlier pioneers who kept it aloft lives on. The employees remember the legends and strive to keep the "Spirit of Alaska" alive.

1. "Jews Discover an Unsung Hero", Christiana Sci-audone, *Los Angeles Times*, June 19, 2004.
2. "Robert Maguire Jr., 94, Pilot Who Airlifted Yemenite Jews, Dies", Margalit Fix, *Los Angeles Times*, June 18, 2005.
3. *Magic Carpet Pilots*, Alaskaair.com.
4. "James A. Wooten, Director of '49 Airlift of Yemeni Jews", *New York Times*, June 3, 1985.
5. Author, interview with Sam Silver, 2013.

1. Sam Silver after his first solo flight, 1938
(courtesy Silver collection).

2. A young Yemenite bride and groom; he was around 12, she was probably 10 or 11. Young marriages such as this were not uncommon among the Yemenites, but shocked the Israelis and British (courtesy Alaska Airlines).

3. Wooten took this photo to prove he could cram 148 people onto a DC-4 and still get it into the air. After the flight, his pilot told him, "never again" (courtesy Alaska Airlines).

4. A Yemenite elder (courtesy Alaska Airlines).

5. Yemenite youngsters in a makeshift schoolroom in Hashed (courtesy Alaska Airlines).

6. Yemenite sisters waiting to begin a new life in Israel. Many Yemenite women were intrigued and delighted by the prospect of greater freedoms offered women in Israeli society (courtesy Alaska Airlines).

7. Sam Silver with Naama Levy. Her mother and grandmother were passengers aboard one of his flights to Israel (courtesy Silver collection).

8. Decendents of Operation Magic Carpet: Warren and Marian's eldest son Warren "Chip" Metzger, Jr., with his sons Warren David and Kenan, and the son and granddaughters of two of the refugees who flew to Israel with Warren Sr., whose names are unfortunately unknown. To their right is the author and niece Elise Metzger, with another granddaughter of the same refugee family. Photo taken at the opening of the Alaska Jewish Heritage Museum (Metzger collection).

9. Part of the Metzger family with Sam Silver (center), pilot on many OMC flights, and Elgen Long, Navigator of "The Ironmen Crew" (Metzger collection).

AFTERWORD

Every kid thinks their parents are heroes. It's a little odd and more than a little wonderful, when you grow up and discover that they really are.

When I was a child, I used to love to sit on the living room floor when the other Alaska Airlines employees came over and listen to them all swap stories.

I don't remember how many times I heard stories about Operation Magic Carpet, although I never heard anyone refer to it that way. It was just, "Remember that time in Tel Aviv..." or "We were coming in over Aden..." or "...about the third trip in the C-46..." Some fabulous, wild adventure followed that would have everyone in the room laughing, though I'm sure a lot of it wasn't funny at the time. It always ended in some grand finale, such as "...coasted into Cyprus on fumes..." or wherever.

I remember my dad telling the story of how, when he and some of the other pilots first arrived in Aden, an overworked British officer, whom Dad thought was in charge of the refugee camp, warned him and the other pilots about the dangers of landing anywhere in Arab territory. What would happen to them if they did —and, worse yet, what would happen to their passengers. The wording was slightly different each time Dad told it, but the gist was always the same. Dad was a sucker for children, and the Yemenite children left a deep impression upon him, especially their big, dark eyes that followed him whenever he walked past.

I remember him shaking his head over the thought that anyone could murder a bunch of helpless, adorable children four and five years old. He never forgot them and spoke of them often.

Our living room is where I first heard the story of how Bob Maguire managed to keep his Yemenite passengers safe during a forced landing in Egypt by radioing ahead and telling the airport that he had smallpox aboard.

It's also where I heard Larry Roger talk about being shot at during approach into Tel Aviv, with his light-hearted, bone-dry delivery... "It certainly gets your attention..."

I've forgotten how many times I heard "the fez story." While I was writing this book, I came across an account of it Dad had written out for someone else. It sounded as if it had been intended for an official record somewhere.

I was shocked when I read that he said it was his co-pilot rather than himself who had done it, thinking to have some fun giving the kids a bit of a scare. So, either my dad lied every time he told the story, or, in this age of hyper-sensitivity, he was trying to avoid giving offense by distancing himself from the incident when recording it. Since Dad was a stickler for honesty, and I never knew him to lie, I assume the latter.

I never tired of Mom's stories of her flights, especially out of Shanghai, ferrying Jewish refugees from China to Israel by way of Hong Kong and Bombay. Or of the way the DC-4 "staggered into the air" while the crew held their breath, gripped their seats, and tried to pretend everything was okay for the sake of their passengers. Or of the nice little old man who stopped to pat her hand, when they disembarked at last in Tel

Aviv, and told her she was "the kind of girl a man would marry even without a dowry."

Or of how the last flight from Shanghai took off to the sound of gunfire coming from the end of the runway as the Communist forces closed in.

For most of my life, I assumed she'd been on that last flight. My research cast some doubt on that, so her second flight out of Shanghai might have been at some other time. A probable explanation is that Mom believed that Operation Magic Carpet covered only the three months from January to March of 1949, and that the flights that happened after that (and prior to) were individual charters. She simply didn't count any other flights she made as being part of the operation. An easy enough assumption to make, considering the secrecy at the time and the subsequent confusion about so many of the dates.

And actually, an accurate one. The name "Operation Magic Carpet" originally referred only to the rescue flights of the Yemenite Jews out of Aden. Only later were the flights from other locations during the same time period lumped together with the Aden flights.

That three month period, which included my parents' wedding in Asmara, was all part of the "Mom and Dad Mythology"; stories that are part of the background and fabric of my life. And as we grew up, my brothers and I stopped really paying attention to it. We took it for granted or dismissed it. It was just ancient history; parents become remarkably un-cool once one hits puberty, and after that, one's own life takes precedence.

In 2007, KTUU TV did an interview with Dad about his role in Operation Magic Carpet. It was shown on TV and printed in the papers in Alaska. I showed copies of the article around to my friends at work and found out that no one I knew had ever heard of Operation Magic Carpet.

In November the same year, Mom and Dad were invited to New York as guests of the Yemenite Jewish Federation of America to a big Gala in celebration of the airlift. They came back with a lot of new friends, great memories, and an award that now sits in my living room. By that time I'd started doing a bit of background research and I learned that On Wings of Eagles —the official name for Operation Magic Carpet—was one of those forgotten, overlooked pieces of history. So I was no longer surprised when no one I told about Mom and Dad's award had ever heard of it. The idea occurred to me, at that point, that this was something I could actually do something about.

I'm a fiction writer and taking on a non-fiction project of such historical significance daunted me more than a little. But it was something that I not only could do, but had to do. I researched, wrote letters, made inquiries to find other surviving crew besides Mom and Dad, and, hopefully, some surviving passengers I could interview. I met Sam Silver, Archie Satterfield, and gathered a lot of good information.

Unfortunately, Dad's health began going south shortly thereafter; he and Mom both died in 2009. Ongoing battles with their illnesses and the health care system ate up my opportunities to work on this with them, and though I tried, I found myself unable to continue with it after their deaths. I put my by-then-bulging files away to wait until the loss was less fresh and went to work on other commitments.

In 2013, I was asked to speak at the opening of the Operation Magic Carpet exhibit at the Alaska Jewish Heritage Museum in Anchorage. Although I thought one of my brothers should have been asked instead of me—after all, they lived right there in Anchorage, and I was in Seattle—I said "yes" and dug out my notes.

Reading through them brought it all back; the magic of the story, the era, caught me up again and swept me away. It revived a lot of the "Mom and Dad Mythology" for me. I read a story or some of my notes and remembered hearing some version of it while sitting there on the living room floor all those years ago.

This is not just a story about Warren and Marian Metzger, Sam Silver, or Alaska Airlines, but about all the people who took part in it. Not just the men and women who flew the overworked, overcrowded C-46s and DC-4s from Shanghai and Aden, over territory where an emergency landing meant probable death. This is also the story of the people who fled from Germany to China, or walked across hundreds of miles of trackless desert and freezing mountain passes on the strength of a whisper and a dream, to ride the Wings of Eagles to a new life in the promised land.

It's a piece of history that must not—will not—be forgotten.

CONNECT WITH DARRAGH METZGER

I hope you enjoyed reading *Alaska Over Israel: Operation Magic Carpet, the Men and Women who Made it Fly, and the Little Airline that Could* as much as I enjoyed writing it. Either way, I really appreciate you reading it! In case you want to follow what else I'm doing, here are my social media coordinates:

Friend me on Facebook: http://facebook.com/darragh.metzger
Follow me on Twitter: http://twitter.com/DarraghME
Favorite my Author's page on Amazon: http://www.amazon.com/Darragh Metzger
Favorite my Smashwords author page: https://www.smashwords.com/profile/view/TFAPress
Subscribe to my blog: http://www.darraghmetzger.com/blog
Connect on LinkedIn: https://www.linkedin.com/darraghmetzger
Visit my website: http://www.darraghmetzger.com
Find my other books: http://www.TFAPress.com

KNOWN PILOTS AND CREW OF OPERATION MAGIC CARPET

This list has been compiled from numerous sources, including pilot interviews, log books, magazine and newspaper articles, and any other documentation. No single and complete source list exists.

For any who have been left off or overlooked, I ask forgiveness. Your participation is deeply appreciated and, like that of those listed below, helped save the lives of thousands of people.

Arnold, Paul
Burke, William
Carlson, Dick
Cheatham, Ralph
Cole, Clarke
Concourd, Wade
Copeland, Tom
Currie, Larry
Cusy, Jean

Edwards, Lyle
Elliot, Red
Epstein, Stanley
Finland, Shaina
Flahart, Larry
Fowler, Bill
Garland, Art
Gessner, Bud
Gjessing, Tony

Grout, Noel
Hall, Bob
Hola, Jerry
Horning, John (Al)
Hudson, Ed
Jones, J.A.
Johnson, LeRoy
Judd, J. Elliot
Karafel, Perry
Kerstiens, Chris
Krawlec, Ed
Land, R.D.
Lang, Milton
Lester, Bill
Lintner-West, Fae
Liscomb, Marian
Long, Elgen
Lund, Bill
MacDonald, Terry
MacKenzie, Gordon
Maguire, Bob
Massey, (?)
Mattiah, John
McCoy, Harold
McFarland, R.T.
McKloskey, Joe
Metzger, Warren

Morris, Bob
Mulleneaux, Hank
Nash, George "The"
Newman, (?)
Ostrander, Thea
Ostrander, Van
Patton, Hershal
Perino, Fred
Peterson, Pete (Al)
Platt, Bob
Raab, Larry
Redlinger, (?)
Roger, Larry
Rutherford, (Bill?)
Sharp, By
Shasky, Sam
Sholton, Bob
Silver, Sam
Stewart (Hal?)
Storey, Bernie
Stringum, Gordon
Stroup, Ray
Thompson, John
Wacha, Floyd
Wheeler, Gene
White, (1st Off.)
Whitting, Dick

BIBLIOGRAPHY

Where possible, I have referenced family papers, letters, photographs, and journals for much of the material on Warren Metzger, Marian Liscomb, and their families. For many of the personal observations, for which no outside verification exists, I relied on personal memories of stories and discussions to which I was party over my lifetime.

Archie Satterfield conducted a series of interviews with many Alaska Airlines employees and alumni from 1970 through 1980, most of which were recorded on tape. He gave me access to these tapes and also his written notes on the interviews he had not recorded or that had accidentally been erased. Some of these interviews are in poor condition; in these cases, I attempted to find verification through his written notes or other sources. In many cases, however, no other source material existed.

Warren Metzger was considered an expert on Alaskan aviation, and as such was interviewed several times during his lifetime. Some of these interviews also touched on Operation Magic Carpet or incidents that occurred during that time. I have made use of those whenever possible.

I also utilized several books and newspaper or magazine articles for general background information and to educate myself about the region and people, without necessarily using them for specific material.

BOOKS / NEWSPAPERS / PRINTED MATERIAL:

Alaska Airlines Annual Report 1948.
Alaska Airlines Annual Report 1949.
Alaska Airlines Executive Committee meeting minutes, March 25, 1949.
Azzam, Abdul Rahman Hassan; "A War of Extermination," *Akhbar al-Yom*, October 11, 1947.
Barer, Shlomo, *The Magic Carpet*, Harper & Brothers, New York, 1952.
Brewer, Sam Pope; "Israeli Blows Stir Arabs To Parleys: Leaders of Lebanon and Syria Confer on Palestine Situation – Other Moves Underway", *New York Times;* January 6, 1949. Courtesy of the Jewish Archives.
Capa, Cornell, ed; *Israel: the Reality*, The World Publishing Company, New York and Cleveland, 1969.
Chang, Jung; Halliday, Jon; *Mao: The Unknown Story*, Anchor, November 14, 2006.
Civil Aeronautics Board Aviation Cases, Report 43-54, *Pacific Northern Airlines v. Alaska Airlines*, September 17, 1948.
Currivan, Gene; "Israelis Fear Loss Of Political War: Tel Aviv Concerned as Pressure Against Jews is Applied in Arab World and East Bloc", *New York Times;* March 26, 1949.
Daniel, Clifton; "Israel-Abdullah Treaty Approached With Caution: Each Party Weighs Effect on Important Groups Opposed to an Agreement," *New York Times;* December 19, 1948. Courtesy of the Jewish Archives.

Eban, Abba; "Modern Anti-Semitism in Europe", *Turning Points in World History: The Creation of Israel*, Greenhaven Press, San Francisco, CA, 2005.

Elon, Amos; "Jewish Pioneers in Palestine", *Turning Points in World History: The Creation of Israel*, Greenhaven Press, San Francisco, CA, 2005.

Executive Committee of Alaska Airlines, Inc., March 25, 1949, Minutes of Meeting

Fix, Margalit; "Robert Maguire Jr., 94, Pilot Who Airlifted Yemenite Jews, Dies", *Los Angeles Times*, June 18, 2005.

Gafni, Shlomo, van der Heyden, A.; *The Glory of Jerusalem: an Explorer's Guide*, The Jerusalem Publishing House, Ltd., 1978.

Hamossadm, Barpal, JDC Tel Aviv; cable to Lt Doctor Schwartz, JDC New York, *Accounts submitted to your Paris office*, October 16, 1950.

Herzog, Chaim and Gazit, Shomo; *The Arab-Israeli Wars: War and Peace in the Middle East*, Vintage, rev. 2005.

Howell, Georgina; *Gertrude Bell: Queen of the Desert, Shaper of Nations*, Farrar, Strauss, and Giroux, New York, 2007.

Israel: The Birth of a Nation, Gilbert, Martin and Beecham, Bernard; A&E Home Video (History Channel), 1996.

Jacobson, Jerome J., JDC Headquarters, Paris; cable to Dr. J.J.Schwartz and Mr. M.Leavitt, *Re: Insurance Aden Flights*, December 6, 1949.

Jaffe, Boris A., Consolidated Tours, Inc.; Letter to Moses A. Leavitt, Executive Vice Chairman of JDC, May 24, 1949.

Keller, Allan; "Operation Magic Carpet", *New York World Telegram* and *The Sun*, May 27, 1950.

Keller, Allen; "Operation Magic Carpet: Airlift Carries 45,000 Forgotten Jews from Feudal Yemen to Haven of Israel", *New York World Telegram* and *The Sun*, April 27, 1950.

Leavitt, Moses A., Executive Vice Chairman of JDC; Letter to James Wooten, June 2, 1949.

Liscomb, Paul Darragh; *Cloud Country*, unpublished autobiography.

Long, Elgen; *On Eagles' Wings: an unknown story of The Magic Carpet*, 2015

Mansfield, Peter; *The Arabs*, Penguin Books Ltd, London, 1976; Revised Edition 1978.

Marguilies, Phillip; "Foreword" and "Introduction to Disputed Ground," *Turning Points in World History: The Creation of Israel*, Greenhaven Press, San Francisco, CA, 2005.

McLellan, Dennis; "Robert F. Maguire Jr., 94: Helped Airlift Thousands of Jews to Israel", *LA Times*, June 17, 2005.

Metzger, Marian Frances Liscomb; *A Life in the Sky*, unpublished autobiography.

Mishal, Nissim, *Those Were The Years... Israel's Jubilee*, Israeli Foreign Ministry, Miskal Publishing, 1998.

Penslar, Derek J.; "The First Arab-Israeli War: 1947-1948", *Turning Points in World History: The Creation of Israel*, Greenhaven Press, San Francisco, CA, 2005.

Satterfield, Archie; *The Alaska Airlines Story*, Alaska Northwest Publishing Company, 1982.

Schmidt, Dana Adams; "Egypt Reports Gains", *New York Times*, January 2, 1949. Courtesy of the Jewish Archives.

Schmidt, Dana Adams; "Full-Scale Attack Reported", *New York Times;* December 27, 1948. Courtesy of the Jewish Archives.

Sciaudone, Christiana; "Jews Discover an Unsung Hero", *Los Angeles Times*, June 19, 2004.

Segev, Tom; "The Makings of History / The Blind Misleading The Blind", *Haaretz*, October 21, 2011.

Sheperd, Naomi; "The Genesis of the Balfour Declaration", *Turning Points in World History: The Creation of Israel*, Greenhaven Press, San Francisco, CA, 2005.

Silverman, Maida; *Israel: the Founding of a Modern Nation*, Dial Books for Young Readers, New York, 1998.

Srebrny Pelz, Margot, JDC London, cable to Harry Viteles, JDC Tel Aviv, *Amendment to our letter of September 8th, regarding Aden Camp*, September 10, 1948.

Stirling Sunset Society, *Stirling: Its Story and People 1899-1980*, Calgary: Friesen Printers, 1981.

Teveth, Shabtai; (1987), *Ben-Gurion: The Burning Ground*, 1886–1948, Endeavour Press, 2016.

Uncredited; "4,500 Flown To Israel: Refugees From Yemen Carried by Air From Aden", *New York Times*, February 24, 1949. Courtesy of the Jewish Archives.

Uncredited; "Adenites Seek Revenge: Tribesmen Reported Gathering to Attack Fortress", *New York Times*, January 31, 1949.

Uncredited; "Entire Yemen Jewish Community Being Transferred to Israel", *The Palestine Post*, November 8, 1949.

Uncredited; "Max Lapides, Lawyer, Served Jewish Agency", *New York Times*, September 1, 1981.

Uncredited; "Palestine Peace: In the Spirit of the Palestine Armistice. Rhodes Shows the Way", *New York Times*, February 27, 1949.

Uncredited; "Relief Seen Near For Jewish DP's: Recovery Of All In Europe Is Likely in Three Years if Help Continues, Warburg Says", *New York Times*, January 2, 1949.

Uncredited; "Tells of Gigantic Airlift Carrying Jews to Homeland. Lang Home on Vacation from Job of Moving Oppressed to 'Promised Land'", *Caledonian Record*, St. Johnsbury, VT, October 26, 1950.

Uncredited; "The Palestine Dispute Sharpens the Clash of Interests in the Middle East. Ruffles U.S. and Britain", *New York Times*, January 16, 1949.

United Press; "Aden Chief Regains Home But Father's Killers Flee", *New York Times*, February 23, 1949.

Uris, Leon; *Exodus*, Doubleday, 1958.

Wooten, James, President and CEO of Alaska Airlines; Letter to Moses A. Leavitt, Executive Vice Chairman of JDC, June 29, 1949.

INTERVIEWS AND RECORDED MATERIAL:

KTUU TV, interview with Warren Metzger, pilot, Anchorage, Alaska, 2007.

Metzger, Darragh; interview with Elgen Long, Navigator, 2013.

Metzger, Darragh; interviews with Sam Silver, pilot, 2008 – 2015.

Satterfield, Archie; interview with Bob Platt, mechanic, 1979.

Satterfield, Archie; interview with Clarke Cole, pilot, 1970.

Satterfield, Archie; interview with James Wooten, President/CEO of Alaska Airlines, 1979.

Satterfield, Archie; interview with John Thompson, pilot, 1979.

Satterfield, Archie; interview with Larry Roger, pilot, 1979.

Satterfield, Archie; interview Sam Silver, pilot, 1979.

Satterfield, Archie; interview with Van Ostrander, Alaska Airlines Director of Purchasing, 1979.

Satterfield, Archie; interview with Warren Metzger, pilot, 1979.

Wooten, James, oral account given before JDC, year unknown.

WEBSITES:

"1948 Arab-Israeli War": http://en.wikipedia.org/wiki/ 1948_Arab%E2%80%93Israeli_War.

"Aden Protectorate": https://en.wikipedia.org/wiki/- Aden_Protectorate.

"Challenges and Inspirations", *Magic Carpet Pilots:* http://www.alaskaair.com/content/about-us/his- tory/carpet-pilots.aspx.

"Operation Magic Carpet", Jewish Virtual Library: http://www.jewishvirtuallibrary.org/site-search?- q=Operation+Magic+Carpet

"Queen of Sheba": http://en.wikipedia.org/wiki/Sheba.

"The Ghosts of Shanghai", Gluckman, Ron: http://- www.gluckman.com/ShanghaiJewsChina.html.

"The Jewish Refugee Community of Shanghai: 1938- 1949", Guest blog by Historicity (Was Already Taken), April 7, 2013: http://beyondvictoriana.com/2013/- 04/07/the-jewish-refugee-community-of-shang- hai-1938-1949/.

"The Shanghai Campaign": http://en.wikipedia.org/- wiki/Shanghai_Campaign.

"Timeline: Israel War of Independence": http://zion- ism-israel.com/his/Israel_war_independence_- 1948_timeline.htm.

"Yemen": https://en.wikipedia.org/wiki/History_of_- Yemen#Modern_history.